Panic Profits

How to Make Money When the Market Takes a Dive

John Dennis Brown

McGraw-Hill, Inc.

New York   San Francisco   Washington, D.C.   Auckland   Bogotá
Caracas   Lisbon   London   Madrid   Mexico City   Milan
Montreal   New Delhi   San Juan   Singapore
Sydney   Tokyo   Toronto

Library of Congress Cataloging-in-Publication Data

Brown, John Dennis.
   Panic profits : how to make money when the market takes a dive /
John Dennis Brown.
       p.   cm.
   Includes index.
   ISBN 0-07-008180-8 (alk. paper).—ISBN 0-07-008189-1 (pbk. :
alk. paper)
   1. Panics (Finance)—United States.   2. Stocks—United States.
I. Title.
HB3722.B76   1993
332.63'22—dc20   93-29849
                                                    CIP

1 2 3 4 5 6 7 8 9 0   DOC/DOC   9 9 8 7 6 5 4 3

ISBN   0-07-008180-8   (hc)
ISBN   0-07-008189-1   (pbk)

*The sponsoring editor for this book was Caroline Carney, the editing supervi-
sor was Stephen M. Smith, and the production supervisor was Suzanne W.
Babeuf. It was set in Palatino by McGraw-Hill's Professional Book Group
composition unit.*

Printed and bound by R. R. Donnelley & Sons Company.

This book is printed on recycled, acid-free paper containing a
minimum of 50% recycled de-inked fiber.

The author is not engaged in rendering legal, tax, accounting, or similar professional services. While legal, tax, and accounting issues cov-
ered in this book have been checked with sources believed to be reliable, some material may be affected by changes in the laws or in the
interpretations of such laws since the manuscript for this book was
completed. For that reason the accuracy and completeness of such information and the opinions based thereon are not guaranteed. In addition, state or local tax laws or procedural rules may have a material
impact on the general recommendations made by the author, and the
strategies outlined in this book may not be suitable for every individual. If legal, accounting, tax, investment, or other expert advice is
required, obtain the services of a competent practitioner.

Contents

8. Adversity's Silver Lining   195

9. Stocks to Buy, Stocks to Avoid   224

10. The 1929 Syndrome   262

Preface

It was while I was waiting for the Meltdown of 1987 to reveal its Deeper Meaning that I began collecting doomsday memorabilia. At that time there was massive confusion in the world's financial markets. They were all in a state of collapse—except those that had shut down to escape the rampant selling. The free world's central bankers huddled in panic by their faxes and phones.

The Advisor struggled briefly to write a headline that would offer an interpretation, but then thought better of it. The story line focused on tomorrow, because the investment letter's readers wanted to know what it all meant for next week. "1000-Point Dow Drop Cures High PE Ratios" was what the editor came up with. Carping critics of the Dow 2700 level had lost their ammo, it advised, for prices had dropped to realistic evaluations.

But having cavalierly dismissed the collapse as yesterday's news, curiosity began to nibble at the editor. A major wire service offered up comparative "worst-day" statistics that included an error so grievous it sent us to the archives to recheck. Curiosity mushroomed: Perhaps a little more research would allow us to weave the events of 1987 with legends of former panics to produce a year-end summary. Or maybe comparisons with the past would fit better into some future letter—say, as part of a crash anniversary roundup. Surely everything would be clear by that time. And so the search for vignettes and meanings of past panics continued.

But when October 1988 rolled around there was not much of a story. It was not 1930. The Dow had not been driven to a new low but instead was plodding along, well over 2100. Of course, at that level it had not even recovered the one-day loss of October 19, 1987, when the Dow dropped from 2246 to 1739. However, the laggard recovery raised other questions. Was it somehow ominous? Not necessarily, for the archives showed that there had been other similarly slow rebounds.

And so the gradual accumulation of clippings, readings, dusty books, and old charts continued. Long library sessions followed, for it is impossible to scroll through the microfilmed events of 1893, say, or 1907 without being caught up in events beyond the financial markets.

In the meantime, the doomsayers were proven wrong, for by August 1989 the Dow had climbed above its peak of 1987. Earlier in this century, it had taken 25 years to recover to 1929 levels. The ghost of 1929 had been laid to rest.

It seemed obvious that 1987 held no Deeper Meaning. There had been no depression, no credit crunch, no failed banks, no blood in the streets. The only unemployment lines were in Wall Street. But surely, it all meant *something*. Frustration set in.

Marching the Panics in Columns

And so the Exchange panics since 1890 were marched up and down the legal-pad pages. There were columns and columns, devoted to damage, duration, convalescence, early symptoms, volume, *dramatis personnae*, historical significance—usually lacking—benefits (if any), and so forth. And when had these crises appeared? Additional columns showed that they had erupted during bull markets, bear markets, depression, boom, and while both parties occupied the White House. There was a frequent divergence from the business cycle.

Common causes were studied and assigned, but there were so many unique elements that they seemed to dominate the listings, making analysis difficult. War and the threat of war, it became obvious, was the one dominant trigger of panic. And then there were those curious implosions, as in 1929 and 1987.

Panics, it seemed, were random and isolated events. As winter follows summer, bear markets both follow and precede bull markets. But panics struck in all seasons, like an unpredictable act of nature.

To make sense of it all, the panics had to be separated and distinguished from the bear cycles. An almanac of major declines, about two dozen important ones since President Benjamin Harrison's administration began in 1889, helped sort out some of the commonalities and differences. The frightening events that triggered panics mostly lacked significance, it turned out, while bear trends, intertwined with depression, unemployment, and commercial crisis, wrote economic history.

Many panics, it developed, paralleled bear market statistics. The great difference seemed to be that panic selling had to be resisted: Buying, not selling, under crisis conditions was the correct strategy, for the reflex profits were automatic. Contrarily, the seduction of buying at lower prices during major declines had to be resisted. Patience was absolutely necessary while awaiting signs that the decline had bottomed.

Patience is of no value during panics. What you see is about what you'll get during crises. The bad news and the distress prices are all immediately revealed. Delay only a few hours and the opportunity will be gone.

Saddam's Invasion Twisted the Thesis

Like every thesis about Wall Street strategy, the one above seemed rather good. And then the Iraqis invaded Kuwait in August 1990. The market responded in its traditional fashion, experiencing huge volumes for about three weeks, while the Dow fell by 14 percent. As it turned out, the decline should probably have been larger, considering the threat to Middle Eastern oil supplies, and the potential for nuclear or chemical bombs from Saddam.

The price declines seemed to argue for purchase. Wholesale disruption of travel plans was an obvious consequence, along with the certainty of higher fuel costs. UAL, a major airline trading at over 160 only a few weeks before, had plunged to the low 90s.

It seemed a classic move, discounting the known problems. Saddam, after all, would probably back down; and if a war in the Mideast did come, he would obviously lose, opposed by the world's great powers.

The reflex from the August panic was predictable, but then new events conspired to drive the Dow beneath the August level. UAL, which had rallied to 119, tumbled to a new low at 84. War was not being discounted twice, but $40 crude, a puffed-up price considering the large supplies available, and brinksmanship in Congress on the deficit limit provided the bears with a platform for a vigorous second-stage assault.

The renewed decline, to 2365 on the Dow, marked an overall loss of 20 percent from the July peak at 3000 and was identified by many as the start of a new bear market. It wasn't, but such was not provable at the time. Panic's attack had been extended in an unusual second wave, and it was too early to rule on its meaning.

And so the charts were again brought out. What other anomalies could be found, where crisis lows were smashed a bit later by a second-stage attack? Such occurrences, it turned out, have not been frequent, but have always been disruptive to the market's psyche. And so other corollaries and theses were collected regarding the nature and course of those exceptional second-stage attacks. Quick money could always be made by a contrarian approach to panic. But there were exceptions of only brief rebounds, mostly in the long-running bear episodes, as in the 1930s. The events of 1990 were another curious exception.

How could one prove the usual opportunities of panic? The changes in the Dow Industrials were impressive, but dull. What stocks, available over the decades, might have been purchased by the average investor in moments of crisis? Hindsight revealed many brilliant performers, but some prescriptive choices were needed. Why not the nation's largest corporation? If the investor was going to buy anything, there was surely some safety in size.

U.S. Steel or General Motors would have been a reasonable selection; they were the no. 1 and no. 2 (and vice versa) industrials for decades. We were in fact surprised at the success of such simplistic stock choices. Even with imperfect timing, they would have rolled up big advances.

Serious money loves bad times, which in this case means deep bear markets. Bear market troughs are hugh profit centers, and generally the investor has considerable time to evaluate and select the probable winners. There seems to be no great secret to stock selection at such times: It is no more difficult than buying no. 1. A breakdown of dependable cyclic winners led to a potential portfolio of names known to every market beginner. And those are the very names that an investor dares to chance under black economic conditions.

Commonplace Stocks
Dominate Big Winner List

The fascinating part of the search for reliable market rebounders was the discovery of how commonplace the really big winners—the "hundred baggers"—were. Such 100:1 successes were not achieved in any single bull cycle, to be sure, but the list of phenomenal winners was amazingly long. They were all superstocks, but none were advertised as such. Since 1950, the list includes such open-book winners as Black &

Decker, Maytag, Gillette, Pepsi, Budweiser, American Airlines, Holiday Inn, and Lord & Taylor. The total includes several hundred names.

The investor needed no technical knowledge, no broker advisor, and no Wall Street insider secrets to have cashed in on any of those tickets. It's not that most of us didn't, at one time or another, own such stocks. What we did was buy, own, and then discard them after we had made 10 points or 50 percent, or whatever.

Discovering the commonplace sources of large market success was part of the learning process that led to this book. Other pleasures included a survey of some of those "slam dunk" inventions that should have made everyone wealthy. And of some of those personal "eurekas" which have occasionally smiled on us all. But how to explain the ones that got away?

Over and over, one finds the startling statistics of the 1930s upsetting theses or overbalancing statistical ranges. Or jogging investors' memories at just the wrong time. We decided to admit that the decade was the equivalent of a financial 100-year flood plain and fence it off by itself, away from the more "proper" sequences and tables. So many of its incidents have been lumped into a special chapter on "The 1929 Syndrome."

Storm Groupies

Some years ago, driving up the coast of Oregon during a heavy winter storm, I stopped for the night in Newport. It was definitely not the "season," and it had not occurred to me to make an advance reservation. I was lucky to get the last room in the inn.

"Where'd all the people come from?" I asked the desk clerk.

"They're storm groupies," he said. "They come from inland whenever there's a big blow along the coast. They walk the beaches, pick up driftwood, or sit by the fire and watch the waves. They just enjoy storms. When it blows over, they'll go back home."

Panics have a similar fascination. No one anticipates such winter gales, but they possess a macabre fascination beside which all the tales of bull and bear market episodes pale. This writer could not let the subject rest.

John Dennis Brown

About the Author

John Dennis Brown is a veteran investment professional, author, and editor with more than 30 years' experience in the field. Formerly a partner and vice president at E.F. Hutton, he was a member of the Chicago Board of Trade and an editor of *The Advisor*. He is the past publisher of George Lindsay's *Market Opinion* and is the author of the recently published *101 Years on Wall Street: An Investor's Almanac*.

Introduction

In the Corinthian palace of commerce called the New York Stock Exchange, the most mysterious occurrence is panic. Of all the events that rule Wall Street's life, panics are the most frightening and the least understood.

There are no warnings of panic. The nominal causes are only vaguely linked to industry and commerce. Panics strike like a tornado in the night, and their swift attack is often compared with other furies of nature—avalanches, summer storms, tsunamis, and so forth.

Panics are intense and dramatic. Their short, brutal attacks are normally triggered by accidents and incidents that imply shocking changes in the economic status quo. War threatens, or a President is assassinated. A vast manipulation or corner fails. Washington administrators ambush a market favorite or suddenly propel interest rates higher. On occasion, as in 1929, the market seems to implode.

Blindsided by events of change imperfectly understood, investors react in an irrational panic, sacrificing both good and bad securities at a fraction of the value seen only days previously. Panics are a psychological phenomenon, not an economic one, and there is no appeal to reason. Only an exhaustion of selling, or a reversal of news, will stay panic's course. A variety of elixirs and palliatives, as surveyed in Chap. 2, have been prescribed for crisis. Some worked, like the delightfully named *Silberzug*, or silver train, which rescued Hamburg in 1857.

Defining Panic the Easy Way

Economists love to weave wordy and sophisticated definitions of panic. We favor the pithy brevity of Charles P. Kindleberger: "...the genus is like a pretty woman...hard to define, but recognizable when encountered."*

*Charles P. Kindleberger, *Manias, Panics, and Crashes*, rev. ed. (Basic Books, New York, 1989), p. 6.

The economists, to be sure, are seeking to define commercial crisis. We are interested in a narrower focus: stock market panics and the bearish sequences of the market, which so often encompass panics.

In former times, commercial stress led to market panic or accelerated the pace of falling markets. Panics and bear markets were occasionally confused, as in the Panic of 1903, which was really a bear market. In this book we try to identify and focus on the sudden episodes of panic that lasted about 20 trading days or less, and that produced a Dow loss of at least 10 percent. One cannot be completely arbitrary, however, and a few episodes of slightly longer length are included, although these tended to be somewhat less intense.

Intensity is the major difference between a bear market and a panic. The worst bear markets have been much worse than the major panics, with the inevitable exception of 1929, but many acute crises have equaled the losses recorded in the minor bear episodes of this century.

It is the psychological impact and intensity that shocks investors, even when the losses are not overwhelming. The collapse of May 1970, triggered by Kent State and the Cambodian war news, dropped the Dow by 14 percent, but it somehow seemed worse than the entire previous decline, which had started 15 months earlier and slashed the average from 985 to 734.

Violent declines of slightly less than 10 percent cannot be arbitrarily excluded. When Germany announced unrestricted U-boat warfare in 1917, the Dow plunged by over 7 percent in one day, and slipped a bit further in the next session. Panic was truly present, for Exchange volume was the largest of the war years, even if the total loss figure was less than our standard. The reader will find more than 90 panics identified in the Appendix, not including those of 1930–1932, which are discussed in Chap. 9.

1901: The Classic Northern Pacific Panic

Meteorologists and weather forecasters, we are told, have their favorite storms, tight and well-defined systems which erupt and slash swiftly across their maps. Maybe just a touch of violence. Financial panics acquire admiration (from afar) for the same characteristics.

Drama, intensity, and shocking speed are part of the classic panics, and perhaps the pattern is best illustrated by the Northern Pacific panic of 1901, which is profiled in Chap. 3. Its drama, which featured a rowdy railroad battle for control of the Northern Pacific (NP), saw the titans of Wall Street faced off against one another. Its intensity remains a legend. The shares of the NP had been accidentally cornered and as they hurdled upward, from 160 to 1000 in a single day, short speculators sacrificed all other holdings, causing a general collapse in both rail and industrial shares.

Volume set a record that would not be matched for more than 20 years, and the collapse and recovery were both unbelievably swift. U.S. Steel, 45 on Wednesday, fell to 24 on Thursday, and recovered to 45 on Friday. The financial storm was over as quickly. By the very next month, the Dow had recovered all its losses and was at a record high.

Panics are so wild and wayward that there is no perfect model. But nowhere do we find an action more classic than that of 1901, accompanied as it was by the high drama which marked the battle between J. P. Morgan and Edward H. Harriman for control of a great railroad system.

Those Devils at the Gate

Chapter 1 surveys the devils at the gate—the many Lucifiers that constantly fork at investors. Bear markets and panics are there, of course, but we also learn about the insidious curse of the market has-been, a silent killer. It is hard to believe, but the giant U.S. Steel company reached its all-time high in 1959, about 2900 Dow points ago. Other victims of the silent killer are examined.

Panics can strike at any time, in bull markets as well as bear markets, in good times, in bad times, at the very top of a market cycle, as in 1919, or at the very bottom, as in 1970. Occasionally, obvious candidates abort or develop in an eccentric fashion, as after Pearl Harbor. These anomalies are surveyed in Chap. 2, which also searches for the possible meaning of these violent events. It is also determined that while panics write financial history for their victims, they seldom carry historical significance themselves.

The benefits of panic are mostly claimed by Pollyannish commentators, but there have occasionally been modest long-term gains for the public. The Federal Reserve System was born, quite tardily, out of the ashes of the 1907 crash. Buyers' panics, socially very acceptable, are briefly noted, along with the famous and often flamboyant *dramatis personnae* that add to the drama of crises.

Searching for the Causes of Panic

The results of panic are easy to detail. The causes, which are examined in Chap. 3, are myriad and occasionally complex, although there is usually a single trigger for the price collapse. War and the threat of war is the most common trigger, but paradoxically, there have been some serious peace scares.

Antibusiness fears have occasionally stirred up great market fright, as occurred in the 1962 Kennedy panic. But a great number of episodes have been totally unique, like the "Cross of Silver" panic of 1896, the Northern Pacific corner, which was successful, if accidental, and more recently, the silver corner of 1980, which failed, despite its billionaire backing.

An Almanac for Bear Markets

Bear markets create more havoc than panics and uncover greater opportunities. When their climax is reinforced by crisis, they present the richest opportunities to be found in the market.

While panics' fright coerces selling, bear markets' seductive pricing lures the investor to the buy side. In each case, the psychology must be resisted, and a contrary option exercised.

While nearly 100 panics with solid credentials can be identified in the past century, there have been only about two dozen bear markets; the exact number depends mostly on the interpretation of some minor Dow theory signals. Chapter 4 presents a bear market almanac and capsules all of the major declines since 1890. These sequences are also measured against the business cycle. A later section of the chapter further distinguishes them from panic, for at times their dimensions, if not their duration, are identical. The 1981–1982 bear market loss was about the same as the convulsion stirred by 13 trading sessions in May 1940, culminating in the retreat at Dunkerque.

Serious money, it will be found in Chap. 5, loves bear markets and always seems well prepared for the selling climax. Patient hoarding during declines is quickly rewarded, for the first-year gains which follow the reversal are the most substantial of the bull cycle.

Watching for the Indicators of Doom

Arriving at a bear market trough with a heavy purse depends on making some hard decisions early on. No one bugles "retreat" when the slide starts, and the natural inclination during decline is to pick up some apparent "bargains" along the way. The trouble is that the cheap get much cheaper in every long decline.

The trick to survival is to recognize when the indicators of doom are sounding the klaxon. There is no perfect indicator of trouble, nor even a perfect parlay of indicators, but even simple technical aids can warn the investor when the barometer is dropping. That is when stocks must be liquidated.

Many defensive tools, such as the popular advance/decline ratio, are reviewed in Chap. 6, along with the Dow theory. Its controversial tenets are seen to offer excellent guidelines, but the theory's signals are often late and certainly not infallible. Its sell signals over the past 90 years are tabulated and examined for efficiency.

Every indicator, even the Dow theory, needs confirmation from other sources for most effective use. The investor can also obtain insight from trend lines, moving averages, relative strengths, and momentum.

Finding a Place for Celibacy

There is an occasional place for celibacy in everybody's life, and there should be prolonged periods of financial celibacy for every investor. The alternative, being invested at all times, fights difficult odds. Over the past century, major declines have occupied the market for a total of 33 years.

That is why the investor must use every trend-seeking missile in his or her defensive arsenal. Without their assistance it is often impossible to judge when a "secondary correction," masquerading as a buying opportunity, is rolling over into the first leg of a new bear market.

The influence of changing interest rates, the utility barometer, divergence between averages, and various sentiment indicators, among other technical aids, are all of assistance in determining when market abstinence may be the best strategy.

Profiting from Adversity's Silver Lining

Panics offer easy profits for courageous contrarians. Bear market troughs offer a silver lining. In both cases, market genius is cash in hand, and no particular wisdom is needed. Although a thoughtful approach will improve on haphazard selection in the reversal month of a bear market, the sure bargains of panic allow no time for reflection—one must seize the moment.

Timing during the days of panic is almost automatically perfect, and crisis contrarians in this century grew rich with household names such as General Electric, U.S. Steel, and General Motors, as tabulated in Chap. 7. It was easy to pull the trigger on such large, solid targets, even on the most stressful days.

The structure and symptoms of panic are fairly easy to assess. Identifying bear market lows is more difficult, and a fundamental scorecard for bear market lows illustrates the statistical divergencies in earnings, dividends, and PE ratios observed at important troughs. A study of those bottom periods shows that in more than half the instances, the investor had over 16 trading sessions, after the cyclic low, in which to enter the market at a quality level—within 7 percent of the Dow Jones low.

Theoretically, speculators can cash in twice on adversity's silver lining, playing the short side of the market during the down trend and reversing the portfolio when conditions improve. It does seem easy, but investors and the average boardroom trader will find such mercurial changes of thinking difficult to handle. The easy profits of short selling are mostly generated by the floor traders. Even the big, well-funded short-trading pools have done poorly in recent years.

Options are equally dicey, but at least the player knows how much might be lost, as compared with the infinity figure for short sales. Those who bait the bear by buying contra-recession gold stocks have often done well during recessionary periods, but other bear baiters have been hard to identify in real time. The sugar issues ran up nicely in 1974, thanks to a large increase in the price of raws, and merger mania. But such contra-moves are hard to anticipate.

A study of Dow theory "buy" signals proves that most other technical indicators are superior in triggering timely buying near bear market lows. Some Dow signals have come nearly a year after the market reversal. On the other hand, the faith to hold positions during a long-continued trend, as in 1933–1937, has been encouraged by the theory.

Rich hope is found for those ultraconservative investors who demand a "test" of the bottom before they'll spend a dime. Following nearly every reversal from a bear market, there has been a delayed buying opportunity for important groups whose cycle low was laggard to the Dow. In 1970, many leading stocks, including International Business Machines (IBM), made new lows in August, although the Industrials held far above the trough of late May.

At the beginning of this century, there were only a hundred or so active stocks at the Exchange. And trades in most unlisted issues were few and far between, in both time and price. Several thousand issues now trade on the Big Board, and there are thousands of other viable issues traded at the AMEX and the NASDAQ. Selection is always difficult.

Stocks to Buy and Stocks to Avoid

When a bear market low is anticipated, the investor needs to focus on stocks with proven rebounding ability. The specific reflex will vary from one cycle to the next, and it's impossible to pick the next rebounding champion, but a study of past cycles suggests a dozen reliable areas. Names and Standard & Poor (S&P) ratings are given for many proven veterans. In the event of doubt, the investor is advised to "draft for the best athlete," regardless of industry.

Cheap stocks, normally regarded as vulgar by investors, are given a green light as the most dependable of all percentage gainers from bear troughs. The caveat to readers is that they must buy a package of at least five or six issues. Betting the farm on a $2 stock is not what intelligent speculation is all about.

Searching for the "Hundred Baggers"

No one has ever forecast and then gone to the wire with a stock choice which turned out to be a "hundred bagger," a 100:1 winner. But looking for potentially big winners may help to overcome some of those market dullards we all find ourselves stuck with. Strangely, the big winners are not expected to be companies of technical brilliance, but those issues which can make life or work easier, or more fun, or tastier, or more entertaining.

Household names dominate the listing of 100:1 winners since World War II, and many personal "Eurekas" of such magnitude have been visited upon us all. How many parents bought Gerber because the kids all grew up on their baby foods? Not a very exciting stock, but $5000 turned into $550,000. My excuse? The kids generally gooped the Gerber veggies all over me.

"Slam dunk" inventions have also built some remarkable fortunes and, as Chap. 8 points out, the investor didn't have to get in on the ground floor to get rich. Even the most dazzling inventions have required more capital, more management, more time, and more marketing than the patent genius or early investors ever expected. Recognition of growing public acceptance, and not early investment in a dream, has been the key to long profits in such inventions as the telephone, Polaroid, and Xerox. There will be many others.

Avoid the Seductions of "Yesterday's Darlings"

Yesterday's market darlings are always seductive, but they are the most unrewarding group to pursue at cyclic turns. They never duplicate their original success. Why bull a stock that everyone is already stuck with and wants to sell? Avoid them. On the other hand, buying panic's most victimized stocks provides a reliable rebound; speculators often target the worst hurt, but they are looking for ultraswift profits and not something to load into the lockbox. Grasping the nettle in such precarious days has always brought quick profits, probably never greater than in the record rally which followed the 1929 crash.

Similar rebounds from extreme circumstances have been quite reliable over the years. Even in the black Watergate days of 1973, reflex moved the market sharply higher despite an ongoing bear market which was the worst since the 1930s.

Fighting the 1929 Syndrome

The worst year in stock market history was 1931, but 1929 remains the benchmark for all that went wrong in the 1930s. Those black legends still haunt investors, although investor veterans of the tumultuous years are mostly gone.

Doomsday advocates and other professional alarmists have used every sharp market decline to trumpet "another 1929," and such posturing has regularly bred fears which crushed potentially splendid investment rewards. Another problem with that earlier era is that the major decline which began in April of 1930 was accelerated by a veritable cascade of panics, which are also reviewed in Chap. 9.

While no market strategy is presumed to be perfect, the 1930–1932 sequence did test the theories of panics' contrarians. Rallies were steep, but ended so quickly that only the most nimble profited. At the end of most three- and six-month periods, even the best stocks showed a loss. Which is one reason why many are still afraid to challenge the violence of panics.

Other anomalies have speared panic recoveries, and even knocked the market down to immediate new lows, in a two-stage attack. These failures are also reviewed. The deflationary market of 1920 also left unimpressive medium-term recovery figures.

Another Meltdown in the 1990s?

The book's final chapter views the market prospects for the 1990s and the potential for another 1987-type meltdown. The most compelling argument against a repeat is that in the aftermath of those decades of huge advances, it has often been difficult to rekindle the bullish mania which inevitably precedes record-breaking air pockets. Certainly, the volatility of the market has been restrained in the first years of the decade.

If the gambling madness which has swept the nation's state treasuries into lotteries and riverboat gambling should continue, there is the chance that the mania might spread to Wall Street. Another threat is the lemminglike rush into mutual funds. "Cash is trash" was the lure to abandon low-paying CDs and jump into funds. Not since 1929 has the Street seen such a rush for investment trusts. In the winter of 1992–1993, the inflow to mutual funds was regularly almost a net $10 billion a month.

Just what might disillusion the avid fund buyers is uncertain, but such manias have always sown the seeds of their own decline. Several small-company funds in early 1993 were forced to close their books to new subscribers, having already doubled or tripled their shareholder list within a few months.

A return of violent inflation would set up new parameters for what the market might do. Fortunately, the experts advise us that such an event is so remote that they don't even have the software to handle it; unfortunately, such confidence offers a contrary warning.

An Imperfect Tool, but the Best One at Hand

Throughout the book, the Dow Jones Industrial Average (DJIA), first computed in 1896, is used as the measure of market change; prior to

1896, the Dow 20-Stock Average is used. The DJIA is admittedly an imperfect average, but it remains the best-known market indicator in the world. For historical studies, it remains the most valuable index.

The senior Dow average—the Railroads—led the market to collapse on many occasions, but the addition of its sector panics would add little to the thesis of crisis profits. The last violent bear leadership by the transportation stocks was in October 1989, when the airline merger mania self-destructed.

Generally, stock prices and index levels have been rounded off, except in instances of historic interest. Point changes for the Dow are mostly ignored, as the advance in that average from 28.48 in 1896 to 3600 makes only percentage comparisons meaningful.

Conclusion

No matter how sanguine we might be about reduced volatility in the 1990s, the fact is that financial mischief always arrives unannounced. Complacency about market trends and values is never warranted, and the lessons of panic will surely be tested again and again during the remainder of this century.

1

The Devils
at the Gate

My former partner, Gerald M. Loeb, said that the battle for investment survival is won by defense. The devils are always at the gate. Buy an auto stock, and Detroit recalls 2 million cars. Buy IBM, and some Texas maverick slashes PC prices by 25 percent. Buy a drug stock, and a $100 million class action suit against the company is an automatic response. Cuts in dividends, bellicosity in Washington, earnings disappointments, strikes, and other Lucifers yap constantly at the portcullis.

However, the only two serious threats to an investor's citadel are panics and bear markets. Panics may frighten an investor half to death, but bear episodes can bleed him to death. The pain of a panic is mild compared to the ongoing torment of a lengthy bear market. Panics blindside investors, but they are quickly over. Bear markets develop slowly but endure. That stubborn erosion—not the lightning strike of panic—is the investor's greatest threat. He is lured into a Maginot mentality, confident because his stocks are A rated, have a large profit cushion, or are thought to possess some special antibear mystique.

The canny investor will handle these two kinds of threats with opposite strategies. Panics strike Wall Street unannounced and, like Warner Brothers' Tasmanian Devil, quickly lay waste to the premises. There is no reasonable exit for the investor; by the time the devil is recognized, he is gone. It's "in your face" at such tense moments. A good offense is the best defense: Buying, not selling, is the proper course.

The best defense in a bear market, on the other hand, is celibacy. Here the devilish seduction is the lure of lower and lower prices. That coveted $40 stock is now 32, and earnings are edging upward. Things look mostly OK, and speculation has quieted. At such times, lash yourself to the mast, for those cheap prices will get cheaper.

Liquidate, if you have the courage. Selling, not buying, is the proper defense in bear sequences.

Comparing Bear Markets to Panics

Panics come with the territory. They are inevitable, unpredictable, and should be recognized as an unwelcome crisis of opportunity—regardless of cause. War scares, assassinations, Presidential health concerns, and banking crises have been among the major causes of short-term stress in the market during the past century. But in nearly every case, prices have recovered swiftly. Sizable rewards are possible with small risk, because panics are straightforward: What you see is what you get. The market immediately discounts the meaning of the news.

In panics, bad news is hawked unceasingly. Bear markets, on the other hand, are deceitful. Banking and political leaders make soothing noises, and brokerage houses pump special situations and defensive stocks. No one bugles "retreat." In bear markets, bad news slips in, whitewashed with the claim that things will be better in the next quarter. Bear markets drag on. Occasional sharp falls are followed by long periods of sideways movement or mild erosion. Investors find themselves hoping for a climax, no matter how nasty, just to end the ordeal.

Preparing for panic is a twofold discipline: Avoid margin trading and maintain a hefty chunk of reserves in cash equivalents—interest-bearing funds, T-bills, and so forth. Only rarely will even the most brilliant student of the market smell serious trouble immediately ahead. But if such insight is found, sell quickly or not at all. A frightened citizen who liquidated stocks on the first day of the Kuwait war in August 1990 would have left the market 400 Dow points above the low reached several weeks later.

Panics are more than four times as numerous as bear markets and have often played the devil's role several times within a 12-month span. There have been only about two dozen bear markets in the past century. Market students disagree on the precise count. Was the reaction of 1953 a minibear, or a secondary correction? Should the depression sequences of 1890–1896 be combined into a single, long-running decline?

Regardless of the exact number, there have been at least 100 major buying opportunities since 1890. Panics guarantee quick money to the nimble. Bear markets guarantee serious money for those who have patiently awaited a major sea change.

Floor traders, professional speculators, and those of a naturally sour disposition will occasionally make "killings" on the short side of the market. But the majority of the Street's legendary bear operators give it all back. Meanwhile, the estates of unknown, untutored small-time investors frequently garner headlines for their patient, million-dollar accumulation of blue-chip wealth.

Arriving at such a state of grace takes only a little luck, but large amounts of patience and the courage to liquidate stock holdings when the boat starts to rock. Unfortunately, it is easier to ride a loser than a winner, so selling discipline is needed. Large beginning sums of money are not necessary to collect serious profits. One can find scores of 100-baggers—stocks that rise a hundredfold—which have bloomed from cheap bear prices. Not many were glamours like Xerox, either.

The opportunities will surely be repeated. Bear markets follow bull markets in repeated cycles. And panics, when the courageous can turn a quick profit, are always lurking.

No investor welcomes panic or bear collapse, for these are the true devils at the gate. But they can be conquered, and the profits of crisis can be astonishingly large.

Beware Sector and Solo Panics

Among the many devils at the gate, snapping at the investor, are the forces of sector and individual stock panics—fierce attacks on a suddenly weak industry or, even worse, a prized individual issue. The clear-cut case for buying stocks in periods of broad panic cannot be validated for sector crises nor for the shares of individual stocks in freefall.

Sector and solo panics are by definition declines that are contrary to the general trend of the market or, in a bear sequence, declines showing marked relative weakness. Often, weakness is partially camouflaged by the counter mood of the broad list.

Computers have encouraged the development of hundreds of group and subgroup indices. *Investor's Business Daily* follows 197. In any one period, several can be found that are in failing health. A half-dozen different types of retailers can be logged, for example, and apparel chains might suffer a slump even as pharmacy issues and the Dow climb to record highs.

In recent decades, important groups such as health care, computers, steels, oils, and autos have all suffered private crises. Such travails are longer-lived than broad panics, and are not so prone to extremes. Prices may finally slip to bargain levels, but the buoyant, automatic reflex which follows panics will be lacking.

Oil Takes a Bath

A surprising sector panic struck the oils in December 1980, though Saudi light crude was teasing the $40 level. While the Dow advanced from a low of 895 in mid-December to 1031 intraday in April, the oils diverged sharply. Standard Oil of Indiana (Amoco) fell from 97 to 51, and Phillips Petroleum lost 38 percent in the counterslide. Only the briefest rally followed.

Gold Shares Hit by Freak Selling Wave

In August 1974, gold shares were hit by a selling wave, uncharacteristic for the "precious" in a bear atmosphere. Homestake Mining dropped from 70 to 30 in just 16 trading days, and *Barron's* gold index was nearly halved. The crash was named the Schaefer Panic, after the veteran gold advisor who had suddenly abandoned his advocacy under mysterious circumstances. Homestake, like the other golds, was an automatic buy; it rose to 56 within two months. But not until 1980, after bullion had gained fivefold, would the South Dakota miner challenge its 1974 top.

It has been argued that important sector divergence, as in the case of the oil stocks in early 1981, is an indicator of trouble ahead for the market as a whole. A reversal of fortune for auto shares, and particularly for General Motors, has often been a bearish bellwether. A sullen withdrawal from bullish leadership by any major group, even if panic is not involved, raises warning signals.

What should you do when your favorite, or a market favorite, takes a big hit? If the plunge comes because of scams, criminal activity, book-cooking, or other scandalous activity, look for a place to bail out. There is no return for such stocks—such as National Student Marketing, Four Seasons Nursing, and ZZZZ Best. Avoid the afterplay of manipulations. There will be no curtain calls.

Selling because of earnings shortages, dividend cuts, massive writedowns, and other discouraging fundamentals is usually overdone, but a dazzling rebound is unlikely, except in cases where the news had been "leaked" early on and was thus discounted. Really bad news often causes a "delayed opening," and a huge downgap. Such stocks may seduce bargain hunters, but beware: Bad news always multiplies. Thus, the 1980 news of a major DES (synthetic estrogen) suit against Squibb encouraged a two-day smash in the stock from 37 to 29, including a multipoint overnight plunge. Even though the company was A+ rated, with a dividend record dating to 1901, the shares slid further, to 24, ignoring a boiling bull market.

An Air-Pocket Virus in Software

An air-pocket virus has plagued software stocks for years, and it doesn't take a computer to figure out why: Earnings consistently, if irregularly, fall short of the Street's hyped expectations. At one time or another, almost every investor has fallen victim to the earnings hacker. Air pockets, however, are not a modern invention, being much older than either the computer or the air age.

An air pocket is just a modern name for an old malady, a solo collapse such as was suffered by the Twine Trust in 1893 and Hocking Coal in 1910. It was no bungee dive from their manipulated heights, for the stocks never rebounded. Solo air pockets are uncommonly dangerous and lack the dependable reflex seen after a broad-based panic.

In January 1993 the biotech firm Centocor unexpectedly announced that it would suspend clinical trials of an important drug. There had been an "excess mortality" among the trial patients, it seemed. The shares were axed by 62 percent within the day. Such merciless price declines, which always come on astounding volume, are like the sickening, invisible air pockets which turn airline passengers into white-knucklers.

No Quarter from
Institutional Sellers

The virus has become more common over the past 25 years, as institutional trading has mushroomed. When that herd turns against a stock, there is no quarter. And it doesn't require excess mortality to trigger the event. A modest change in earnings expectations can slash dozens of points off a high-priced issue.

A reasonable reflex action usually follows such stampedes, but lurking above the market are the sell orders of all those who were left behind plus those institutions anxious to sell on even a modest rally; they don't want to be seen with "yesterday's darling," now shunned by their peers. One can leaf through the chartbooks of the past several decades and locate hundreds of air pockets which were not recovered for years.

None illustrates the danger more vividly than the graph of gold in January 1980. On January 21, the London Fixing was at $850 an ounce. On the following day it was $737.50. Within a week, the figure was $560. The air-pocket gap below $850 was never filled.

Solo air pockets for stocks, like those for commodities, are ridden with danger, even for the most daring against-the-grain speculators. Ugly-looking gaps too often are followed by a substantial new low or worse, Gaposis II. When a stock turns uniquely weak in a market that is stable or rising, the weakness always persists longer than was originally anticipated. Only a drastic haircut, psychological and not fundamental, should encourage chance taking.

Investors need eyes in the back of their heads. There are not only bear markets and panic markets to contend with, but sector defections. Plus those solo dives, which hurt the most, because it seems that every stock is going up, except yours.

Selling the Family Jewels

Regardless of the state of the market, there are always some holders who never sell. "Can't afford to pay the taxes," is a common excuse. Or perhaps the shares really are the family jewels, and liquidation would involve a psychological trauma. "After all, grandfather founded the company, you know." It's easier to do nothing.

There is no perfect answer on how to handle long-term holdings during periods of market stress. What of the lucky investor who bought Xerox for around 42 (adjusted) in the 1966 collapse? By early 1970, the shares were priced at 116, despite a savage bear market. Ignore the trend and hold on? Or sell? There is no perfect answer. Xerox, although it was a premium growth stock, was badly hurt in the spring break. The result was something more than a trading turn, from 116 to 65. But believers were rewarded: The stock soared over 100 points by 1972, to 172.

Obviously, such shares should never leave the lockbox. But then, one of those unhappy "what ifs" occurred, and Xerox and 49 other Nifty Fifty stocks took a bath. Shares of the copier maker fell below 50. A long-term chart suggests that they should have been sold sometime in 1973, as a trendline was broken. But never mind, they would surely rise again.

Of course, they didn't, at least not by much. Xerox should never have been sold in its secular advance through the 1960s. But as with every stock, there finally did come a time to sell. Following a reflex rally from the 1974 disaster, the stock turned sideways; in 1981, when earnings of $7—almost six times the figure for 1966—were assured, the stock fell beneath the 1966 low. In 1982, earnings dropped and Xerox sold at 27.

Market Has-Beens

"Defense, defense" is on every investor's mind, but few give thought to the ultimate hazard: Sooner or later every stock becomes a market has-been, even though the company survives.

Remember your favorite stock of 20 or 30 years ago? Is it still no. 1? The aging process is slow, but inevitably market senility creeps up on every company. The changes may be disguised with a few face tucks, and a new product or two, but generally the process is irreversible.

The railroads, as we shall see, are a perfect sector example. But their sad departure from market power was long ago. There are plenty of modern industrial and mercantile examples in the likes of International Harvester, IBM, Johns-Manville, Sears, and Xerox.

Unlike most of the ailments which strike down investors, the has-been virus is slow-working. It doesn't destroy capital overnight or even in a few years. It won't break your wallet, but it may break your heart. The investor who stubbornly refuses to believe that the tide for a stock or industry has, indeed, turned will be seriously handicapped. We are not talking here of market revulsions against fads and fashions, such as double-knits, hand-held calculators, and "go-go" stocks, which often occur almost overnight.

Rather, we are concerned with the epochal reversals in the relative strength of traditional market leaders. U.S. Steel reached its all-time high in 1959, about 2900 Dow points ago. General Motors peaked in 1965. They have been market has-beens ever since. Good money has been made occasionally by trading these popular and well-known securities, for the companies have enjoyed many prosperous seasons. But a market which has gone from Dow 700 to Dow 3600 has been much more profitable for those who recognized along the way that market leadership had passed to other groups. The old guard was gone. Why fool around with a stock that hasn't made a new high for 20 or 30 years?

Looking for the Causes
of "Has Been"

The causes of dehabilitation are varied. There have been cases of management Alzheimer's, such as struck down Montgomery Ward after

World War II. Management had a flawed vision of the future and hoarded its cash for the depression which was surely coming. Meanwhile, Sears hustled out and built a lot of new stores. Ward would forever more be no. 2.

Often, someone built a better mousetrap, or perhaps a protective patent expired. Archaic labor practices and union intransigence helped do in others. Depression and hard times knocked others out of the box when, strapped for sales and capital, they lost all momentum. The 1930s killed the great automobile builders Pierce-Arrow and Auburn. The former company never found the funds in 1933 to put its new *Silver Arrow* on the assembly line, and went out of business. Only five hand-made models were ever constructed. Auburn, a $296 stock in 1931 after some bullish pranks, succumbed in 1937.

At other times, even the most powerful financial corporations saw their tide of industrial empire turned by events which they seemed barely to understand, as when the perception of quality deserted Detroit and leaped the oceans to the assembly lines of Germany and Japan. Occasionally, new inventions or better processes levered veterans aside.

It may seem discouraging, but every stock market listing eventually becomes a market has-been. Unfortunately, none of us can immediately recognize the symptoms. It is only when the stock begins to show severe relative weakness against the market that suspicions are aroused. Sometimes, a full market cycle passes before the divergence becomes obvious. Only rarely has a single, cataclysmic event, obvious to all, been the cause. More often, it is a parlay or even a trifacta of developing pressures that erases market leadership. Companies don't disappear from the financial manuals overnight, but are gradually weakened until forced out by some viable and relatively young upstart. Others continue a life of quiet desperation, dreaming of a comeback.

Decline of the Smokestack Axis

An investigation of the insidious dangers of investing in market has-beens can find no better place to start than along the smokestack axis, from Detroit to Pittsburgh. That heartbreak land has witnessed scores of leadership abdications in the past few decades.

U.S. Steel, formed in 1901 by J. P. Morgan as an amalgamation of 170 companies, was at that time the world's largest producer of iron and steel. Morgan's "trust of trusts" was a billion-dollar corporation that commanded a 60 percent share of the market. It was the crown jewel of Morgan's empire, and for decades it boasted the very strongest backing on the floor of the Exchange. However, that support dissolved while Eisenhower was still in the White House.

The Pittsburgh giant charted its all-time high at $108\frac{7}{8}$ in August 1959 (see Fig. 1-1), when office equipment and technology stocks such as IBM and Texas Instruments were beginning to seize market leadership from the heavy-industry veterans.

Cheap imports and the innovative mini-steel plants helped do in the steel giants. In 1982, the Pittsburgh veteran made a serious move to diversify and latched onto Marathon Oil and its fabulous West Texas production. Otherwise, the track record would be worse. In 1987, the best price for U.S. Steel was 59, compared with the 109 peak of 1959 (both before a 3:2 stock split).

Even today the historic steel company remains the largest steel works in the nation, and the world; it produces about 11 percent of the domestic output. But it has been a market has-been since 1959. From that year until 1974, it fell persistently, even though the Dow climbed from 678 to 1052. At the end of 1972, with the Dow at 1020, within a few points of its record high. U.S. Steel closed at 31, less than a third of its peak 13 years previously. With the exception of the period from 1974 to 1976, Big Steel has been a market laggard, not a leader. Steel's best relative performance of the past 35 years came in 1974, when the stock actually advanced despite a devastating bear market, and its strongest rally peaked in 1976 when the stock reached a high of 89, before adjustment.

Doubtlessly the seeds of below-average performance were sown long ago. Some say that it all started after World War II, when Japan and Germany were forced to replace their battered steel plants with modern mills, while America's industry lived mostly with dinosaurs of the past. But the cutting edge has been in steel substitutions, where strong new plastics and aluminum have elbowed into steel's dominant position on the auto assembly lines, as well as in other markets. Mini-mills and cheap foreign competition have brought deep hurts. It's a far cry from the early years of this century

No other stock has ever dominated activity on the New York Stock Exchange the way U.S. Steel did. Not only was it the largest American corporation in the first decades of this century, but it claimed the very strongest backing from institutions and banks. It was the single best barometer of the market. "How's Steel?" was the eternal question among traders.

A study of early volume records for the corporation shows Steel's amazing dominance. In nine years through the first two decades of

U.S. Steel: World's Largest Manufacturer of Steel

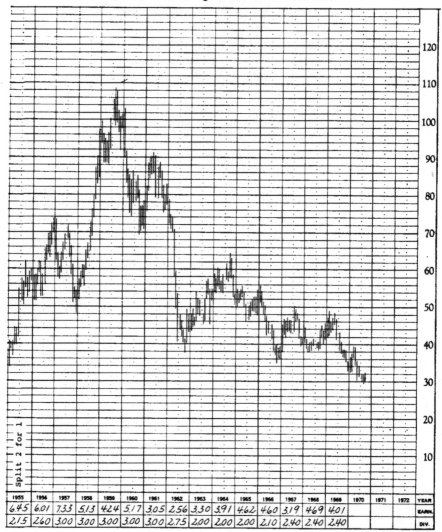

YEAR	1955	1956	1957	1958	1959	1960	1961	1962	1963	1964	1965	1966	1967	1968	1969	1970	1971	1972
EARN.	6.45	6.01	7.33	5.13	4.24	5.17	3.05	2.56	3.30	3.91	4.62	4.60	3.19	4.69	4.01			
DIV.	2.15	2.60	3.00	3.00	3.00	3.00	3.00	2.75	2.00	2.00	2.00	2.10	2.40	2.40	2.40			

Figure 1-1. U.S. Steel, the most famous corporation in America in the early decades of this century, became a market has-been in 1959. Its stock price peaked at $108\frac{7}{8}$ in August of that year; earnings were $4.25. (Both figures are unadjusted for subsequent stock splits.) (SOURCE: M. C. Horsey & Company, Salisbury, MD.)

this century, trading in U.S. Steel common amounted to at least 10 percent of total activity on the NYSE, a figure never approached by any other stock.

In four of those years, over 20 percent of Exchange trading was in Steel common shares. And there was also a solid investor interest in the $7 preferred. In two years, activity in the preferred exceeded that of the common shares. The enormous concentration of trading in Steel shares ended in the early 1920s, when a roaring bull market added a lot of new fancies to the speculative list. By 1929, Steel's volume amounted to only 2 percent of total activity.

Peak activity had come in 1917, when it commanded an unbelievable 26 percent slice of stock exchange trade. That was a wild year, what with Germany's U-boat attacks and America's declaration of war, so there was ample room for both bulls and bears. The Steel shares, 119 in January, fell to 99 in the submarine panic, but then climbed to 137 in May as the market boomed once again. Autumn price controls on steel products cooled the enthusiasm, and the Pittsburgh shares slumped to 80. The entire common capitalization, just over 5 million shares, turned over nine times as Steel's volume climbed to nearly 48 million.

Those were the old days. Since 1959, it has been an unending twilight zone for the market star of the early twentieth century. For a time in the 1980s, U.S. Steel could gloss over its problems with the help of Marathon's Yates Field crude. Now that the steel and oil operations are separate (USX-Steel and USX-Marathon), Pittsburgh must fight on without the cushion from oil.

General Motors: Searching
for Past Glories

Lyndon Baines Johnson was President when General Motors posted its all-time high. Presidents have come and gone and a half-dozen bull markets have churned past since General Motors reached 113¾ in October 1965. At the time, the Dow was well below 1000. In the roughly three decades since, the Dow has nearly quadrupled, but General Motors' best effort was 101 (unadjusted) shortly before the Kuwait war. In the raging bull days of 1987, its high was 94. General Motors has been searching 30 years for its past glories.

Obviously, the stock is a market has-been, even though the firm regularly boasts the highest sales of any American company, $132.5 billion in 1992. Still, investor hopes perennially surround the company. The contrarians argue that GM's shrinking market percentage will stabilize and that the giant sales base will then be translated into more consistent profits. Then market luster and leadership will surely return.

It's always possible, of course, but a succession of elixirs, including restructuring, new auto plants, new cars (the Saturn), exotic acquisitions (Hughes Electronics and EDS), new management, downsizing, and so forth, have not changed the has-been mathematics. At its early 1993 high, GM stock was only at par with its 1983 peak, when the Dow was 1285.

How did it happen? It began with the new reality that swept through Detroit, starting in about 1965. In the next five years, automotive product imports increased sixfold. Many of the imports were small, and price was a factor. But Detroit's reputation for quality had been sinking for years. There were too many clinkers and clunkers coming off the assembly lines. No one wanted a car made on Monday, reportedly a day of high absenteeism and other problems. Steering wheels sometimes fell off in showrooms. Ralph Nader raised a howl about safety.

There would be no relief. As the years wore on, new safety and pollution legislation were laid on the auto makers. A bit later, it would be airbags. The energy crisis brought mileage legislation from Washington, which encouraged small-car production. But by the time the industry geared up for the second-generation Pintos, the gasoline lines disappeared and the American public reneged on its lust for gas-savers. Recalls became epidemic, and auto imports continued to soar. Foreign passenger cars sales reached $60 billion in several different years.

In 1993, General Motors bit another bullet. Bowing to new accounting rules, it announced the largest yearly loss in corporate history. The $23 billion figure was ballooned by booking massive retiree health-care costs for the years ahead. Some thought it was the last bullet, for the shares climbed to their highest price in several years, the 1965 equivalent of nearly 100.

Figure 1-2 shows the all-time high for General Motors, made over a generation ago. Although it is the nation's largest industrial corporation, its stock remains a market has-been, far below the top of 113¾ (unadjusted) recorded in 1965. Its sales in that year were $21 billion, and earnings were $7.41 per share.

In recent years the company has lost market share, not only to imports but to its Detroit rivals, and its enormous sales, over $130 billion, have failed to spur the stock's indifferent market performance.

Today the tony parking lots hold a lot more Lexuses than Cadillacs, and even the lower-priced Japanese cars have the reputation for supe-

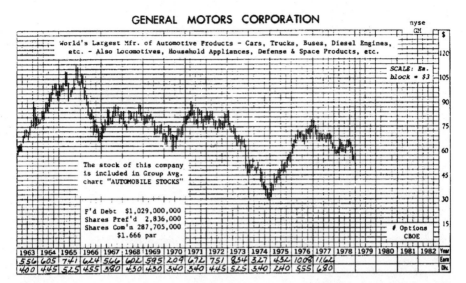

Figure 1-2. General Motors, the world's largest auto manufacturer, recorded its all-time market peak nearly 30 years ago. (SOURCE: M. C. Horsey & Company, Salisbury, MD.)

rior quality. Maybe Detroit's only hope is for a federal indictment on foreign auto dumping. But if so, say the experts, look for more sticker shock on American cars.

Rails Surrender Market Leadership to Industrials

Fifty years before U.S. Steel and General Motors surrendered their market leadership, the railroads packed it in. Typically, the surrender to new market forces was neither immediately severe nor immediately recognized.

The Dow Rail Average (now the Transports) is the senior market average, much older than the Industrials. It was the more important of the two until about 1910, for up to that point the railroads were the largest industry in the nation. As late as 1911, railroad securities predominated at the Exchange, aggregating over 55 percent of the total listings, although that was well down from the figure of 10 years previously. Until 1915, the Rail average was above that of the Industrials.

Market leadership, however, was slowly being surrendered, and in the war boom of 1915 the industrial group became the unchallenged speculative leader. But old ways die hard, and even in the late 1940s many elderly investors demanded a daily quotation rundown on the rail stocks.

It was not the epidemic of receiverships in 1893 that made market has-beens out of the rail securities; the rails' greatest-ever period of prosperity followed that depression. Rather, it was the iron grip of the state railroad commissions and the Interstate Commerce Commission (ICC) that shunted investor interest in other directions, beginning in the early 1900s: Overregulation threatened profits. Additionally, there was a sudden cornucopia of new industrial securities, available because of the trustification mania, which lasted from 1898 until early 1903.

Existing concerns were bought at extravagant prices, consolidated into giant trusts, and loaded on the public. It was the great opportunity for promoters, and they were not slow to take advantage. Competition for the established rail securities eroded in the face of massive offerings of exciting amalgamations in steel, steamships, farm equipment, and locomotives, along with a large amount of coattail trash.

All the new consolidations were heavily watered, but they were seductive because they were priced at "reasonable," two-digit levels. The average investor was hard put to buy even 100 shares of the leading rail stocks, which were much higher priced.

Modern corporate policy is to keep the firm's stock price at a modest level by means of stock splits and stock dividends. A lower price tends to broaden the shareholder base and creates a loyal consumer cadre. A century ago, there was considerable corporate pride in high-priced stock. The average high price for 35 leading rails in 1891 was 73; there were 11 issues over 100 but only four priced below 20.

At the beginning of this century the great railroad names were mostly at 100 or higher. The list included the Central of Jersey, the Chicago, Burlington & Quincy, the Chicago, Milwaukee & St. Paul, the Chicago & Northwestern, the Chicago, Rock Island, and the Chicago & Omaha. That's only through the "C's," but it does show that Chicago was a popular terminal for a lot of important rail stocks. The New York, New Haven was a $200 number, while the New York Central entered the new century at 125.

The long-term strength of the railroads ended in 1906, climaxed by the speculative Harriman boom. The Dow Rail Average, at its 1909 peak, would fail to reach the 1906 top and would fail again in the bull markets of 1916 and 1919. The 1906 transport peak would not be exceeded until 1927!

In 1914, the has-been maturity of the American rail era became more evident when many long-term investment favorites, including the Baltimore & Ohio, the New York Central, and the Illinois Central, fell below the levels of 1907 and 1901, while the Industrials held substantially above those earlier troughs. More indicative was the fact that in 1915, for the first time, the Dow Railroad Average fell below the level of the Industrials. During the previous 20 years, the Industrials had typically been at about two-thirds of the Rails, though in 1902 and 1903 it had slumped to a 50 percent discount. Continuing the silent kill, the Rails in 1921 fell to their lowest level since 1898.

The worst was yet to come. The automobile would do in the viability of the railroads, causing far more damage than stodgy and sometimes crooked management, featherbedding unions, and overregulation and overcompetition. Passenger traffic peaked in 1920. By the early 1920s, the highway lobby had the states up to their ears in highway bond issues. The new roadways sucked both passenger and freight traffic from the heavily taxed rail systems. Airline competition lay not too far ahead.

On January 1, 1929, the Rail average was only 10 percent higher than it had been in January 1906. The subsequent depression collapse would not be recovered by that average for 35 years. Important market milestones celebrating new highs—1906, 1927, 1964—were separated by decades.

Has-Beens Can Make Comebacks

There were brilliant individual exceptions, to be sure. The long-haul western roads and the heavy-traffic coal routes provided solid success stories. The Northern Pacific (NP) steamed from 5 to 55 between 1949 and 1959. That run was not all railroading, however, for oil discoveries in the Williston Basin focused attention on the line's vast land holdings. The move was thought so uncharacteristic of the rails that Dow Jones arbitrarily sidetracked the NP right out of the Rail average, of which it had been a member since the 1880s.

Even has-beens make occasional extraordinary, if generally temporary, comebacks, as U.S. Steel did in the mid-1970s. The largest annual railroad advance in history occurred in 1958, when the average gained 63 percent. The storied St. Paul and the North Western both tripled during the year.

The Aluminum Co. of America (Alcoa), adored by the early growth cult of the 1950s, flew to 134 in 1957, when it was valued at about 38X earnings, an unconscionable figure at the time. But Alcoa turned into a rare immediate has-been, and the stock did not match its 1957 peak again until the 1980s, when, sufficiently revived and rested, it made a run from 22 to 80, the latter high occurring in 1990.

Earlier, General Motors had nearly foundered in its 1920–1922 slump. In 1920, aided by an artificial corner in the stock, the shares sold at 42. By 1922 they were near 8. In the meantime, well-regarded Studebaker had climbed far above its 1920 peak, but by then the erratic management of General Motors' founder, Billy Durant, had been replaced by the brilliance of Alfred Sloan, and the future looked less uncertain. Still, the shares needed help, and in an uncharacteristic move for a class stock, a 1:4 reverse split was used to jack the share price higher. By 1926, GM had topped its 1920 high. The stock would be a leading driver in the last years of the bull market, despite having spent about four years on the suspect list for has-beens.

Famous Has-Beens from the Dow Jones Industrial Average

Alcoa, General Motors, and U.S. Steel are not the only Dow Average members that have stressed out as market leaders since the 1950s. International Harvester, the giant farm-equipment trust put together by J. P. Morgan in 1902, peaked in 1966 and now struggles under the Navistar banner. Johns-Manville topped out in 1971. International Business Machines waited until 1987, when it peaked at 176. Six years later, it traded at near 50.

These stocks have all been, at one time or another, among the great market leaders in the years since World War II. What of earlier giants that were important enough to be included in the very select DJIA? There were only 12 Industrial "blue chips" until 1916; then the roster was expanded to 20 and, finally, in 1928 to 30 names. It has always been a narrow list, by presumption made up of the important and representative leaders of American industry. Many, such as American Tobacco, survived for decades. Now stricken from the average by the antismoking campaigns, American Brands, which grosses over $20 billion a year in cigarettes, snack foods, liquor, and so forth, remains a market leader despite its exile from grace. But who remembers American Cotton Oil, Laclede Gas, the Pacific Mail, American Spirits, or the locomotive stocks, American and Baldwin, all one-time Dow stocks?

When the average was expanded and revised in 1928, Mack Truck, Victor Talking Machine, and Wright Aeronautical were important enough to be included among the elite 30. Hudson Motors, Nash, and

Studebaker, all historic auto names, were included in the Dow at one time, as were such wildly diverse companies as Central Leather and Remington Typewriter.

Radio Corporation of America (RCA) joined the Dow 30 in October 1928 and became a has-been exactly one year later, one of the speediest declines ever. In 1932, another soon-to-be has-been, Nash Motors, made it into the listing for the second time and replaced RCA.

All of the companies named were market leaders at one time or another, and many of them still survive in one form or another. But for one reason or another, they all lost their leadership qualities and became market has-beens.

The Devil is always at the gate.

2
Our Mysterious Panics

Nowhere is it written that stock market prices have to go up. And when prices go down, there is always the chance that a market "correction" will turn into a bear episode—or a panic. The latter crisis remains the least predictable, least understood, and most mysterious of all the events that affect Wall Street's life.

Every investor yearns for a return to the equity values of the last bear market—and a satchel full of cash. Panic prices carry no such lure, but panics are an inevitable if irrational part of the market experience, and participants should learn how to respond, for the record of reflex profits following panic is nearly perfect. We do know that panics strike with lightning speed and that their violence can occur in any phase of the business or market cycle. Their swift passages are also the best remembered of all financial legends; the famed Northern Pacific panic of 1901 lasted barely two days. They cannot be eliminated by the Securities and Exchange Commission, the Federal Reserve Board, or the New York Stock Exchange, for they are a natural part of the market's life.

Panics inevitably appear at the most awkward moment, striking swiftly on the heels of a shattering accident or incident, such as President Eisenhower's heart attack in 1955. Occasionally they implode, as in 1929. Blindsided by surprise, the individual investor finds the easiest escape is a surrender to fear.

Quality provides no insurance against loss. And since the stock market has no conscience, panic treats the possessions of widows and orphans as harshly as those of plungers. In 1987, for instance, Borden, Inc., A+ rated and with a dividend record dating back to the turn of the century, fell from 54 to 30 within three days. There were no rumors that "Elsie" and friends were about to go Chapter XI. The stock's earnings, having doubled in the previous six years, were expected to rise again sharply in 1988—which they did.

Such abrupt declines, fearsome as they are, provide reliable buying opportunities, for they are quickly done and the bad news is immediately discounted. The patient suddenly revives and last rites are canceled. In the case of Borden, crushed from 54 to 30 within a few days, the stock rallied to 49 within two weeks and traded as high as 57 in the spring of 1988. Automatic profits are the rule for those investors who sense that the financial storm is passing.

Identifiable panic conditions in the market may last only an hour, spurred by, say, a canard about a Presidential heart attack, but here we are concerned mostly with instances where, by arbitrary selection, the leading stock market average fell by 10 percent or more within about 20 trading days or less. Often the violence was over within a week. Few of these collapses carry historical significance off the Street, though high drama and intensity may rank them among the classic declines.

The most spectacular panics convert what appears to be a normal correction into a frightful fall, as happened in 1929. But nearly 30 bull market panics can be identified where a brief disaster was quickly overcome, freeing the market to race to new high ground.

Panic has often accelerated bear episodes, most frequently in the 1930s, and has been a frequent companion of cyclic lows. While the biggest bear market in history ended in 1932 with barely a whimper— as did the war sequences of 1917 and 1942—the popular conception is of a high-volume, spike low. The panic action of May 1970 affords a dramatic example. And *Sputnik I*, in October 1957, provided a traditional climax following the extended "triple top" of 1956–1957, illustrated in Fig. 2-1. Such rare reversal formations show three peaks, widely separated, at about the same level. Regardless of volume anomalies, however, bear market and panic climaxes are much easier to identify than topping action.

The Search for Meaning

The treachery of panic lies in psychological shock and a sudden reversal of expectations. Financial philosophers and economists have long searched for a meaning for panic. A sensational collapse attracts microscopic study. Past panics are recalled and tabulated, for a centu-

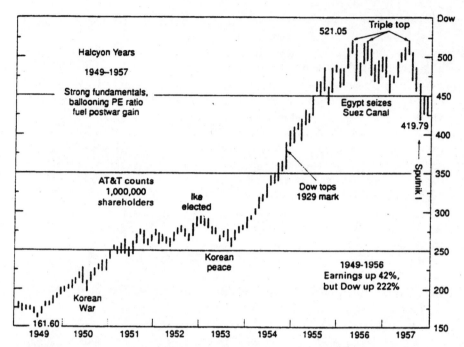

Figure 2-1. The Dow Industrials' second longest bull market ended in the complex triple top of 1956–1957. Fifteen months separated the first and last efforts to overcome the Dow 521 level. The lengthy advance had previously been interrupted by an unimpressive Dow theory correction in 1953 and a pair of panics, caused by the Korean War (1950) and Eisenhower's heart attack (1955). In each instance, the Dow recovered to a record high within a few months. When the shock of *Sputnik I* climaxed the sharp decline of 1957, the Dow had lost only 28 percent of its stubborn postwar gains. [SOURCE: John Dennis Brown, *101 Years on Wall Street* (Prentice-Hall, Englewood Cliffs, NJ, 1991), p. 134.]

ry of detailed statistics makes comparisons easy. Unlike the fears sparked by a listing ship or a loud shout in a crowded theater, the measure of stress in a financial storm can be calculated instantly. Still, the 1987 meltdown, an implosion similar to 1929, remains an enigma despite a lengthening shelf of scholarly toil. Computer wizardry has yet to solve any of the riddles of panic.

Panic is akin to a violent act of nature, which may be caused by a mysterious reaction to global temperatures, winds, barometer readings, ocean currents, and so forth. On Wall Street, an uneven mixture of interest rates, politics, war threats, White House and economic news, currency rates, internal technicals, and corporate fundamentals—to name a few ingredients—mysteriously explodes into a financial tornado.

In theory, a model for stock market panic might be constructed, but how would one input the Street's psychology and the overnight rollover from greed to despair? Explanations and rationales for panic abound. Meanings are often lacking.

Why do panics occur? Panics often follow portents of ruin. War threatens. Sensational but poorly understood economic or political events challenge confidence. A political leader dies or is assassinated. Gold movements create currency chaos. A commodity corner collapses. The resulting price change may be no more than 10 or 12 percent for the leading average, but the surprise, drama, and intensity of decline causes investors to freeze. Individual stocks outperform the Dow to the downside, and reason is overwhelmed by fear of the unknown.

When do panics occur? Frequently, if irregularly and unexpectedly. A darkening economic sky usually foreshadows a bear market, but a panic is a psychological phenomenon, not an economic one. Panics occur in every phase of the market and business cycle, often striking under conditions of high optimism and strength, but shocking crises can also appear after months or even years of decline. In the spring of 1932, after 30 months of bearish momentum, the market was once again battered. Macy's, 255 at the 1929 peak, plunged from 57 to 36 in March. By June the retailer was at 17.

What is the significance of panic? Panics write financial history for their victims, but it is often difficult to find long-term significance in them. The nightmare of 1987 is remembered chiefly for its fright. There was no recession, and no banks failed.

Infrequently, panic signals the end of an era, but such realizations are always tardy. The wholesale trustification of American industry came to an end in 1903, in the episode called the Rich Man's Panic, but contemporary viewers saw it only as a lull, caused by all the "undigested securities" lying in the vaults of investment bankers and their insurance company allies.

Historical significance makes no difference to the sacrificial lambs; widows and orphans suffer right along with speculators. No crisis of the past century had more impact than that of the autumn of 1907, although that event was not the most devastating market blow of the year.

The Legacy of 1907

The convulsions of 1907 spurred New York State to the first legislative investigation into the fabric of panic. Washington, not to be outdone, mounted its own highly publicized committee hearings into the "money lords." And from the ashes of 1907, the Federal Reserve System was born. At the White House, President Theodore Roosevelt was seen to compromise his antitrust rhetoric in a trade-off to halt the financial crisis.

Certainly, no other year experienced the variety of crises seen in 1907. Within nine months, the market was rocked by three panics, all different in both cause and effect.

The year is best remembered for the Panic of 1907, but that autumn episode did less damage to stock prices than the earlier attacks. The year's menu of trouble was the broadest of the century. It included a brutal bear raid in March, a worldwide credit crunch, two failed copper corners—in the actuals and in the shares of a pool stock—and a highwayman's fine of $29 million levied upon Standard Oil (Indiana). In those days, $29 million was serious money.

The year also saw a mounting gold crisis, multiple bank suspensions, a currency famine, and the hijacking of one of the nation's largest steel companies by U.S. Steel, despite the antitrust rhetoric from the White House.

Before it was all over, J. P. Morgan would be both damned and hailed. But he emerged as the lender of last resort as he rallied banking pools time after time to slow and then halt the financial bleeding. Morgan's leadership calmed the bank runs, saved New York City's credit, knocked 90 percent call money in the head, and sandbagged the levees around the NYSE, which were being attacked from two sides— by market panic and by an epidemic of failing banks.

The Street's high drama ended in mid-November. By that time there had been secret trips to Washington, gold shipments from London, blocks-long lines of desperate depositors, a premium on currency, and heavy use of Clearing House certificates. Secretary of the Treasury George Cortelyou had been intimately involved, racing by late train to New York and transferring sizable federal deposits to the leading banks.

The March Collapse

The year had started badly. In early January, Standard Oil was indicted for coercing rate rebates. On January 27, at a Gridiron Dinner in Washington which was attended by Morgan, President Roosevelt castigated the "money barons" for blocking his reforms. A worldwide shortage of capital, born in the Boer and Russian-Japanese wars, was jacking interest rates higher. Four percent railroad money was gone, and refinancing could be done only with short-term notes on which the yields ranged from 5 to 7 percent.

Stocks eased off the market peak, made on January 7, but volume was light following the heat excited by Roosevelt's comments. On the last day of February, the Dow closed at 90.54, less than four points below the previous year-end level. What lay ahead included the worst intramonth decline between 1893 and 1929. The average lost nearly 17 percent by March 25, when a Morgan-backed pool rallied the market and cut the loss to 11.5 percent by month-end.

The price collapse had been helped along by several bear pools. Daniel Reid of the Rock Island line and the veteran speculator, Judge William H. Moore of Chicago, were members of one clique operating mostly against Edward H. Harriman's rails, which included the Union Pacific, Southern Pacific, and Illinois Central, among others. According to *The New York Times*, "a powerful group of speculators in control of almost limitless means...had planned a comprehensive campaign against prices."

The campaign won an enormous victory for the bears. The Union Pacific, 195 the previous autumn, was hammered down from 172 to 120 in the first 14 days of March. Steam rails were not the only victims. Tammany Hall's pet, the Brooklyn Rapid Transit subway (BRT), fell from 71 to 45 in the same period. Before the month was out, favorites of Morgan, Hill, and the Guggenheims would also be bloodied. Steel dropped from 45 to 32, and the Great Northern from 163 to 126; the latter had been 348 in the previous year. American Smelting, controlled by the Guggenheim brothers, was melted down from 140 to 104.

Accusing fingers pointed in many directions. William Jennings Bryan took a populist stand and blamed the railroads, despite their horrific market losses. Andrew Carnegie attacked "Wall Street gamblers." A bit later, Lord Rothschild said that London holders had been induced to sell through fear of President Roosevelt.

The triggering event for the rather mysterious collapse at mid-March was disappointment over a proposed conference between rail chiefs and the President. J. P. Morgan, bound for Europe, had visited the White House on Monday, March 11, and suggested the possibility of Roosevelt's consulting with railroad leaders. It was thought that the conference was agreed to, but no official invitation was forthcoming. The cold shoulder convinced investors that the railroads were in trouble not only at the state level but in Washington as well.

Mass liquidation hit the rails—still the leading business in the country—and then spread across the board; the Dow was cut by nearly 12 percent in the two-day period ending March 14. Frightening rumors, a handmaiden of every panic, were floated. Harriman, it was said, had sold Morgan's firm 200,000 shares of Union Pacific at 110, ten points under the market on the trade date.

Still, there were no brokerage failures, as there had been after a smaller decline in 1903 and when a Morgan-sponsored banking pool came to the aid of the market. Late in the month, it was found that the heavy liquidation was gone, although new lows were scratched out by both Dow averages.

The March collapse was classic in its intensity, much worse than the more famous fall crisis. In the autumn slump, the worst one-day damage suffered by the Dow was a loss of less than 3 percent. On March 14, the Industrials were crushed, losing over 8 percent—the biggest loss between 1899 and 1929. In the October–November period, only three days had volume of over 1 million shares. In March there had been 15, including three when activity ran over 2 million shares.

So if March was so bad, why does it get no respect? First, it lacked the drama of the autumn—the bank failures, the Morgan presence, the currency shortage, the failed copper corners, the all-night meeting of the city's most important financiers.

Second, it missed the staging of autumn's commercial crisis, played out in a nationwide arena of unemployment (Bethlehem Steel had summarily laid off 7000 workers), bankruptcies (including Westinghouse), and a currency famine. To make matters worse, harvests were late and aggravated by a shortfall of financing at the country elevator level; the stricken money-center banks could not remit country-bank funds. In Portland, Oregon, "wheat money" was issued to provide liquidity in the city. A bushel of grain stored in a bonded and insured warehouse was valued at $1.50, and one "wheat" dollar could be issued against it.

Rail Speculations: The Beginnings of Trouble

March's market disaster was restricted to the financial centers, and targeted the Harriman railroad empire. Interest rates were rising, financing was tight, and the greedy rail speculators of late 1906 were trapped. The roots of trouble lay in the "Harriman market." The Union Pacific chief had taken the riches received in the splitup of the Northern Securities holding company and plunged them into other rail securities. Starting in August 1906, about $129 million was spent on the likes of the Baltimore & Ohio (B&O), Illinois Central, Atchison, St. Paul, North Western, New York Central, and St. Joe, creating a bullish frenzy.

Dividends were raised by the Union Pacific, the Southern Pacific, the Atchison, and, a bit later, the Pennsylvania, sometimes in a secret fashion which allowed insiders to reap immoderate profits. The increase in the Union Pacific dividend, from $6 to $10, and Harriman's massive buying convinced the public of better things to come. The Union Pacific, trading at 155 in early August was predicted to rise easily to 200. The Southern Pacific, at 65, was expected to go to 100. On August 20, volume at the Exchange rushed to nearly 3 million shares, a figure which would not be matched for 10 years. Margin trading was heavy. The mania would prove costly, and its fallout would be long. The Dow Rails high of 1906 would not be surpassed for 21 years.

Acute market distress disappeared after the March attack, but the rally was poor. The reflex ended in May, with the Industrials regaining less than half of the winter loss. The world's money malaise would not go away. Gold emigrated, particularly to France. Europe's central banks hiked their discount rates. In London, where British consols (perpetual bonds) had sold in March at their lowest level since 1876, the rally in the bonds was not worth a farthing.

Standard Oil Fined $29 Million

At the end of July, the Dow was barely two points higher than its worst spring price. If the market couldn't go up, it was time to fall again. On August 3, the crusty Judge Kenesaw Mountain Landis, who would later become commissioner of baseball and bench Babe Ruth, shocked business by levying a monster fine on Standard Oil, found guilty of receiving rebates on oil shipments from Whiting, Indiana, to East St. Louis. The levy: $20,000 each on 1492 counts (or tankcars). The draconian judgment, over $29 million, would be overturned a year later, but alarmed investors pushed the Dow down by 11 percent.

Standard Oil fell to its lowest price in 10 years. Pressure was again brought against the Harriman favorites, and there were rumors that American Sugar would face a fine only slightly less than the Standard Oil figure. In London, it was reported that John W. Gates was "bearing" consols, and the Bank of England unexpectedly raised its discount rate on August 16. But the "Roosevelt slump," the second of the year, ended within three weeks.

Shortage Fears Spur
Copper Mania

Aside from the Harriman rails, the most intense speculative mania of the previous two years had attached itself to copper and the copper shares. The employment of electric current for transportation, illumination, distribution of power, and the transmission of words and speech was seen as wondrous. "The rapidity of growth in these [electric] fields is probably unsurpassed in any other branch of human activity," was the giddy praise of a Census Bureau bulletin. Stock manipulations in the mining shares found eager disciples. Some talked of a worldwide shortage of copper.

United Metals, a Perth Amboy, New Jersey, metals refiner and sales agent allied with Standard Oil interests, had initiated in March a prodigious copper-hoarding effect, acquiring over 140 million pounds by September. But the corner failed, and the asking price of 25 cents suddenly fell to about 13 cents. Copper shares, with a single exception, lost their bullish fascination. A congressional committee would later determine that the purpose of the corner had been to unload mining shares under the umbrella of "25 cent" copper.

The one "copper" stock that could ignore the collapse in the price of actuals was United Copper, formed by F. Augustus Heinze and Charles W. Morse to mine the speculative ores of Wall Street. It was a pool stock, incorporated for manipulation and not mining, and its October collapse would lead directly to the third panic of the year. Both Heinze and Morse had powerful enemies on the Street. Heinze, whose only asset at one time was "a hundred lawsuits" against the most powerful mining companies in Montana, liberally rewarded friendly judges and legislators in that state, and in 1906 the Rockefeller-controlled Amalgamated Copper (which owned most of Anaconda) surrendered the court fight and bought off his claims for a figure estimated at $15 million. Morse had earlier promoted the "Ice Trust" and controlled large sectors of coastal shipping. The success of his American Ice company was partly due to Tammany graft, which gave him monopoly privileges on New York City docks. Later it was determined that large stockholders in the ice company included the notorious Tammany boss Richard Croker and New York Mayor Robert Van Wyck.

Another Failed Corner

Heinze and Morse subsequently gained control of several banks, such a relationship being an important aid to their "investment" activities in the likes of United Copper. Despite an eroding market, its shares crept higher in October. On Monday, October 14, the stock astounded the Street by leaping from 30 to 60. Heinze and Morse plotted further pain for the shorts and demanded delivery of all shares due them, including those from some of their false allies. But the price doubling of the previous day attracted stock from every vault in the country. Like many another desperate manipulation, the pool had only "almost cornered" the market. In the last few minutes of trading on Tuesday, the stock cascaded from 60 to 36. On Wednesday, it plunged to 10.

On the surface, it was just another failed speculation, and not an important one at that. But enemies of the two men encouraged the rumor that their banks might be embarrassed. Anxious depositors lined the street early the next day, and Heinze's Mercantile Bank applied to the Clearing House for help. On Friday the Clearing House forced Heinze to resign in return for banking aid.

On Saturday, Morse was similarly excised from his banks and trusts. The nouveau trust banks were disliked by the establishment because of their unfair competition. The trusts had minuscule cash reserve requirements and were able to lure depositors because of their ability to pay high deposit rates. Such freedom from regulation encouraged promotional ownerships and adventuresome lending practices. Few trusts belonged to the Clearing House.

A Worsening Panic

On Monday, Morgan's National Bank of Commerce announced that it would no longer act as clearing agent for the Knickerbocker Trust. Fifteen million dollars were promised to shore up the beleaguered Trust, but the credits were betrayed and on Tuesday Wall Street banks withdrew millions before the man on the street realized that the rules had changed. The Knickerbocker, stripped of cash, closed its doors shortly after noon, its failure being the largest in history.

The Wall Street Journal observed that October 22 was the worst day of panic since 1884, a statement which mirrored the banking problems rather than the situation in stocks. Exchange volume on the 22nd was the largest of the autumn crisis but totaled only 1.36 million shares, and the Dow's loss of less than 3 percent was small compared with the 8 percent decline of March 14.

But runs spread to every bank in the city. It took an emergency cash transfusion on Wednesday afternoon to keep the doors open at the Trust Company of America, and on Thursday the Lincoln Trust required an immediate advance of $1 million. "Slow pay" was the order of the day at the wickets, and cashiers took extraordinary care and time in counting out depositors' funds.

At the NYSE, call money went to 100 percent and then to 125 bid with no offers, and the desperate Exchange was on the verge of an unscheduled closing; brokers could not meet their stock clearing commitments or pay monies due clients. But Morgan, the National City Bank, and First National Bank helped round up $23.5 million and then another $10 million later in the day, saving scores of brokers from bankruptcy. Secretary of the Treasury Cortelyou deposited $35 million in the New York banks; it was to be reloaned to the trust companies, as they were not eligible for direct federal deposits.

On Saturday, the Clearing House tardily announced that it would again issue Clearing House certificates. Stock traders tried to stop the bleeding. Westinghouse had fallen from 103 to 35 within two days upon news of its receivership, and the Pittsburgh Stock Exchange had suspended activity. Morse's Chicago ice company had melted down from 52 to 26 in a single day.

At the Clearing House, members rushed to exchange their frozen collateral for certificates in order to reduce their clearing balances. On Monday, a new loan supplicant, New York Mayor George McClellan, appeared hat in hand at Morgan's home. The city needed $30 million for current obligations, including salaries. Municipal default seemed certain by the weekend without new funds.

Morgan was up to the task, but Tammany Hall was reined in as part of the deal. A special committee would be appointed to eyeball the city's accounts and disbursements. On Tuesday, the banks bought $30 million in city bonds, but the municipal paper was then turned over to the Clearing House in return for an equal amount of certificates, which were credited to the city's accounts at the First National and National City Banks.

Fading the Panic: Odd-Lotters Buy Heavily

In the meantime, anxious depositors had again queued up at the Trust Company of America and the Lincoln Trust, among others. Many had been in line all night. Lockbox rentals soared, as those lucky enough to have been early in line cached their currency, which continued to command a premium paid by cashier's check. Shares mostly held their own in the last week of October, steadied by heavy odd-lot buying, a typical phenomenon of panic. Substantial under-the-mattress funds had been found, for *The New York Times* reported on November 1 that odd-lot purchases in the previous 10 days had totaled 2 million shares, equivalent to over 30 percent of the reported volume.

Such odd-lot demand seems unbelievable today, but even at 1907's panic levels, average prices were much higher than in the 1990s.

Standard Oil was near 400, and Calumet & Hecla, having fallen from 1000, still cost $53,500 for 100 shares.

Bank depositors were more chary than the odd-lotters. Runs continued, as did the currency famine. The improvised solution was to call again for help from J. P. Morgan, who had become the financial czar of the city. On November 2, he summoned leading bank executives for a Saturday night meeting at his mansion. Gathered in the imperial library at his home on Madison at 36th were the trust company chiefs, so far notably uncooperative in the crisis, and the heads of the major institutions. Needed was about $25 million to fill up the depleted vaults and restore confidence. Morgan was determined that the trust companies should at last come to the aid of their own.

Also needed was an answer to the vexing problem of Tennessee Coal & Iron, whose collateralized shares were a loose cannon threatening yet another liquidity crisis. A pool organized by John W. Gates had swept up the floating supply of stock with the intent of selling the ore-rich firm to Morgan and his U.S. Steel company. There was a nominal, "pegged" market at 130, but there was also a huge margin loan against the stock at the firm of Moore & Schley, Schley being a member of the Gates pool. The firm's broker loans, about to fall due, totaled about $25 million, collateralized by slumping stock values including 157,700 shares of the Tennessee stock, which probably could not be sold for more than 90 under prevailing conditions. The lending institutions, including the Trust Company of America, Moore & Schley, and the entire financial establishment, were in extreme peril.

The Clearing House bankers and friends gathered in the East Room while the captive trust heads were herded into the treasure-filled library. Morgan and a clutch of his Cuban Santa Clara cigars retired to the sidelines. His was a field marshall's role—to receive, evaluate, and rule on suggested defenses planned by a brilliant staff. By 5 a.m. the trust companies, under duress, had agreed to a $25 million loan to aid their brethen.

Sacrificing "Bet a Million" Gates

In the East Room, a preliminary plan had been worked out which would also require $25 million—but not in cash. Morgan would encourage the U.S. Steel company to take up the shares of Tennessee stock with an issue of its own 5 percent gold bonds; the banks would be delighted with such an upgrading of collateral. By Sunday night, the proposal begged only one question: antitrust.

That evening, a special train rushed Judge Elbert Gary, president of the steel company, and Henry Frick, Andrew Carnegie's former partner and a director, to Washington, where a breakfast meeting was scheduled with President Roosevelt. It was apparently represented to the President that the relief of the Tennessee stock was the only means of halting the financial crisis. In any event, Roosevelt was seen to waive his populist principles in exchange for a lender of last resort, and the good news reached the Exchange minutes before the opening bell.

Morgan's coup for the steel company was seen by some as blackmail; it was most certainly piratical. It gave him a double satisfaction, for the takeover enriched Steel at gunpoint pricing and sacrificed the noisome John W. Gates's thin margin position in the Tennessee stock. Gates, a major Street player for the previous decade, has been called the greatest gambler of the period and was known as "Bet a Million" Gates. He didn't die broke, but retreated to Port Arthur, Texas, terminus of the Kansas City Southern, of which he was a director. He was also a director of The Texas Company, which had a refinery in that city.

The weeks of strain and anxiety were nearly over, though the Dow would suffer a bit more, falling to a low of 53.00 on November 15. But the average then reversed and closed higher for the month, by which time the panic was ended and the circulation of certificates immensely reduced.

That late-autumn period in 1907 has often been called the most severe financial crisis in the nation's history. But the impact on the stock market was much less severe than that of March.

Central Banking Hastened

It was the stock market convulsions of autumn, however, that moved financial history. For the first time, a New York State legislative investigation was launched into the affairs of Wall Street. Governor Charles Evans Hughes, later a Supreme Court justice, appointed a committee in late 1908 to investigate the affairs of the Street. The committee reported in June 1909 without having heard any seriously damaging testimony.

The most far-reaching result was linked to the establishment of the Federal Reserve System, finally legislated in 1913. From the privatized resolution of the problem of 1907 would arise a central banking system as the nation's lender of last resort.

Morgan, who was 70, was tired of standing always at the gates, and his influence helped pass the Aldrich-Vreeland bill in 1908. It provided for more flexibility in the issuance of national bank currency. The

National Monetary Commission was authorized to study the nation's banking system and recommend needed changes. Step by step, the road led to the Federal Reserve System, with some political stops along the way.

Congressman Charles A. Lindbergh of Minnesota would father a resolution (and also the aviator) to investigate the great powers of finance. It established what was called the Pujo "money trust" committee, named after its head, Arsène Pujo, the Louisiana senator. The Reserve bill finally passed in 1913 and the Board's organization began in August 1914, just in time to assist with the next financial crisis, at the beginning of World War I.

Morgan's role in halting the 1907 route was generally admired, though Senator Robert M. La Follette of Wisconsin mouthed a populist myth that the panic had been caused by financiers who had "deliberately brought on the late panic, to serve their own ends." If La Follette was correct, the immediate results were distressing. In December 1907, Morgan's partnership account was debited almost $6.2 million as his share of the firm's losses for the year, according to a Morgan historian. A significant additional loss was carried forward.*

The Great Train Wrecks of 1893

While its end results were not as far-reaching financially as those of 1907, the commercial crisis of July 1893 forced harsh changes on the railroads and helped lead the nation's largest industry into its greatest period of prosperity. Few other crises, besides those of 1907, have ultimately worked such benefit.

The trigger for the rails' problems came in the business collapse of midsummer 1893. Treasury gold reserves had fallen to their lowest level ever as Europe liquidated her American credits, fearful of the silver dollar's falling value. The proceeds were converted to gold and called home. Almost every ocean liner that left New York was carrying American bullion.

A credit squeeze was on. Hoarding widened and currency sold at a premium. The New York Clearing House opted for the issuance of loan certificates. On June 26, the Indian mints were closed to the free coinage of silver, and the metal plunged from 82 to 62 cents an ounce

---

*Vincent P. Carosso, with Rose C. Carosso, *The Morgans, Private International Bankers, 1854–1913* (Harvard University Press, Cambridge, MA, and London, 1988), pp. 614–615.

within days. President Grover Cleveland called for a special session of Congress to repeal the Silver Act. The West's silver-mining industry was doomed.

Aspen Turns into Ghost Town

Commercial depression swept the country. Credit was frozen. Railroad, mining, and factory unemployment soared. Rail loadings slowed to a trickle. In Aspen, Colorado, the country's largest silver-mining center, prosperity expired, never to return to the likes of the Smuggler and Mollie Gibson mines. Mining employment there, over 2500 barely a year earlier, fell to about 150, mostly in caretaker jobs for closed operations.

July's collapse of the Dow 20, amounting to over 18 percent, would write the worst monthly loss for any Dow average until October 1929. The railroads, more or less ignored in the May collapse, were savagely attacked. Both the Atchison and the Union Pacific lost 50 percent off their June highs. The Missouri Pacific fell from 35 to 17 during July, and the Northern Pacific went from 13 to 7. A few of the industrials were again smashed. General Electric, near to the receiver's gavel, fell from 73 to 30 during the month.

During the last week of July, the Erie, a perennial financial cripple, entered receivership for the third time, and call money rose to $\frac{3}{16}$ percent per day. A hastily organized banking pool resolved the crisis, and the market ended its panic phase, although the rail news would worsen. Figure 2-2 shows the summer market crisis of 1893.

Spidery Branch Lines
Ruin Railroads

The railroads' downfall lay in circumstances of depression. But they had been preparing their own doom for nearly a decade. A frenzy of expansion in the late 1880s, when 40,000 miles of new track were built, had mainly enriched promoters and shady construction companies and was the undoing of the carriers. The expansion, much of it spidery branch-line extensions, had ballooned mortgage debt and fixed charges. Various manipulations and combines, such as the Philadelphia & Reading anthracite monopoly, led to further credit problems. The Reading had failed in the spring of 1893, a generally prosperous time.

Before the year was over, there would be 74 railroads involved in bankruptcy or foreclosure proceedings. These immeasurably expand-

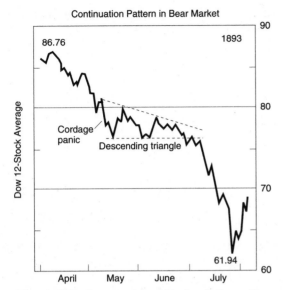

Figure 2-2. Commercial crisis struck the nation in the summer of 1893. Clearing House certificates were put into use in June, but by July cash commanded a premium to certified funds. Heavy foreign selling and an emigration of gold encouraged the July panic, which climaxed when the Erie Railroad went into receivership.

ed the horizons of railroad lawyers. Every class of stock and bond was represented by a phalanx of attorneys, as were the roads' claimants and creditors. Almost 30,000 miles of rail line, nearly one-third of the nation's total, were posted at the courthouse.

In the last five months of 1893, the list of new victims read like a scroll of Western movies. In August, the Northern Pacific was placed in bankruptcy. In October, it was the Union Pacific's turn, and in December, the Atchison, Topeka & Santa Fe, with its 9300 miles of line, was stricken.

Receiverships Key to Later Rail Prosperity

But much good would come of the rail crisis. Overexpansion was ended, partly because the Western frontier had vanished. James J. Hill and the Great Northern ended the century's big expansions, completing to Seattle in 1893. Rail mileage laid down in the last half of the decade would average barely 2600 miles per year. Branch lines and exorbitant leases were excised. Fixed charges were slashed, to the dismay of bondholders, who were forced to take lower coupons and also a reduction in maturity principal. The iron fist of the Northern Pacific's receiver squeezed down interest payments by 50 percent.

When they were finally free of the wringer, the roads were able to capitalize on the prosperity that bloomed in 1897. The advance of the Dow Railroad average in the 1896–1902 period would not be surpassed for 90 years, not even in the 1920s. The Atchison's price would advance 2500 percent by 1901. The gain for the Northern Pacific: 6 to 150—and that is before the famous corner exploded its price to 1000 in 1901. Lesser names such as St. Louis & Southwestern were up more than 10-fold.

As for the lawyers, they were mostly looking for another calling. In 1901 only four railroads entered receivership, and only 73 miles of track were involved.

Panics Favor the Autumn Trimester

We have not seen any cyclical study of panics, and we doubt one could make order out of them. Historically, however, they have occurred most often in the autumn, when the efflux of harvest credits from the money centers to country banks cause seasonal credit stresses.

The establishment of the Federal Reserve System in 1914 helped smooth out the pattern, but autumn malaise reappeared in the 1950s. One can count 20 panic periods in the years since 1954. Of these 20 downers, 15 began in the four months August through November. This may be because of September's notorious calendar record—the worst of any month—or because October has so often been a "bear killer." The only sure conclusion is that lightning has struck the Exchange on a disproportionate number of occasions during that autumn trimester.

With regard to the occurrence of panic within the market cycle, it shows up most frequently in bear episodes, accelerating but often terminating the downward trend.

Nearly 50 bear market panics can be identified since 1890, even after excluding the unique 1929–1932 period. Such incidents cause great pain, but are not so traumatic as the mind-altering experiences that blindside bull markets. Bear market players are, after all, always on notice that the bad news will probably get worse.

In October 1979, the Fed struck a weekend blow against inflation and the Dow collapsed from the year's high to the year's low within about a month. The drama of that bull market setback is recalled as the

"Saturday Night massacre." Several years later, with a bear market already in place, the average was knocked for a similar loss in the early autumn. But a sharp slump in an already slumping market is not the stuff of legend. Though the credentials of the decline were almost identical with those of 1979, the bear incident lacks cachet.

A panic climax to an aging bull market has made that final turn of the card into a fortune builder, for those who dared. Eighteen bear markets have ended thus, as they reversed the down cycle to up. The last classic double hit was in May 1970. The summer rally that followed that year was impressive, up 21 percent, led by the popular mobile home stocks. Champion Home Builders, 8 in May, tripled by Labor Day. Figure 2-3 shows the 1938 climax to a bear market, which had already suffered an epidemic of crises in the previous autumn.

Figure 2-3. The collapse of late March 1938 was typical of the "bad" panics of the past century. Within 14 trading days, the Dow lost 22 percent, struck down when Hitler forced Anschluss on Austria. The intensity of the decline was similar to 1893's commercial crisis, 1899's "Black Week," the collapse of March 1907, and the Dunkerque retreat, among other swift and infamous routs.

The war scare gave impetus to defense stocks, and Lockheed flew from 6 to 38 within the year, while Douglas Aircraft, winging on hopes for its new DC-3, rose from 31 to 81.

The 1938 crash was aggravated by Dow theory selling and the psychological blow resulting from the average's drop below par. It added up to a "bear trap," and the ensuing 12-day rally was spectacular. The false peace hopes of the autumn's Munich conference climaxed the final advance, a rare intrayear bull market, with a gain of 60 percent. That figure was almost double the two-year advance of 1966–1968.

Panics can come in bull and bear markets, and in both bad and good economic times. Earnings declines, dividend cuts, negative court, FDA, and EPA decisions, strikes, White House malaise, political surprises, war and the threat of war—all lay in wait for the investor. If it's not the outside threat, there are inside traps—pools, manipulations, program trading, and bear raids. The most mysterious and disturbing crises are those ignited by implosion, as in 1987.

Killing Bull Hopes: "The Terminators"

One would think that panics striking a market already weakened by a bear sequence would be more fearsome than a crisis attack on a bull market. This does not seem to be the case: The psychological reaction to bull market panics is more traumatic. This is because such downdrafts represent an overnight reversal of the prevailing mood. Panics in bear markets may do as much damage, but if investors are equally stressed financially, they are better prepared emotionally, being already traumatized. It's just one more blow.

The Silver Crisis of 1980 and the Saturday Night massacre of 1979, both part of the 1978–1981 bull sequence, were more frightening than the November crisis of 1973, although that bear market episode did more damage. Eisenhower's heart attack in 1955 shook confidence and slammed the market with the biggest volume since 1939. In April 1915, the surging Industrials registered their largest monthly advance ever, 18 percent, and thus the market was sensitive and vulnerable to any bad news. The *Lusitania* was torpedoed just one week later.

Market fears cannot be measured accurately, although relative volume and intensity are of some help. But many of the most frightening panics have been terminators which wrote *finis* to a bull market. In

Table 2-1. The Terminators
Panics That Killed Bull Hopes

Year	Bull market high	Panic began	Dow loss before panic (%)	Dow loss in panic (%)
1895	Sept.	Dec.	9	16
1899	Sept.	Dec.	2	23
1916	Nov.	Dec.	5	14
1929	Sept.	Oct.	13	40
1937	March	Sept.	9	17
1946	May	Aug.	10	16
1987	Aug.	Oct.	8	31

such cases, sudden catastrophe demonstrated conclusively that the game was over. The most famous example is 1929.

That October smash was a convincer. Many frightening crises have come under similar circumstances, as an apparent correction turned terminator. In each of the incidents, listed in Table 2-1, the bull market was already over the hill, but the decline was not yet large enough to create fear. It was then that the terminator panic struck.

With the exception of 1929, the losses prior to the terminator action were uniformly mild, not serious enough to arouse bearish suspicion on price alone. The March–August time span in the 1937 experience appears long, but bullish hopes had been renewed in August when the Dow rallied to within 2 percent of the March high. A similar double top was registered in August 1946. In 1929, the Industrials had been within 8 percent of the September high only a week before the panic began.

These terminator panics, all of substantial size, are logged as part of the bear markets which they confirmed. But they were fearsome occurrences, for at the moment of execution, the markets appeared to be in the process of an orderly correction. They all struck while the bull market was assumed to still be in progress, and thus remain among the most frightening of all such incidents. All the price declines were of significant proportions.

Bull Market Panics Reverse Quickly

The 1920s are remembered as a stock market rose garden, but there were some tumultuous downsides. In the spring of 1926, an ignorant

and excited bullish constituency, attracted by record pool manipulations, was destroyed when the Interstate Commerce Commission
(ICC) unexpectedly rejected the five-way Nickel Plate consolidation,
spiking yet another merger craze. The Cleveland railroad was
derailed, falling from 163 to 130, while the Erie, another participant,
lost 29 percent of its value. Typically, the worst day of panic, March 3,
saw record volume.

The autos were hit hard, and General Motors fell to four times its
projected 1926 earnings. But the bull market panic was quickly done,
and the Dow would eke out a new high in the early autumn, by which
time GM had doubled.

In late November 1928, Treasury Secretary Andrew Mellon
launched an attack on speculators, and the market suffered a breathtaking drop. On December 7, *The New York Times's* financial columnist
wrote that "many of the new crop of traders will have their first
acquaintance this morning with margin calls." Radio Corporation was
smashed from over 400 to 293 within the week. But by the end of the
month the Dow was at a new high, 300.00.

Quick recoveries to new highs have been a feature of bull market
panics, but the rebound after 1978 was agonizingly slow. The Dow
had scored a two-year high at 908 in September, but by October it
was below 800, crippled by rising interest rates, margin problems, and
the customary evil rumors. It was whispered that a large
brokerage firm's computer was 24 hours behind in monitoring undermargined accounts. Not until July 1980 would the average top Dow
908. Gasoline lines, inflation, Tehran hostages, the Afghanistan
invasion, and the Saturday Night massacre conspired to make convalescence slow.

Over 30 panics have temporarily enjoined bull markets. Some have
been among the most spectacular in history. The mood swing is truly
frightening, but under bullish circumstances it seems to clear the air,
freeing the market to race ahead into new high ground. The torpedoing of the *Lusitania* in May 1915 provided such action. Although the
event seemed to threaten war, the crisis was over in little more than a
week. American Locomotive was a grievous victim, falling from 61 to
38 within a few days. But the Dow rose to a new high in the following
month, and the engine maker followed in September.

The Flower Panic of May 1899 and the Lawson Panic of 1904 tripped
up major advances near the turn of the century, and since World War
II, the Eisenhower Panic and the Silver Crisis of 1980 provided classic
bull interruptions.

Nursing Panics: Elixers and Palliatives

At the New York Stock Exchange, a most effective elixir for panic has been to padlock the barn. The longest Exchange closing came in 1914, at the start of World War I, when activity was basically suspended from July 30 until December 12. Trades could be made at July's closing values or higher, but the only issues wanted were a few proven war babies, such as the sugars. An outlaw "gutter" market sprang up which accommodated those who had to sell securities. Price fell steadily during the early autumn, reaching an October low in the outdoor market.

In 1873, the Exchange was padlocked because of the Jay Cooke panic, closing at noon on September 18 and not reopening until September 30. Rumors of a closing in October 1987 helped fire the panic embers of that ordeal, but the last time the safety valve was used came following President John Kennedy's assassination in November 1963. Trading was halted immediately after news of the tragedy was received on Friday afternoon, and the Exchange remained closed on the following Monday. On many other occasions—as in the 1907 panic and at the beginning of World War II—proposals for closing the Exchange were rejected.

"There Oughta' Be a Law"

Congress has yet to outlaw panics and bear markets, but from time to time it has hatched bizarre proposals to assist price maintenance. In 1933, after the July panic, Senator Elmer Thomas of Oklahoma characterized the "market racket" as second only to the kidnapping racket. He proposed to cure the problem by having the government—presumably the Post Office—calculate the price range in which stocks might legitimately fluctuate. Too low might land the stock bootlegger in Leavenworth. Too high would catch only a wink, apparently, for within several months, Thomas was arguing for mandatory currency inflation.

Representative Adolph Sabath of Illinois was another who abhorred a two-sided market, and he frequently tilted at short sellers. In 1947, irked by the postwar market decline, he proposed that the proceeds of short sales be taxed 5 percent. But both here and abroad, attempts at price fixing and bans on short sales have proven ineffective palliatives.

Since 1934, margin rates have been officially controlled and often adjusted in reaction to stock prices. But even prior to the Securities

Act, well-managed brokerage firms acted in the same fashion. After the disastrous October slump of 1937, the Federal Reserve Board (FRB) cut initial margin rates from 55 to 40 percent. By 1946, wild speculation had urged the rate up to 100 percent, but that figure was cut in 1947 and again in 1949. Market migraines in 1958, 1960, 1970, and 1974 were also treated with margin reductions.

Clearing House Certificates

Until the advent of the Federal Reserve System, stock market panics were generally caused or accompanied by commercial crises. Banks failed or at least suspended payment to depositors. Trade bankruptcies multiplied, as did unemployment. Interest rates rocketed. Call money sometimes approached 186 percent, plus various other "points," bringing the cost to nearly 200 percent or higher.

Currency usually sold at a premium. A dollar in currency might command $1.03 to $1.05 in certified check funds. In the crisis of 1907, millions of dollars in currency changed hands at the outdoor market, the Curb, where there were no listing requirements and contracts could be executed on any wager of chance, including stocks.

When illiquidity reached such a stage, the elixir of choice was Clearing House certificates, issued by the New York City Bank Clearing House. They were a time-proven palliative, first used during the Civil War.

By the time of the 1907 currency famine, the efficiency of the certificates had led to nationwide popularity, and they were even issued in small currency denominations, spreading into public use. San Francisco was the leader in such small issues, with over $7 million in small-face certificates outstanding. In New York City, however, the smallest certificate was for $5000, and most were for $100,000. Nationwide, nearly a half-billion dollars in cash substitutes were created, including the "wheat money" issued in Portland, Oregon, against stored grain.

Clearing House paper came into heavy use again in the war crisis of 1914, as the Fed was not yet quite in operation, and found a role in the winter banking crisis of 1933.

Bankers' Pools

Yet another elixir used to stay or relieve panic were bankers' pools, generally conceived to add liquidity to a call-money market under siege. The pools pushed funds into the call market, and the very prospect of such reserves could ease stress.

Often, the pools had a vested interest in "saving" certain important stocks. The most famous syndicate was launched in the 1929 crisis, when J. P. Morgan and five other institutional players (plus the Guggenheim brothers) anted up $250 million in a direct effort to support stock prices. While they effected some trades in popular market leaders, their most energetic buying was for those on their own client or portfolio list. The Guggenheims' American Smelting was on the list, but U.S. Steel, still the favorite among Morgan's investment banking clients, received the largest dollar support. It was followed by American Telephone & Telegraph (AT&T) and American Can.

Mega-millions and the Morgan mystique accomplished little, however. Richard Whitney, who led the pool's floor operation, made his first pool bid on October 24. It was for U.S. Steel—205 for 25,000 shares—when the previous best bid was 195. He didn't get the order completely filled, but he received a lot of floor attention and turned the market temporarily. Pool or no pool, Steel was trading at 150 by mid-November.

But 1929 was a very special year. Earlier pools had been more successful. The elder Morgan's $25 million pool in 1907 is a historical legend, and in 1902 he and friends had put together a $50 million syndicate at a time when no such figure was needed. It became known as the "faith cure," for though not a penny was loaned, the huge reserve calmed the autumn credit crisis and blunted fears of a bear raid based on Germany's drive for a naval base in the Caribbean. A $10 million money pool in 1899 broke the call rate from 188 to 6 percent within days.

"Encouraging Words" by Politicians

Such stock and credit-propping combines have never been able to halt a crisis, but they have usually encouraged a psychological reversal. "Encouraging words" have not been so successful, for neither talk nor logic has been able to turn the tide of panic or bear markets. But words of encouragement have proved irresistible to politicians, Street sources, and economic gurus during crisis moments.

President Herbert Hoover has been ridiculed for over 60 years because of his optimistic statements of October 1929: "The fundamental business of the country...is sound," he told the nation on Friday, October 25. Latter-day ridicule stems from the events of 1930–1933, for business, unlike the stock market, was not on the ropes in 1929. U.S. Steel announced that nine-months earnings through September were $15.82, compared with $8.17 for the same period in 1928, and declared an extra dividend, as did American Can.

Autumn extras were also declared by such blue chips as Consolidated Gas and Standard of Jersey, which were also Dow stocks. American Telephone's earnings were $12.57 in 1929, versus $12.11 in the previous year, and its shares would record a price advance for 1929, despite the travails of the fourth quarter. Hoover's error was not in weighing business fundamentals, but in confusing them with a stock market trend.

In late April 1970, President Richard Nixon was quoted by an authorized spokesman as saying, "Frankly, if I had any money I'd be buying stocks now." The Dow would fall 14 percent in the next month.

"Circuit Breakers"

Dow 3600 has mostly erased the vivid memories of the 1987 meltdown, when the doomsayers were again proven wrong; it was not "1929 again."

The events were akin for only a few days. Unlike the early 1930s, the public, irked by CDs that barely yielded cigarette money, has flocked back to stocks. "Cash is trash" has been the startling rationale.

The significant divergence from the 1930s script has given investors assurance about the future. Market reforms, it is argued, will stay catastrophe. Calm and reason will be legislated. The principal reform has been the installation of "circuit breakers." When the Dow Industrials fall (or rise) 50 points in a session, restrictions are placed on computerized program trading, which many believe aggravated the crash of 1987. When the Standard & Poor's 500 futures contract, traded on the Chicago Mercantile Exchange, falls 12 points (about 96 Dow points), a 30-minute time-out is whistled. If the S&P falls 20 points, it is "limit down" and can trade no lower for the rest of the day.

If the Dow falls 250 points, trading stops for one hour. A 400-point drop (ouch) brings a two-hour recess and, hopefully, the end of the day's trading. Declines of that size haven't occurred since 1987, so the efficiency is yet to be tested. Other improvements have been effected in operations, communications, and capital requirements. Over the decades, many specialist firms have been buried by extraordinary selling pressure against their books. Minimum capital requirements are now up 10-fold from the level of a few years ago.

Will all this halt Meltdown II? Not necessarily. Commodity speculators, who have suffered many more panics than equity players, know that a halt in trading because a market is down a daily "limit" only postpones the pain. It may open down the limit for several more days. And the new specialist capital requirement, $1 million, is not a heavy-duty shock. The NYSE has geared up its computer systems for a billion-share day. That doesn't mean better prices—you'll just receive those disappointing reports back faster than a few years ago.

Panics Can Yield Benefits

The benefits of panic are more evident to sideliners and philosophers than to the victims. Crises write financial history but often lack historical significance. They are, however, a natural market event.

News can't always be all good, and when it is unexpectedly bad and the market is extended, herd fear takes over. The flight for safety breaks all the rules, smashes down the fences, and sacrifices the margin lambs.

Panic always improves the fundamentals of the market, though it's a cruel cure. The 1929 crash came partly because the Dow was at a lofty fundamental level—19 times earnings. A few weeks later, at the autumn low, the multiple was an attractive 10 times earnings, and from there a rally of historic proportions began.

Panics sometimes save the Street from itself by arresting mad speculations before they overwhelm the entire market. A *New York Times* editorial following the Northern Pacific panic took the view that the 1901 crisis had a silver lining for a nation grown addicted to reckless speculation. "The country will be safer and happier and more prosperous in the autumn than it would have been if the reaction had been deferred," was its Polyannish conclusion on May 10, 1901.

Panics often uncover cancer which might have later killed if it continued undetected, as happened in the Grant & Ward scandal of 1884.

By accident, some panics have influenced events in a beneficial and significant fashion. A market crash in the summer of 1896 was stirred by the silver inflationists and their Presidential candidate, William Jennings Bryan. The collapse frightened the East and solidified opinion against the Silverites. Sound money survived, helping to bring a return to prosperity.

The Federal Reserve System was born, tardily, out of the commercial crisis of 1907, and the SEC was established partly because of 1929 and the recurrent crises of the early 1930s.

The Rich Man's Panic of 1903 benefited the public, though not the Street. Huge, watered consolidations had been foisted off on the public for years. Monopolistic combinations, it was hinted, would provide enormous profits. But such was not the case, and the monopoly game suddenly ended when the public would buy no more. And so the bankers' vaults became crammed with sheaves of unsalable securities. The trust mania was discredited and retired, relieving the public of a costly pioneer plague of initial public offerings (IPOs). Wall Street, of course, would develop a new pitch. Copper, seen as the prime beneficiary of the electric age, became the new market darling.

It can also be argued that the bitter smash of July 1893 had redeeming value, although it toppled the nation's railway lines, one after the other, until 74 of them were in the lawyers' hands. But the restructuring which was forced upon them had longer-term benefits, as seen earlier.

The benefits of panic are obvious for shorts in stocks and index options. And also for those who, for whatever reason, were smart enough or lucky enough to be out of the market. Time after time, they have been rewarded with marvelous opportunities. One has only to glance at those downward spikes on the market charts of the past 125 years. Almost as dependably as the seasons, two or three periods of turmoil roil the market in each year.

The benefits of panic are only accidental and usually long in realization, and they are therefore seldom recognized by the average investor. But such crises are a natural, if irrational, part of the market. Every investor will eventually be victimized. Like sandtraps on a golf course, panics are a part of the game, and the investor must learn to cope.

Buyers' Panics

Buyers' panics are socially more acceptable than the sellers' variety, but they are rare and of brief duration, what with gravity and the universal urge to cash profits.

For those reasons, upscale excitements have a difficult time recording a 10 percent change within a couple of weeks, figures easily achieved on the downside. On Sunday, March 31, 1968, President Lyndon Johnson revealed that he would not seek reelection and would deescalate bombing in Vietnam. For diverse reasons, the announcement was received with glee, and the Dow opened on a huge volume gap, advancing by 8 percent in just nine trading days. Xerox, the decade's growth leader, also gapped and sprinted from 229 to 288. The Dow's gap would not be filled until the summer of 1969.

Battling inflation, President Richard Nixon in August 1971 unexpectedly declared a 90-day freeze on prices, wages, and rents, and the surprise created a similar large gap to the upside. The Dow climbed by over 7 percent in 17 trading days, but skepticism regarding the program set in and the gains were all lost by late October.

These were both buying panics, but they failed by far to match gains of earlier upside phenomena. The outbreak of World War II in September 1939 created a bull classic, with the Industrials gaining 16 percent in only nine days; it was a paradoxical response to war. Curiously, just one year earlier, Munich's promise of peace had pushed the Dow up over 17 percent in 14 days. In all of these bullish bubbles, widespread assumptions and expectations had been suddenly reversed, a symptom common to selling panics.

President William McKinley's "prosperity" reelection in 1900 brought a loud hurrah from the Dow, as it seemed to settle the silver problem. The average climbed 13 percent in the next 12 days. Perhaps it was the excitement of the nation's first auto show, which debuted in New York that same month. It boasted a full menu of power: 19 gas cars, seven steamers, six electrics, and a pair of hybrids. There were no automobile stocks to trade, but American Steel and Wire was a proven swinger, and it jumped from 36 to 48 within a few days. Many other issues, such as Colorado Fuel & Iron (CF&I), the Erie, Katy, and the Northern Pacific had virtually doubled since September on GOP hopes.

Apparent bear market lows and panic climaxes have also encouraged aggressive short-covering and sharp, high-volume runups. In the late summer of 1982, interest expectations suddenly improved and a remarkable stock rush began, although there had been no crisis to mark the end of the 1981–1982 sequence. On August 13 the Dow lifted off its bear market low at 777, and by month-end it had reached 901, accompanied by record-breaking volume. Never had daily trade approached 100 million shares. In the last two weeks of August, there were five days far above that figure. The quick gains were so immoderate as to seduce early selling, which would prove a serious mistake, as the month was an exception to the contrarian views of panic. Fortunes lay ahead, though some stocks, such as Merrill Lynch, had already exploded; the brokerage house had run from 21 to 35.

In the last several decades, institutional herd runs have been responsible for buying panics, as in the record-breaking advance of January 1976. Some superwaves have lasted nearly 90 days, but the classic patterns are short.

In January 1987, 12 consecutive days of institutional panic advanced the Industrials by 9 percent. A long-wave buying panic actually occupied the entire first quarter, as the market whistled by Dow 2000, 2100, 2200, and 2300, while smashing all volume records at the Exchange.

Such prolonged displays are atypical by past standards, but the institutionalization of the market will encourage a repeat when bullish frenzy rises again. The case for selling into them is not as clear as the mandate for buying into downside crises.

Most of the short, sensational buying panics have come as reflex from a market driven into a deep hole by massive liquidation and/or a psychological crisis. The last such action followed the 1987 meltdown. Previous intense advances include the double-digit gains listed in Table 2-2, all recorded in less than 20 trading days.

One of the biggest daily advances in history was overwhelmed by the crash events of 1929, which surrounded it. On October 30 of that year, bargain hunters shot the Dow Jones Industrials average up over 12 percent. This was short of the 15 percent gain of October 6, 1931, however, which celebrated the end of the "Sterling Crisis." That depression advance was only one of many extraordinary short-term

Table 2-2. Almanac of Buyers' Panics

July 26–Aug. 4, 1893	Plus 13% in nine trading days. Reflex from panic which accompanied Erie bankruptcy.
Dec. 18–Jan. 2, 1899	Plus 17%. Rebound from Boer War fears.
Nov. 25–Dec. 6, 1907	Plus 15% in nine trading days following end of commercial crisis.
Feb. 25–March 22, 1920	Famous corners in Stutz and General Motors helped boost market 16 percent in 22-day recovery from February break.
Dec. 8–Dec. 31, 1928	Bulls return with vengeance after shocking one-week bear raid which robbed RCA of more than 100 points. Dow gain: 17%.
1929–1932	Multiple buying panics sparked by short covering. In one November week in 1929, the Dow jumped 25%. A 27% gain was counted in 16 trading days of October 1931.
March 15, 1933	FDR policies announced during bank holiday encouraged "one-day" gain of 15% when NYSE reopened.
March 31–April 16, 1938	Rebound from war scare. Dow up 22%.
Aug. 31–Sept. 13, 1939	Buying frenzy following Nazi invasion of Poland. Recalling World War I boom, traders rushed Dow up 16%.

gains which interrupted the bear market. Other notable one-day panic advances occurred in the relief from the Northern Pacific corner, and the bear raid on the Harriman rails in March 1907. All the gains were well over 6 percent. With the exception of 1987, there have been no comparable one-day bull events since 1939.

Some of the eventful "up" days provided a good opportunity for contrarians. None was as fateful as that of September 1939. The Industrials would scratch out another few points, but they would not rise seriously over the September 5 level of Dow 148 until February 1945.

Dramatis Personnae

Presidents, bankers, and scalawags, though not necessarily in that order, have held leading roles in market panics. The most obvious case is General Dwight Eisenhower. Then President, he suffered a heart attack after playing 27 holes of golf in Denver. Within about two weeks, the Dow fell by nearly 12 percent, intraday.

Such innocent guilt is unique. A smoking gun is usually at hand. In 1895, President Grover Cleveland sent a message to Congress that seemed to threaten war with Britain, and a five-day collapse followed during which U.S. Rubber fell from 36 to 21. President Theodore Roosevelt's brusque treatment of railroad representatives helped encourage the bitter bear raid of 1907, which saw Schloss-Sheffield Steel crushed from 68 to 42 within two weeks.

Panics have often been named after their lead character or the compelling accident or incident. Thus, the Lawson Panic of 1904 was named after the notorious speculator and financial muckraker Thomas W. Lawson, and James R. Keane had his name attached to several routs. Many Presidents have been blamed for short-term disorderliness in the market, but the extraordinary distress caused by President Cleveland's gaffe is commonly known as the Venezuelan Panic.

The Silver Panic of 1896 is also known as the Bryan Panic, after the Democratic Presidential nominee. Several battles are intimately associated with market spasms—the Boer War defeat for the British at Colenso and Dunkerque. And a pair of famous vessels, the *U.S. Maine* and the *Lusitania,* are remembered in the lexicon of panic.

England's House of Baring is the only investment banker stuck with the black bean, caused by their widespread credit speculations in Argentina; 1890 is remembered as the Baring Panic in both London and New York.

The Panic of 1903 is a misnomer. It was actually a year-long bear market, but the terms panic and bear market were often used interchangeably at the time.

James R. Keene, a master manipulator known as the "Silver Fox," triggered several panics, usually after he had already shorn the lambs, as in his 1893 machinations in the shares of the "Twine Trust," National Cordage. Active since the 1870s, his last great coup left his coat-tailers in the Columbus & Hocking quite destitute in 1910.

Near the turn of the century, even J. P. Morgan was blamed for some nasty market spills. His lust for the Northern Pacific inadvertently caused a great smash in 1901, and in 1902 he overplayed the trustification mania with a steamship trust—which foundered—and helped bring on the investment bankers' headaches of 1903.

The "radical" Woodrow Wilson frightened conservatives even before his 1913 inauguration, but the market impact was slight compared with the "Peace Scare" he helped thrust upon the market in late 1916, when the Dow slumped by 18 percent within a one-month period. That December's crisis was a watershed event, for the Dow would not recover its losses until mid-1919.

Boston's Charles Ponzi speeded the summer deflation of 1920 when his easy-money schemes collapsed; and in 1929 England, a bloke named Clarence Hatry did the London Stock Exchange in, what with counterfeit stock certificates and the like. London's distress was a secondary cause of the autumn weakness at New York. A speculator much larger than life fell victim to silver's siren call in 1980, and Nelson Bunker Hunt's name was added to the list of those who have almost single-handedly brought chaos to the Street.

The occupant of the White House has a daily opportunity for financial mischief, and it is to the credit of all of the Presidents of the past 50 years that they have usually cautiously chosen the timing and wording of their public statements. But not always. John F. Kennedy, a model of public calm in the days of the Bay of Pigs, the Berlin Wall, and the Cuban missile crisis, managed to get into a shouting match with the steel industry in 1962, bringing on a bitter market reaction.

And Richard Nixon, usually careful in his public utterances, was less guarded on tape. And so Watergate's aftermath ravished the market in the early autumn of 1974. Curiously, the steepest decline occurred after Nixon had resigned and fled to California.

Bear markets, on the other hand, lack a colorful stage bill. President Kennedy did get his name attached to the spring panic of 1962, but he escaped the onus for the bear sequence which had started in December. Watergate is closely associated with the decline of 1973–1974, but that sequence has never been called the Nixon market, though the GOP would have been happy with that title credit for earlier gains.

Presidents Hoover and Franklin Roosevelt had their names attached to the respective depressions of their administrations, but not to the market results. And while President Theodore Roosevelt was widely blamed for the railroad troubles of 1907, we have seen few references to a "Roosevelt market."

The most common Presidential market references are to the "McKinley" and "Coolidge" markets, but both were bull sequences.

The Structure of Panic

Expect no more than four days of hard panic, though crisis conditions may last somewhat longer. There were only three, slightly separated, in 1899, and but a day and a half during the Northern Pacific crisis. The first, and worst, crisis of 1907 put only two days of intense heat on longs, though the climax followed nearly two weeks of steady erosion.

Two-day climaxes seem to dominate the panic model, though sometimes the pattern is relieved by a sideways action followed by a renewed attack. The exceptions have been nasty. In May 1940, when Sitzkrieg turned to Blitzkrieg overnight, driving the Allied troops to the beaches at Dunkerque, the Dow marched down in three steps. They were spread over 10 trading days in May, during which the Dow fell 23 percent. Figure 2-4 shows the panic and the action of early June, when the average slipped to a new low, creating a "bear trap," since a swift reversal began immediately.

Volume on May 21 was the largest of the war years, nearly twice that registered in the aftermath of Pearl Harbor. Many stocks were knocked down from the year's high to the year's low within the month, but despite the war's unceasing bad news, some would recover enough to exceed the April–May peaks. Bethlehem Steel was one. It was an 89-to-63 victim of the panic, but by year-end it was near 95.

The Dunkerque panic could have lured an investor into a premature buying decision on the first of the two big-volume, big-down days, and a buyer would not have recovered the Dow price until September. But such traps are rare.

The underlying principle of panic is fear. The road to fear is never the same. Sometimes, as in 1917, the emotional impact is exhausted within a day or so. At other times the agony drags on, as in May 1970. In most sequences there will be several days of hard selling, often widely separated, in which the Dow suffers a daily drop of 2 to 5 per-

The Dunkerque Panic

Figure 2-4. The most violent market downdraft of World War II occurred in the 1940 events leading to Dunkerque and the evacuation of Allied troops from the beaches. May's panic spun out of a lengthy "line" formation, which had reflected the war's stalemate since the previous autumn. On May 21, volume at the NYSE was the largest of the decade. In a deceitful move on June 10, the Dow fell to new low ground, only to swiftly reverse, having created a "bear trap." Despite the fall of Paris in mid-June, the market responded normally in the aftermath of crisis, advancing by 21 percent within four months. The collapse of May discounted the war's black news for the subsequent 18 months. Not until Pearl Harbor would the Dow penetrate the Dunkerque low.

cent. In 1946's September plunge, which lasted for 13 sessions, there were four hits of between 2.3 and 5.6 percent. The first day of crisis was the gravest, and the final slump—although it did not mark the end of the autumn travails—did the lightest damage.

   More commonly, the next to last day will be the most frightening, and the final session of the episode will see reduced volatility, except when a key reversal takes place, as in May 1962. Thus October 19, 1987, not October 20 (when the crash ended) is remembered as the day of horror. Expect a pressure package of five or six hard "down" days at the end of the episode; there will occasionally be a rally session of poor quality in that last week. The 1987 meltdown was accompanied by five consecutive days of aggressive selling, including October 20, when the low was recorded but the market accomplished a key reversal, ending with a higher close.

Since the end of World War II, similar hard-driving finishes of about five days can be observed in charts for the 1980 Silver Panic, in 1973, 1970, 1962, 1960, 1957, and 1950. Ike's crisis wound up with four downers at the end, but Harry Truman's panic expired quietly in terms of volume and volatility. It was a rarity.

The market climax of October 1974 was a stretchout, with the Dow falling for 11 consecutive days. In December, however, the Industrials wrote the final panic figures for the year on a more traditional basis, with four tough down days separated by a two-point closing rally just below the Dow 600 level.

Peak volume sometimes comes at the very beginning of a panic, often on the second day, as in 1946 and 1950, or at the final climax. In 1980, the final day of panic saw the Dow close lower, but a late move on enormous volume had rallied the Dow almost into plus territory, after it had fallen to its lowest intraday point in five years. Although the Dow would make a modest new low in April, all of the weak holders had been liquidated in the day's volatile, high-volume action.

Endings: What to Look For

Panics end, well, in panic. High volume, high volatility, and desperate declines mark their passage. They have often aggravated the final stage of a long bearish episode, but pure double jeopardy has not been seen since 1970.

Near the turn of the century, a terminal panic was a reliable indicator of the end of a bear trend. In 1890, 1893, 1896, and 1907, crisis conditions hastened the end of a bear decline. In September 1900, however, the Industrials—in a private bear market for about a year—broke with tradition in a low-volume turn. Trade in August, barely 4 million shares, was the slowest between 1897 and 1912.

Bear market reversals come from an exhaustion of selling, by attrition, as in 1900, 1932, and 1942, or by a high-volume shove from panic. Only infrequently does news play a role, for news breaks will not turn a bear trend much before its natural maturity. In 1957, however, the report of Eisenhower's decision to stump the country on economic, missile, and defense policies spurred a furious reversal of the *Sputnik I* decline. It was the "most vigorous rally of a generation," according to *The Wall Street Journal*. And in 1982, word that Salomon Brothers' interest-rate guru, Henry Kaufman, had turned friendly to the interest-rate structure was an important factor in the reversal.

Occasionally, a festering financial sore is lanced and the relief from suspicion and worry triggers a final trough. In 1893 it was the Erie receivership, and in 1903, the announcement that U.S. Steel had reduced its dividend, a long-rumored threat. The collapse of a great rail manipulation in 1910 killed another transcontinental rail dream, amid crisis conditions, but after the July liquidation the Rails would advance for the next two years.

Panics' finales are easy to spot, marked as they are by a frenzy of excitement. Bear markets tend to expire quietly, and their end is often little noted. It is only when a sudden excitement of buying returns and finds no cheap stock that a price explosion signals a new bullish era. The super price and volume expansion of late July 1932 is the best example, but January 1975 and August 1982 put up some dramatic figures. In each of these classic instances, the largest volume came after the market low.

In panics, on the other hand, peak volume usually accompanies the climactic low except when the collapse has been front-ended by some appalling news. Such triggers push activity to an early peak, as happened after Eisenhower's heart attack.

Panics write their own tickets. Bear market endings are more circumspect, with high volume present only when crisis pricing strikes in the final act. Low volume has been much more common. If one considers the three-month decline of 1990 as a bear market, the figures are typical. Six days of war-panic selling in August each went over 200 million shares. When the sequence ended in October, the volume for the last five days averaged only 149 million shares.

Don't Panic

"Don't panic" is the best advice in a panic, for the opportunities of crisis on Wall Street are legendary.

The driving forces of financial storms are easily understood, for they translate immediately into chaotic pricing. In turn, the violence raises the specter that scandalous revaluations—insider cheating, failed manipulations, hidden deals—lie ahead. Otherwise, why would the market be so bad?

The essence of panic is fear, and it creates an avalanche of prices, destroying reason and logic. Buy, sell, hold tight? All the pressure is on the individual to surrender unconditionally, and join the overpositioned, undermargined speculators in a selling stampede.

It is the worst possible time to do so, for within a day or so the storm will subside. The proven risk in times of panic is selling; the proven opportunity is in buying stocks.

Finding a No-Brainer

The lasting memory of panic will be pain, but for those who respond properly, the lasting result will be opportunity rewarded. Good timing at such moments, as in March 1980, is more reflex than thoughtful. The stock you almost bought last month at 45 is at 27 and sinking. Take a chance. The risk at 45, you now know, was at least 18 points. At 27? Probably two or three points, at least for the time being.

Ignore the doomsayers crying "It's 1929 again." The statistics of gain for stocks bought in those panics that terminate bear markets are awesome, but lesser crises—the Black Mondays, Fridays, and even Saturdays—are reliably profitable. Buying at such moments is a no-brainer, requiring little market knowledge or wisdom, only courage and a heavy purse.

Panic conditions don't give a lifetime free pass. There is always a bear market somewhere over the horizon, but contrarians get a leg up on the inevitable rally.

For an example of a no-brainer, consider the results of buying just one stock in the days of panic, say the nation's no. 1 corporation in terms of sales. That would have been U.S. Steel through the late 1920s and General Motors thereafter. Steel's record in 11 run-of-the-mill panics between 1901 and 1927 was splendid. The simplistic choice doubled in the aftermath of the 1901, 1904, 1908, 1926, and 1927 setbacks, for example. General Motors did even better in its heyday.

Other no-brainers of superior performance can be found, but an everyday choice like Steel indicates some of the potential. The rewards come from contrary action, not from a sophisticated or complex market strategy.

Every panic of this century—except two—has seen the Dow higher one month after the climax of crisis.

3

War, Peace, and Other Panic Triggers

A hundred years ago, market dislocations were generally blamed on commercial crises and the resulting currency shortages, but this is no longer the case. Bear markets now are usually blamed on worsening economic conditions—or a perception of them. The longer they endure, the greater despair grows. The 1973–1974 bear market, successively flailed by Watergate, the OPEC cartel, and inflation, ended only when prices seemed to signal the end of Western civilization. Such a malaise of spirit is different from the acute fear of panic episodes, and ordinarily is more damaging. A survey of scores of panics, detailed in the Appendix, measures damage figures and duration, but cannot capture the intense fear that marks these incidents.

At one time it was believed that there is a certain periodicy to commercial crisis and its attendant market disruption. Thus, the land panic of 1837 was followed 20 years later by the Ohio Life failure. The crisis of 1873, when Jay Cooke went to the wall and the NYSE suspended operations, came ahead of time, but the Civil War was presumed to be the cause of the irregularity, for the Panic of 1893 appeared on schedule.

But then the Rich Man's Panic of 1903 disrupted the timetable again, along with the rationale, for this time there was no commercial crisis. The autumn smash of 1907 was the last of the classics, and it was the third crisis of that year. Wall Street gave up on the theory of periodicy. Panics strike when they like, with or without reason.

The causes of panic are myriad. The most common trigger, and probably the most easily understood, is war—or the threat of war. But peace, or the threat of peace, can also trigger a panic. Some panics are caused by hidden flaws in the market: Various forms of dishonesty, even if they had been suspected previously, can trigger a panic when they are exposed. Political and financial events may also trigger panic, and sometimes the balance of the market is suddenly upset by an event so unusual that it does not fit into any natural category. In this chapter we will examine some of these many panic triggers.

Concealed Rottenness in the Market

Often there are concealed flaws in the market structure. Wrote Thomas Paine, panics "bring things and men to light, which might have lain forever undiscovered." Chicanery, fraud, counterfeit stocks, high-leverage gambling, and dishonest financial reporting have been exposed time after time in the relentless light of panic, to the sorrow of the guilty and innocent alike.

Such was the case in 1884 when a market rout followed exposure of the crimes of Ferdinand Ward, a "young Napoleon," who was the operating partner in Grant & Ward, a brokerage firm which included ex-President U. S. Grant and his son. Sadly, the President was ruined, though he had no part in the day-to-day operations of the firm. It was not the panic which had caused the mischief, however, but Ward's Ponzi-like manipulations, which had cheated the many clients who had invested because of their trust in the President. A handful of other defalcations were also uncovered by the slumping prices, to the longer-term benefit of the Street.

Weak underpinnings sharpen the course of panic. John Stuart Mill wrote over 125 years ago that "panics do not destroy capital, they merely reveal the extent to which it has been previously destroyed." This broad damning fails to fit many exotic cases, however, and was written with financial crises, rather than those of the stock market, in mind. Many panics have struck Wall Street when the economy was enjoying the most favorable conditions, and would continue to do so.

War and the Threat of War

More than any other political or financial event, war raises the possibility of radical changes in the economic order. Munitions and other war goods shoulder out less vital trade. Commodity prices boom.

Inflation fears seize upon prices. Interest rates climb, for the credit demands of belligerents are insatiable. Fears of new taxes, shortages, and large-scale industrial dislocations cloud the economic horizon. World currency markets turn violent. In such panics the causes are obvious: The potential implications are clear to all.

Every important war threat (except for World War II) has triggered selling in the market. Even foreign conflicts have pressured the market. War and the threat of war involve grave risk, and cautious investors skip to the sidelines. The short-term drive is usually to lower prices. After Iraq invaded Kuwait, the Dow fell by 14 percent in 15 sessions. But against-the-grain buying proved profitable, as it had in previous war scares.

When World War I began, the NYSE forestalled continued panic by closing down the Exchange. Recurrent war threats during the 1930s— in China, Abyssinia, and Central Europe—kept the New York market on tenterhooks, much as the Balkan and Moroccan crises had kept the European bourses in turmoil in the period before 1914.

The paradoxical buyers' panic at the outbreak of World War II, the exception to war-fear selling, was inspired by memories of the huge gains in the early years of World War I, when America was quartermaster to Europe's armies. Brokerage firms in 1939 nudged the forgetful by rushing into print statistical reviews of the big winners of 1915–1916. Table 3-1 shows the market's nervous response to wars and the threat of wars. With one exception, every war or war threat of the past century has brought a sudden drop in stock values. Curiously, the worst of such slumps, the Venezuelan Panic, occurred a century ago.

The Venezuelan Crisis

In December 1895, President Grover Cleveland seemed to threaten war on the nation's biggest creditor, England. The underlying cause of the theatrical episode was a decades-long border dispute between Great Britain and Venezuela, in which arbitration appeared to be refused by Britain. Cleveland viewed such intransigence as an excuse to chime the Monroe Doctrine. In his "Venezuelan message" to Congress, he promised to resist British "aggression." The potential loss of British credits was deemed serious, and the market convulsed, dropping 16 percent in a week. General Electric fell from 32 to 20.

Fortunately, the Presidential bluster quickly evaporated, and the crisis lasted only a week. GE spurted to 40 in February. Though the script now seems buffo-opera, the December 20 drop of 8.5 percent would stand as a record rail loss for 36 years.

Table 3-1. War and the Threat of War
Panic Lows versus Later Prices

War scare	Date	Panic loss (%)	Dow* gain after crisis low		
			3 months (%)	6 months (%)	12 months (%)
Venezuelan crisis	Dec. 1895	16	11	12	6
Sinking of the *Maine*	Feb. 1898	11	15	34	51
World War I	July 1914	12	NA†	13	46
Austrian Anschluss	March 1938	22	35	43	38
Invasion of Czechoslovakia	April 1939	20	10	23	24
World War II	Sept. 1939	0	8	9	(4)
Dunkerque	May 1940	23	16	21	3
Korea	July 1950	12	16	23	28
Kuwait	Aug. 1990	14	3	18	23

*Dow 20-Stock average in 1895.
†NYSE closed.

The Sinking of the *Maine*

Barely two years after the Cleveland crisis, the sinking of the U.S.S. *Maine* in Havana harbor pushed the market into anther war-related crisis. The panic lacked the intensity of the 1895 episode, but the losses were similar and the reflex opportunities proved greater. The "Cuban problem," a festering insurrection against Spanish rule, had agitated the United States for the previous few years, fanned by the jingoistic New York press. The sinking of the *Maine* on the night of February 15, with a loss of 268 lives, excited the nation into a war fever.

"Destruction of the Warship Maine Was the Work of an Enemy," was the headline of the *New York Journal* on February 17, though no such charge was ever proven. The initial reaction to the loss of the *Maine* amounted to 11 percent for the Dow, with that low being reached on February 24, when the highest volume of the war months was recorded. A lower Dow figure was seen in March. Panic conditions, however, were not prevalent throughout the period, and did not reappear in April when a state of war was finally declared.

Caribbean operations which might fall victim to the fighting were hit hard. American Sugar dropped from 139 to 108, and Pacific Mail from 35 to 21. Southern Pacific, which operated steamship facilities from its New Orleans terminus to New York, was a bigger loser, dropping from 30 to 12.

But such losses were minor compared with the gains which would come swiftly once the amazing American field successes in the "splendid little war" were evident. On May 1, the Spanish Asiatic Squadron in the Philippines was destroyed. Colonel "Teddy" Roosevelt, with others, charged up San Juan Hill on July 1. The Queen Regent's fleet at Santiago, Cuba, was sunk July 3, and on July 26 Spain sued for peace. By the end of August, the Industrials had climbed 41 percent from the April low, equal to the rocket-advance pace of late 1982.

Individual issues richly repaid those who had ventured purchases in the spring turmoil. Pacific Mail reached 46 and Union Pacific more than doubled, as did Southern Rail and the BRT. American Cotton Oil nearly tripled, from 16 to 46, and the Southern Pacific rose to 35.

A rousing GOP victory in the fall elections helped boost the ambitious Roosevelt into the New York governor's chair, and renewed the market's vigor, which had been sapped by delays in the peace process. Madrid had stalled final negotiations, hoping that an international group might soften the proposed terms of the Treaty of Paris, but no such aid was offered. Afraid that further dilatory tactics might encourage the impetuous Yankees to add the Canary Islands to the war's prize list, the Spanish commissioners signed the treaty in December.

The Outbreak of World War I

Britain's losses in the Boer War, which began in 1899, tumbled prices in New York, but it was the fear of credit losses to London (to be discussed later), and not the war events themselves, which caused the sharp decline of that year. The Russian-Japanese war of 1904 had little impact in New York, being so far removed, and the recurrent European crises in the following decade only affected New York because of the mischief they worked in the European bourses.

The outbreak of World War I in July 1914 was, of course, something else. The Exchange was the first American casualty. On Friday morning, July 31, minutes before the scheduled 10 a.m. opening, the Exchange governors voted to suspend operations, an extreme and controversial measure that had last been ordered in 1873. At that time the war was less than a week old, and in fact it was not yet a world war: Only Austria and

Serbia were in it so far. It had been a month since the assassination of Austria's Archduke Ferdinand at Sarajevo, but Austria's ugly ultimatum to Serbia on Thursday evening, July 23, had spurred financial anxiety in Europe. A panic spread rapidly, with a drumroll of bourse closings. On Monday, Vienna, Brussels, and Budapest closed. On Tuesday, trading was suspended at Paris, Toronto, and Montreal. Amsterdam, Berlin, and St. Petersburg shut down on Wednesday, Rome and Edinburgh on Thursday.

On Friday morning, as New York slept, the London Stock Exchange was closed, an act unthinkable during the Napoleonic wars. Europe's sellers focused on New York, the only world-class market still open. Investors everywhere wanted to convert paper assets to gold, or currency. Short sellers saw opportunity, if only to hedge against stocks frozen in other markets.

While the week's action had not been disastrous, Thursday's performance had been ominous: The Dow had fallen by 7 percent, the largest daily loss since 1907. General Motors, 94 the previous Saturday, had dropped as low as 55. Bethlehem Steel had lost a quarter of its value since Monday. American shares were battered as the news from London worsened. Fifteen stock-exchange firms had failed in the City, and British consols had fallen to $69\frac{1}{2}$, the lowest price on record.

In New York, the week's distress was heightened by the fact that many blue-chip rails had slipped beneath the worst levels of the 1901 and 1907 panics. Among the cripples, besides those issues mentioned on page 25, were the St. Paul and the North Western. The great "transcontinentals," like the Atchison and the Union Pacific, were far above earlier lows.

On Thursday afternoon, however, the consensus of a bankers' group meeting at J. P. Morgan was to keep the Exchange open, despite the fact that the NYSE was being swamped with selling orders for foreign accounts. What was inevitable on Friday was a tsunami of liquidation washing westward across the Atlantic. The cables of crisis were pouring into New York; England and the continent held an estimated $6 billion in U.S. securities, and war-frightened investors were determined to realize their credits. "Some of the offerings," it was reported later by the *Chronicle*, "consisted of enormous blocks which were to be sold absolutely without limit as to price."

In a crisis session at 9:45 a.m. on Friday, the governing committee of the NYSE voted its most momentous decision in 40 years. Less than four minutes before the opening gong, a message flashed on ticker-tapes across the nation that the Exchange would not open on that day and would be closed until further notice. All other major U.S. securities exchanges followed suit, as did the cotton exchanges. The Chicago Board of Trade, however, remained open.

It was a traumatic decision for the NYSE. The losses of late July had been exceeded many times. But if the Exchange had not closed on that Friday, it would not have lasted the weekend without a record panic. On Saturday, Germany declared war on Russia, and then, on Sunday, invaded France without any formalities. Within days England was also at war, and in hindsight the decision of July 31 seemed brilliant.

Editorialized the London *Times* on Monday, "Feeling this stupendous task of absorbing all the world's business, the New York Stock Exchange decided to close indefinitely," thus avoiding an avalanche of liquidation. It was that suspension, not the extent of the preceding decline, which makes the 1914 war panic fascinating. The suspension, of course, created nearly as many problems as it solved.

Those financial markets which remained open were convulsed. The British pound, long stable at the $4.87 level, quickly advanced to $7, a figure never seen before or since. The Bank of England's interest rate leaped from 3 percent to 10 within three days. A prodigous rise occurred in most commodities, cotton excepted. The September wheat option at the Chicago Board of Trade rose from 76½ cents on July 14 to $1.12 on August 31. The New York Clearing House circled the wagons once again and on Monday August 3 authorized the issuance of Clearing House certificates for the settlement of interbank differences.

The Exchange had sought to construct a great cofferdam, to save U.S. stocks from a flood of liquidation. Immediately, however, leaks sprang up. On Monday, the president of the NYSE was forced to issue a warning about "wildcat brokers." The board quickly approved its own cumbersome means for limited trade. Buy/sell orders had to be processed through its clearing facilities, and transactions could be executed only at or above minimum levels—the closing prices of July 30. Within days, a rudely organized outside or "gutter" market sprang up, for there were thousands of investors who wanted to sell, and some who literally had to.

Trade was generally light, and the war news from the Allies was generally bad. Still, by September, the free-spirited brokerage industry was chafing at restrictive trading rules. But the Exchange held firm, though there was increasing business in the outdoor market. In early October, the news from the front worsened, and the confusing economic picture encouraged many firms to reduce, defer, or eliminate dividends. U.S. Steel, the nation's largest corporation, stunned its holders by cutting the quarterly payout from $1.25 to 50 cents.

It was at this time, in the third week of October, that securities prices reached their low for the year. Such pricing was not generally reported by the press, and *The Wall Street Journal* did not publish the outlaw stock tables, regarded as "illegal and damaging to the general economic welfare," until April 1, 1915.

Fortunately, other records were available, and investors could measure the extent of the autumn crisis and its delayed panic. On July 30, the eve of the long trading holiday, the Dow Industrials had closed at 71.42. On October 28, the 12-stock average hit its 1914 low, unofficial though it may have been, when the index was 66.19.

Thereafter, unofficial pricing steadily improved. The Curb market approved a resumption of trading in November, and the Exchange reopened on Saturday, December 12, though with restrictions on those "international" stocks that were widely held abroad.

Panic had been given a reprieve, and the reprieve had been turned into a full pardon. The Dow closed four points above its level of July 30 and would not challenge that low again until 1932. General Motors, having traded to 55 in the summer panic, sold as high as 85 on December 12, while Bethlehem Steel's July–December "holiday" gain was from 30 to 47, the latter price being its highest for the year.

Within months, Wall Street would become the financial capital of the world, and American paper—stocks, bonds, and paper currency— would be perceived as preferential to any European counterpart.

The Sinking of the *Lusitania*

Great tragedies often suggest large conspiracies. The sinking of the *Lusitania*, like Pearl Harbor and the assassination of John Kennedy, has attracted a conspiracy cult, suspicious of every detail. It is agreed that the Cunard liner, holder of the Atlantic Blue Riband for speed in crossing, was torpedoed off the southeast coast of Ireland at 2:10 p.m. on May 7, 1915, by a German U-boat. It took only 18 minutes for the 32,000-ton vessel to sink, and the casualties totaled 1198. Of the 198 Americans aboard, 128 perished. Other facts are still disputed.

The *Lusitania* was carrying a mixed cargo of passengers and contraband, including 4,200,000 rounds of .303 ammunition for Britain's Enfield rifles, and there were charges that other explosives had been concealed. On the day of the ship's sailing, a travelers' warning had been published by the German Embassy; vessels flying the British flag were liable to destruction in the war zone. Had the liner been deliberately sacrificed to rouse anti-German sentiment in the United States? Conspiracy theorists felt that the ship, which had not received escort into the Irish Sea, had been carelessly risked by Winston Churchill, First Lord of the Admiralty.

Fascinating as are theories about the concealment of 6-inch guns, loaded shells, and Canadian troops in mufti, the indisputable historical fact about the sinking is that in America the incident began a subtle tilt toward the cause of the Allies. Previously, British arrogance on the high seas and a large German-American population had offset U-boat horrors, and the soapbox orators of Times Square had been split in their allegiances. After the *Lusitania* disaster, their vocal support swung toward England, as did the sympathies of those parts of the country that were not determinedly neutral.

The initial reaction to the tragedy was general outrage and, on Wall Street, panic. On Friday, May 7, early rumors of the sinking were indifferently received, but a Cunard bulletin, reported on the news ticker about 1:30 p.m., ripped the bottom from the market. Bethlehem Steel was a typical victim. It had reached a record high in the morning at 159, but after the tragic news sank like a stone to 140 and then, on only 500 shares, plunged to 130. Panic swept across the floor, and 600,000 shares were traded in the final hour. Until late March, there had been only one occasion in 1915 when daily volume had reached that figure.

Friday's action was relieved by a sharp rally in the last half-hour, as further reports indicated that the ship's casualties were light. But Saturday morning brought *The New York Times* and a black eight-column, three-line headline detailing the tragedy. Westinghouse, 108 in late April, opened the day at 82, down 10, on 6000 shares—which was then a large block.

On Monday, a selling wave battered the Exchange, spurred by rumors that President Woodrow Wilson had been assassinated. Pressed Steel Car was smashed down to 40, off 12 points. Bethlehem Steel lost 16. A final end to the stressful period came on Friday, May 14, with the *Times* Industrial index having fallen by 14 percent. American Locomotive had dropped from 61 to 38, and Maxwell Motors had slid to 35 from its peak of 54.

By then the floor had decided that America would not enter a war because of the sinking of a British ship, despite editorial blasts in the Eastern press and Theodore Roosevelt's eagerness to raise a brigade and again charge up some faraway San Juan Hill.

The tragedy became a political football. Diplomatic notes were penned and studied for 18 months with no final solution until overt acts by Germany convinced the public and even the idealist peacemaker, Woodrow Wilson, of the inevitability of war.

A trigger event had caused a fearsome panic, though it had not thrust the United States into war. But it had wrought a decisive change in the moral support for the Allies. Because of the tragic cause of the panic, the conspiracy theory, and the watershed change in war sympathies, the *Lusitania*'s loss gained historical significance.

The convalescence from the liner's loss is of financial interest. By the third week of June, the Dow was at a new high, a record bounce from panic. Bethlehem Steel was accelerating even more rapidly. The stock, which had been 46 in January, was 125 at the May low, 246 in July, 346 in August, and reached 600 in October.

Another U-boat sinking, that of a cross-channel French packet, the *Sussex*, in March 1916, caused some difficulties for the runaway market at the New York Exchange, but facts concerning the tragedy were confused and slow to be revealed, and the modest 10 percent decline carried little drama.

The U-Boat Panic of 1917

Woodrow Wilson, re-elected to the Presidency in 1916 on the slogan, "He Kept Us Out of War," played his last peace card on January 22, 1917. Following a month of negotiations with both the Allies and the Central Powers, he went before Congress with his plan for "Peace without Victory."

The goal was noble and possessed Wilson, but it was a lonely dream. Neither of the belligerent powers were agreeable to any such idealistic solution and, in fact, the German high command had already plotted an unrestricted offensive by its U-boat fleet.

On Wednesday, January 31, at 4 p.m., the German ambassador presented himself to America's secretary of state and advised that unrestricted submarine warfare would be resumed immediately. Neutral shipping, whether armed or unarmed, would be attacked without warning in the German war zone.

For the stock market and all but Wilson, the die was cast. At the Exchange, the decline on February 1 was the worst in 10 years, with the Dow down 7 percent. Prices of both averages fell further on Friday. On Saturday, stocks were swept disastrously lower, only to reverse and close higher for the day. Volume exceeded a million shares, a rarity for the short session. Suddenly the U-boat panic was over, although the Dow had lost 10 percent intraday in just three days.

Individual stocks outperformed the Industrials to the downside. The Atlantic, Gulf & West Indies Steamship line, a natural target, dropped from 122 to 90. Morgan's long-troubled Atlantic blue-water trust, the International Merchant Marine, was cut nearly in half. Commodity stocks, threatened with a blockade on exports, were mauled.

Cuban American sugar lost a third of its value, as did American Hide and Pittsburgh Coal. The market had suffered through an earlier winter panic, the peace–war unsettlement of December, and the U-boat proclamation pushed the winter's loss to 26 percent, equivalent to a minor bear market.

Although Wilson refused to seek a declaration of war, he felt compelled to break relations with Germany and declare that an overt act would force him to seek war. He would be quickly accommodated.

The Zimmerman Telegram.   On the first day of the market break, the *U.S.S. Housatonic* was sunk without warning. On March 1, the bizarre contents of the "Zimmerman telegram" were revealed; *The New York Times* gave it a banner headline. Zimmerman, Berlin's foreign minister, was caught red-handed seeking an alliance with Mexico, his coded message to Ambassador Johann von Bernstorff in Washington being compromised. Germany promised to help Mexico regain Texas, New Mexico, and Arizona.

On March 18, three American ships were torpedoed without warning, with a heavy loss of life, and almost on the same day came news of the Russian revolution and the abdication of the czar. The ways of democracy, or so it seemed, could now be served by all the Allies.

On the evening of April 2, Wilson appeared before Congress and asked for a declaration of war. America's age of innocence had ended, but such innocence as was lost had already been discounted by the market's February plunge. The Dow was higher on the war's eve than it had been in late January. Both the war act and the war itself would be, for a time, market nonevents.

The 1930s: Preparing for War

Looking back, war and the threat of war were as much a part of the 1930s as world depression. Japan invaded China and Italy overwhelmed Emperor Haile Selassie and Ethiopia. Minor and major war panics intruded regularly upon the market.

Nazi rowdies attempted a coup in Vienna in July 1934 and assassinated Premier Dollfuss in the Austrian chancellory. While the putsch failed, it raised war fears and pushed to climax a summer setback caused by communist-inspired labor troubles on the San Francisco waterfront and the general strike called in that city. German troops reoccupied the Rhineland in the spring of 1936.

In March 1938, Hitler's Austrian Anschluss stirred serious war fears in a market already shocked by the Exchange's expulsion of President Richard Whitney; to millions of people, he had epitomized the NYSE. New rumors swept Wall Street just a year later as the Nazis marched into Czechoslovakia.

Such persistent anticipation of unfavorable news can discount even the fact of war, it was soon to be proven.

The Onset of World War II: A Buyers' Panic

An extraordinary opening chapter to World War II was written in the world's financial markets. Fear and panic have often been the hand-maidens of war, but in 1939 there was no fear in the bourses of the world, and the panic was on the part of buyers.

When World War I broke out, there had been only sellers. Every major exchange in the world was overwhelmed by liquidating orders, and all were forced to suspend activity. But when Germany invaded Poland at dawn on Friday, September 1, 1939, it stirred a buying spree in New York, on the Continent, and in Tokyo. There has been no such similar market response in the past century, but no other war has been so long discounted.

The Dow Jones, which had been at 131 in late August, posted 156 by September 12. In Tokyo on September 4 (the NYSE was closed for Labor Day), the trading was so violently bullish that the afternoon session had to be canceled so that brokers could balance their trades. In New York on Tuesday, September 5, the Rails ran up over 10 percent, one of their best advances ever, and the Dow spiked up by more than 10 points.

Investors and traders remembered the glory year of 1915, when the Dow had scooted to its biggest gain in history. At that time the United States had also been a neutral, and war's export demands had promoted scores of astounding gains. Bethlehem Steel, for example, advanced from 30 in the "gutter" market of October 1914 to 600 just 12 months later.

For those investors in 1939 whose memories were short, brokerage houses rushed to print statistics on the awesome gains of American stocks in that earlier war. The numbers did encourage a certain hyste-ria. General Motors, another giant of the earlier war, had gained 1445 percent, from 55 to 850. Commodity stocks had enjoyed their tradition-al war play; South Porto Rico Sugar had been a 28–240 winner.

There seemed no reason to change the bets in 1939. Bethlehem Steel rushed up from near 50 to 100, gaining over 14 points on September 5. Wright Aero flew up 24 points in a single day. Most "war brides" enjoyed their happiest days during the short September honeymoon, for the Dow had already registered its high for the year—indeed, its high for the next five years.

The events of September 1939 remain an exception in the market archives of war, but it was the giddy buyers who erred in breaking the pattern. The buyers' panic, which lasted less than a month, was a classic bull-trap. Hitler would be dead before most of the coveted "war babies" would show a profit. For some "obvious" speculative choices, such as United Aircraft and Sperry, the wait would be longer—until the 1950s.

The brutal blow of the Dunkerque evacuation in May 1940 decimated such favorites of the previous September. Dunkerque was an epochal event in financial as well as military history, and its effects are discussed in detail in Chap. 8.

Pearl Harbor: The Panic That Didn't Jell

There are probably one or two minor panics each year which don't jell completely, even if they have the right ingredients. The events of Sunday, December 7, 1941, and the following fateful days are part of one such curious episode.

Pearl Harbor's infamy has been engraved on the memory of every American. The loss or severe damage to six of our finest along Battleship Row and the destruction of half the island's air fleet, all within a few hours, staggered the nation. While the military groped for a response, financial leaders struggled to get a handle on what U.S. involvement in the war would mean. Only 18 months before, events leading to the Dunkerque evacuation had ripped the Dow for a loss of 25 percent—and the nation had been only a spectator to that tragedy.

On Monday, December 8, the Dow fell barely four points. In 10 of the previous 12 years, the record daily loss had been more severe. But the news would worsen. Three days later, two of Britain's mightiest warships were sunk off Singapore, lost to air power. And despite the warning of Pearl Harbor, General Douglas MacArthur's scarce B-17s were destroyed by bombing attacks in the Philippines.

By mid-December, the Japanese were established on Luzon and had already overwhelmed Wake Island and Guam. It was a disastrous entry into war. But when the Dow's December low was marked on the 23rd, the 14-day decline had cut the Industrials by less than 9 percent.

Why didn't the panic quite come off? Conspiracy theories of prior knowledge of the attack at high levels of the FDR administration don't really explain the resilience of investor psychology to the massive dose of bad news in December 1941. One must assume that during the 19 months since Dunkerque the market had discounted America's possible participation in the war. The only surprise was that the trigger was pulled in Tokyo, not Berlin.

There had been apprehension about Japan's intentions, to be sure. Relations with Japan had become increasingly strained over the previous decade, as she had thrust brutal army after brutal army into China, all in the interests of "self-defense." In late 1940 she had aligned herself with Hitler and Mussolini in the Tripartite Agreement. Her reward: a sphere of interest known as the Greater East Asia Co-Prosperity Sphere. In early 1941, an American volunteer group, the Flying Tigers, irked Tokyo by giving air assistance to China.

In late July, President Roosevelt declared an economic embargo on war supplies to Japan, halting shipments of petroleum products and scrap iron. To many, the move was tardy; America's East Coast drivers were already suffering a coupon fuel shortage, while Japan had virtually cornered West Coast aviation gas. Enraged by the embargo, the island militarists pushed their troops into Saigon and southern French Indo-China. Borneo and its oil riches would be next, the pessimists claimed.

They were wrong. Pearl Harbor would be next, after an autumn of rancorous diplomatic tilting which helped conceal the Imperial Navy's plans for the treacherous strike across the northern Pacific. It was not war, but the route by which it arrived at America's doorsteps that surprised the market.

And so the shock of Pearl Harbor left no historic scars on the market. In market archives, 1941 remains unique because of the panic which did not jell. The sharpest slump of the year had come in the early winter, when a curious consensus of military experts warned that the Nazi invasion of England would surely come in the spring of 1941. In that ignored crisis, stocks fell by nearly 12 percent within a one-month period.

Postwar War Panics

In the first major conflict after World War II, war returned to Asia when North Korea invaded its southern neighbor in June 1950. The panic sell-off that followed, which lasted about three weeks, was the only severe market hit between late 1948 and Eisenhower's heart attack in 1955. Otherwise, the Cold War era produced no severe shocks to the market, and the gradual immersion in the Vietnam swamp also lacked sharp market impact.

Saddam's invasion and threat to Middle Eastern oil dropped the market sharply in August 1990, and the initial panic low was knocked out in October as the specter of inflation and $40 crude frightened investors who had resisted the first selling rush. By the following April, however, victory had been won for the United Nations, and the Dow was at a new peak, above 3000.

The Menace of Peace

The stock market has often been charged with being schizophrenic. As we have seen, war and the threat of war have repeatedly set off panics. But so has the threat of peace.

1916: The "Menace of Peace" Smashes the Market

The 1916 Christmas season was the most prosperous in America's history. Serving as the neutral quartermaster to the warring armies of Europe had provided the nation and the stock market with tremendous profits.

In the previous year, the Dow had enjoyed its largest gain in history, a record which still stands. An enormous favorable trade balance was running about six times the prewar figure. Following the example of U.S. Steel, many corporations announced generous Christmas bonuses. Newspapers were swamped with consumer advertising. In *The New York Times*, the automobile section was crowded with display ads for now long-forgotten marques—the Chandler, Cole, Hupmobile, Mitchell, Saxon, and Velie. Automobile production, as yet unhampered by any war restrictions, was up 194 percent from the 1914 level. General Motors, already a legendary market driver, had sped up from 55 in July 1914 to 850. Given the great prosperity, the buyer's biggest problem then, as now, was how to get in the fast lane. A feature in the auto section explained to motorists "How to Get out of the Big City and Connect with Roads for Important Points."

In early December, the *Times* 50-stock average was only a couple of points below the year's high, reached in late November. While there had been rumors of a peace offensive during the autumn, serious initiatives had not begun until after the Presidential election of November. Both President Wilson and the Germans, who had just captured Bucharest, felt that the timing was good for an overture of peace. On December 12, Berlin made its pitch, creating a sensation in the market. The Dow lost 4 percent on the largest volume since 1907. Rumors swirled through the market, though the peace proposals were, at best, received cooly by the Allies. The new Russian government immediately rejected "premature peace."

A sharp rally was halted dead late on December 19, when Britain's Prime Minister Lloyd George seemed to leave the peace door open. In the meantime, Wilson's own peace note had been "secretly" forwarded to the belligerents on December 18; its text was released on the night of December 20. Thursday, December 21, was the most tumultuous day since 1901, with a volume of over 3 million shares—the largest figure in the 24-year period between 1901 and 1925.

The peace note smashed stocks at the opening. GM opened on 50,000 shares, down 6; it was one of the largest blocks in history. War stocks were dealt mortal blows. But the peace scare was just for openers. At mid-morning, the news ticker reported that Secretary of State Robert Lansing had said the country was drawing near to war. Instantly, peace scare turned to war scare, and the downrush accelerated. By the day's end, the Dow was down 15 percent from its level just two weeks earlier. A schizoid headline in the *Times* said it all: "Peace and War Talk Hit Stocks."

The war stocks had been hurt worst. Central Leather, 114 on the previous Monday, collapsed to 75. Bethlehem Steel lost 72 points on a few hundred shares, closing at 500. Cuban Cane Sugar traded down to 43; its early December peak had been 70. U.S. Industrial Alcohol was a 138–95 victim in the same time period. U.S. Steel had fallen from 124 to par, while Crucible Steel, 96 a few weeks earlier, fell to 50. On Friday, Lansing's "I was misquoted. Sorry" jumped stocks back up to where they had been Wednesday, a 5 percent gain, but the market's psyche had been transformed and the advance of 1914–1916 ended. War in Europe had been bullish. Peace in Europe had been bearish. But the United States at war in Europe was even more bearish.

Almost immediately, there were charges of "peace tip profits." Washington insiders, it was claimed, had used early information of the peace moves to instigate short-selling campaigns. Secretary of the Treasury William McAdoo, the President's son-in-law, Bernard Baruch, who would become war production czar, Jesse Livermore, the legendary speculator, and even German Ambassador Bernstorff were mentioned among the suspected profiteers. A Republican member of

Congress introduced a bill to investigate the alleged speculators, but it was lost in the Democratic majority.

Rails Swoon after V-E Day

Another major "peace" panic occurred in the summer of 1945, following V-E day. While the Industrials were relatively unaffected, the Dow Rails took a beating. The pathetic performance of the carriers during the 1930s was recalled, and their average fell 15 percent in just over a month, reaching a low in August following the informal surrender by Japan. Such widely spaced rails as the B&O, Canadian Pacific, and Gulf Mobile & Ohio lost about one-third of their value during the postvictory swoon, although the average and most lines would struggle to a new high in late autumn. Perhaps it was an indicator. In the 1946–1949 bear sequence, the carriers' loss of 40 percent would be much more decisive than that of the Industrials, down 24 percent.

The Influence of London

A century ago, the London Stock Exchange was the world's largest, a truly international market (which New York has never been) in such exotics as Kaffirs, Colonials, Indians, American rails and the tea plantations of the East. Great Britain was America's largest creditor, and her capital had built many of the leading U.S. railroads.

"How's London?" was the first inquiry into market prospects each day, for the City's quote had an immense influence on prices. Most leading rails were traded dually, and arbitrage was common and practical; a round-trip telegraphic exchange required only about four minutes. Thus, it was inevitable that London sometimes led or pushed Wall Street over the brink.

The Baring Crisis

The Baring Crisis of 1890 affords an early example. For a century the House of Baring had been England's leading investment banking firm, and it had close and historic ties with New York. Troubles at Baring led to a convulsion on Wall Street in the autumn of 1890.

"Gaucho speculations" were the cause of Baring's downfall. The firm had invested both its customers' money and the firm's capital in financing huge credits in Argentina. A second Western Frontier, it was postulated, would develop in that country. Although warnings of peril had been published as early as 1888 in *The Economist*, the situation became sticky in the early fall of 1890. London was forced to cut and run from its American investments in order to try and save the Argentine credits.

The Bank of England came to the rescue, aided by a gold loan from the Bank of France, but not before London selling and a bear attack on the Northern Pacific and friends had stripped the New York market. The Dow lost 14 percent during the November crisis. North American, a holding company for the Villard rails, crashed from 34 to 7 within a few days. The NP dropped from 28 to 17 in the same period.

The Boer War

Wall Street's first panic of the decade had originated in the pampas of Argentina. Fittingly, the last crisis of the 1890s also began abroad, even farther from New York than Argentina. War in the Transvaal between the Boers and Britain erupted in early October of 1899, and within weeks England's dismal record was being duly reported by a young war correspondent named Winston S. Churchill.

Speedy cable facilities encouraged swift repatriation of British capital. Despite its foreign origin, the panic was true to form in its intensity, in the swirl of ugly rumors which attach to every crisis, and in the fact that vague clues of trouble had been available for months. Britain's "Black Week" leaped the Atlantic in December 1899. The continuing war losses had worked sharp mischief at London, and British capital sought to redeem its American credits despite bad pricing, as apprehensions rose concerning U.S. gold losses, dear money (the call rate went to 186 percent), and fresh defeats in the Transvaal.

The Dow fell 23 percent in 13 trading days, and volume at the climax was the third largest in history. The loss of nearly 9 percent on December 18, following news of the defeat at Colenso, would not be exceeded until 1929.

Newly formed industrial trusts were the prime targets, for such "fancies" had no background of earnings or performance. John W. Gates's American Steel & Wire and Morgan-controlled Federal Steel both lost over one-third of their value. American Tobacco fell from 118 to 79.

Frightening rumors, encouraged by short sellers, swamped the Exchange. When one firm suspended, an act much predicted, then, "in its usual harum-scarum way, Wall Street hurried to a belief that all circulating rumors of bad import must be true." General Electric and Westinghouse were said to face antitrust charges. Boston banks would suspend activity because of copper finance problems. Baltimore banks were in trouble under the load of the Seaboard railroad consolidation. Queen Victoria was dead. And so on.

The rail stocks rewarded the panic buyers with the usual quick fix, recovering their losses within a few months. The Industrials rallied vigorously, but they could not match the carriers, and the divergence continued into the autumn. War was the excuse for their collapse, but they had been suspect for months. There were too many stocks of uncertain value, a result of the trustification mania which had begun in 1898. James R. Keene, a bear during most of the year, had correctly predicted trouble earlier when he declared that the market was in the "ebb tide of a speculative sea."

Not until 1931 would events in London again cause such distress in New York. In September of that year England abandoned the gold standard, and the U.S. market plunged to its worst fall of the 1930s. Like other crises of the Depression period, this "gold panic" is surveyed in Chap. 10.

Even when the Exchange was not spooked by London, there were plenty of in-house entanglements to cause troubles. The Northern Pacific and Stutz corners, the Twine and Hocking bubbles, and the 1933 Whiskey Pools were all bull manipulations which were shattered by a sudden collapse. Such artificial risks played a great part in Exchange activity until the very eve of the SEC formation.

Antibusiness Fears

Antibusiness attacks have occasionally blind-sided the market, but fortunately the rhetoric of Washington has outpaced the action.

The fears have had multiple roots. Concerns about tariff reductions, the Interstate Commerce Commission, antitrust measures, liberal Presidencies, investigative committees, and even out-and-out antibusiness campaigns have often chilled the market and sometimes brought panic.

When Woodrow Wilson, whom the *Commercial & Financial Chronicle* termed "radical," was about to assume the Presidency, he panicked the market with a Chicago speech which seemed to portend painful changes for business. Lower tariffs and an income tax were already discounted in the impending political changes at the White House and in Congress. But the President-elect's antibusiness speech frightened the Street.

A few weeks earlier, naively concerned that businessmen might start panic to prevent the enactment of reform legislation, he had promised them a "gibbet high as Haman." The intemperate threats continued, and on January 11, 1913, speaking to the Commercial Club of Chicago and an audience which included J. Ogden Armour and Cyrus H. McCormick, he lashed out at men who had restricted credit and conspired to establish monopoly. "I cannot deal with you...you have got to clear yourselves before the general jury."

The weekend threat signified to some the beginning of a general assault on property, and the market took it poorly, falling sharply on Monday and over the next week. The pace then gentled and by February, Wilson's right-hand man, Colonel House, was conferring with Wall Street leaders in an effort to mend the fences. The toll on the Dow had been modest, just over 10 percent.

Six years earlier, in March 1907, President Theodore Roosevelt, a bull-in-the-china-closet Republican, had caused great damage by shrugging off a meeting with the nation's rail leaders which J. P. Morgan had worked hard to arrange. Legislative hostility toward the railroads had already impaired investment confidence, and Roosevelt's affront worked swift damage.

One year later, Roosevelt fired up his antitrust batteries again in a speech before Congress. His attacks on business, including a letter to the ICC urging more vigorous action, helped peel back the Industrials by 11 percent. Rail followers were offended at the new campaign, since the Seaboard Airline and Chicago Great Western had just slipped into receivership. Twenty-two other roads would also go to the courthouse in 1908, a year of anomaly—a depression for commerce and a raging bull market for stocks.

In 1948, the only market panic related directly to a Presidential election result struck after Harry Truman's upset of Tom Dewey sent a Democrat to the White House for a fifth consecutive term. The disappointed Republicans saw the win as a victory for antibusiness forces, for the New Deal had not been forgotten, nor Truman's unsuccessful veto of the Taft-Hartley bill. Truman was not seen as a "smoke-stack" man, and the heavy industry stocks fell sharply. Chrysler dropped from 61 to the year's low of 51, and the railroads declined by 16 percent during the election month. The stubborn bear market was extended for another seven months.

The Kennedy Panic

The showdown between President John F. Kennedy and U.S. Steel in the late spring of 1962 ignited a classic panic, dramatic and of short duration. It brought the most confrontation with the White House since the 1930s and spurred the perception that the President was antibusiness.

At the end of March, the United Steelworkers Union and the industry had agreed to a new labor contract with no general wage hike but some fringe increases. On April 6, U.S. Steel announced price increases averaging $6 a ton, a move which infuriated Kennedy, who had thought the pact, which he had helped implement, was completed on the basis of no price increases. A seething Kennedy described the price action as "wholly unjustifiable and irresponsible" and ordered the Attorney General, his brother Robert, to begin a grand jury investigation. The steel industry, of course, saw another side to the picture. Earnings in 1961, a good business year, had been less than half the average figure for 1955–1958 and something less than those of 1950, so modest price increases seemed justified.

Though the price raise was rescinded, the market took the charges of antibusiness bias seriously and headed south. The free-fall continued through late May, peeling 22 percent off the Dow's value. In the final convulsion, on May 28, the Industrials suffered their largest point loss since 1929. The rebound from panic, however, was muted, and most group indices fell further in June, when the Dow low was 536 as compared with 577 in May.

Fearful of the fallout from White House anger, investors continued to liquidate steel holdings into the autumn, with the group's final low coming during the Cuban missile crisis. Issues such as CF&I, Lukens, U.S. Steel, and Republic all lost half their value in this nonrecession year. It might have been worse. Many bloated stocks of 1961 suffered more harshly. Addressograph, a 110-to-39 loser, and Bell & Howell, smashed from 70 to 16, also made their lows in October.

One-of-a-Kind Panics

Often the balance of the market is suddenly tilted by an event so unusual that not even perennial bears might have imagined it. These one-of-a-kind wipe-outs are so unexpected that they can turn euphoria into a selling frenzy overnight. They challenge cataloguing, but they attract intense curiosity.

Two unique incidents—the unraveling of the Twine Trust and the Hocking Coal manipulations—are discussed in Chap. 10 because they provide rebound statistics which are rather less than perfect.

Here are some of the other famous "uniques."

The Cross of Silver

Few political speeches have stirred the nation like that of William Jennings Bryan, the "Boy Orator of the Platte," at the Democratic convention of July 1896:

You shall not press down upon the brow of labor this crown of thorns, you shall not crucify mankind upon a cross of gold.

Bryan's ringing words, a battle cry for free coinage and a 16:1 ratio between silver and gold, catapulted him to the Democratic Presidential nomination, in a race that pitted him against Republican William McKinley. Bryan's speech cleanly split the sound-money men of the East from the agrarian and mining inflationists and splintered both political parties. "Silver Republicans" and "gold Democrats" would each nominate their own Presidential candidates.

The sound-money men had thought the silver matter laid to rest in 1893 by the repeal of the Sherman Silver Purchase Act. Though the election-year market problems are now largely forgotten because of the larger political and currency considerations, Bryan's impassioned appeal to inflation sentiment frightened Wall Street. Haunted by ghosts it thought deposed, the market reacted in panic, falling 19 percent from the postconvention high to an early August low. London sold the market, and dollar proceeds were converted to sterling balances. Gold emigrated.

Bryan had been labeled "The Great Commoner," a battler for agrarian and populist reforms. But in his first strike at the Presidency—he was to be his party's nominee again in 1900 and 1908—his campaign was one-dimensional. By late August the hysteria of the Silverites had become a handicap, and Republic hopes brightened. The Industrials responded and shot up 36 percent in just three months. Tennessee Coal & Iron, 27 before the convention, slumped to 13 but reached 33 in November.

Southern Rail preferred, which had lost nearly half its value in the panic, falling to 16, recovered to 33. In Chicago, however, "heedless speculation" in Diamond Match and New York Biscuit helped bring failure to the Moore brothers; the Chicago Stock Exchange would be padlocked until November.

On November 3, William McKinley and his friends ended for a generation the Silverites' political threat. The Silver Crisis had played a role in scaring the electorate to the side of sound money. Higher grain prices and "McKinley prosperity" would then kill the issue for most.

But for Bryan and his friends there remained the paradoxical fact, not yet faced, that the Nebraska Democrat had nailed his party to "a cross of *silver* which the party had to bear through three successive Presidential elections," long after the issue carried any economic or political reality.* It was one reason why no Democrat would be elected to the White House until 1912.

The Flower Market

In 1899 the curiously named "Flower market" was the victim. Ex-Governor Roswell P. Flower of New York was the most celebrated bull of the late 1890s. In early 1898 he had declared himself a bull on America and American stocks. As a leader of the constructive forces on the floor, he had the thorough approval of such allies as the Rockefellers, Vanderbilt, and J. P. Morgan. He was, however, often opposed by some powerful speculators on the floor, including James R. Keene.

The conclusion of the Spanish-American war gave his force and followers great momentum. Though he was active in the steam rails, his greatest success came in manipulations of the Brooklyn Rapid Transit—a treasured plaything for both politicians and speculators—in New York Air Brake, and the Chicago Gas trust.

His successes were astounding by the measure of any era. New York Air Brake, which had only 62,500 shares outstanding, was bought at auction in 1898 for $5–$6 a share and bulled to 200. The BRT, purchased near 20, was marched almost without interruption to 140. Peoples Gas netted over 200 percent. It was estimated that $100 million had been added to the value of the "Flower" stocks, an inflation boosted by the Dow's rise of over 70 percent from the time of the *Maine's* loss.

It was a period of feverish mania, fueled by strong pools and the excited creation of vast new industrial trusts, all heavily watered. Noted the *Commercial & Financial Chronicle* in January 1899, "The public is in the market and its capacity for absorbing securities seems at the moment unlimited."

Flower's following was successful and thus quite enormous, but when he unexpectedly died of a heart attack at a country club in Eastpoint, Long Island, there was a vacuum of leadership. New York Air Brake, 185 on the eve of his death, wilted on the next day to 135, compounding the grief of his followers. Actually, Keene had already launched an attack on the Flower favorites; Air Brake had been 204 in late April. Federal Steel, a creation of Flower and the Standard Oil crowd, had been ramrodded to 75 from a low at 46 in February; it slumped to 50. The Dow's loss in the three week decline of May was 11 percent.

*Page Smith, *The Rise of Industrial America*, Vol. 6 (McGraw-Hill, New York, 1984), p. 548.

The collapse of the "Flower market" seems to mark the only occasion in the past century when the death of a noted speculator caused such panic. Neither the passing of Jay Gould, James J. Hill, nor Edward H. Harriman caused any appreciable damage to stock values. Though the Dow would inch to a new high in September, it was only stage dressing. For the public, Flower's demise meant the withdrawal of solid support in a lot of conspicuous stocks and a suspicious revaluation of the prospects of the scores of newly organized trusts.

The $1000 Northern Pacific Corner

The classic model of high drama in panic remains the accidental Northern Pacific corner of 1901, which drove the shares of the railroad from 160 to 1000 within a day. It was not only unique but a true classic, for it was short, brutal, and followed immediately by a brilliant rally. Daily volume peaked at a level which would not be exceeded for 24 years. Its protagonists were the titans of Wall Street, locked in a rowdy railroad brawl for control of the Northern Pacific.

The crisis was over within three days. It was a microcosm of the paradoxical fear and opportunity of Wall Street's legendary crises. U.S. Steel sold at 47 on Wednesday, May 8, at 24 on Thursday, and bounced back to 45 on Friday.

The trigger event was not the typical collapse of a market favorite, but a rocket shot which propelled NP common stock from 160 to 1000 on Thursday morning. That bizarre advance was possible because the stock had been accidentally cornered. Fueled by a desperate short interest, the unprecedented gain created a selling panic in all shares; the men trapped in the corner threw all other possessions overboard. The Southern Pacific was axed from 50 to 29 within the morning. American Telephone & Telegraph, even then a blue chip, fell from 130 to 99, its record intraday decline.

Though the crisis had exploded without warning, the storm had been building for a year in a struggle to gain control of the Chicago, Burlington & Quincy (CBQ). The Burlington's line into Chicago was coveted by both Edward H. Harriman's Union Pacific and James J. Hill's NP–Great Northern combine; neither group had direct access to that vital rail center.

Hill, backed by J. P. Morgan, won out; the NP acquired the stock and thus became proxy for control of the CBQ. Harriman's request for a cooperative position was denied and he secretly began buying shares of the NP, in which his adversaries lacked full control. Learning of his move, the Hill forces launched a reckless buying campaign in their own stock. Morgan cabled from France to buy 150,000 common shares at market (there were only 400,000 outstanding). Additional short sellers, convinced that the Northern Pacific was far overpriced, were seduced.

An estimated 140,000 shares had been sold short, and the bears suddenly found that there was no place to borrow the stock for delivery. The railroad antagonists demanded every share owed them. "He who sells what isn't his'n must buy it back or go to prison" was the old adage. And so a corner, unintended and unwanted, stirred the market to panic.

Thursday, May 9, was a day of doom for longs in the market and shorts in the surging railroad. For investors with reserves and calmness, it was a day of extraordinary opportunity. By noon, Northern Pacific had reached 1000, where 300 shares were bought in a cash trade. Meanwhile, panic convulsed other quality stocks. The electric railroad, Manhattan Elevated, though far removed from the western battle, fell to 83 from its previous close at 122.

Around noon, a lightning reversal was achieved when the Morgan forces and Harriman's Kuhn, Loeb bankers agreed to a truce and announced that shorts would not be bought in that day. The announcement sparked frenzied buying. U.S. Steel bounced from 24 to 40, and the Atchison recovered from 43 to 67. It was too late to help the bull pool whose failure had contributed to the railroad's morning bloodbath. Northern Pacific again countered the market's trend, closing at 325, down 675 points from its noon peak. It would fall further, to 150, on Friday. Table 3-2 capsules some of the historic price gyrations.

The averages also suffered immoderate damage from Wednesday's closing level to the intraday low Thursday morning. The Railroads, which would remain the higher priced index until 1915, fell from 111.62 to 88.63, a drop of 21 percent; their loss from Monday had been 25 percent. The Industrials' overnight drop to 60.58 amounted to 16 percent.

May 9 buyers reaped rich profits, but the spectacle frightened the public, which turned away from the market. The unique panic had been unnatural, not caused by dear money or calamity, but by the determination of two powerful forces to control a rail property. A sensational banner headline in the *New York Herald* said it all (see Fig. 3-1).

The panic remains a classic because of its unprecedented violence and drama, particularly the smash of Thursday morning and the startling afternoon reflex. The participants were Wall Street barons, giants of finance and railroading, and the prizes they sought were among the

Table 3-2. Northern Pacific Panic
Leading Stocks, May 6–10, 1901

	Monday high	Wednesday close	Thursday Low	Thursday Close	Monday– Thursday extreme loss (%)	Friday close
Atchison, Topeka	89	78	43	67	⁻52	74
American Smelting	61	57	40	53	34	50
Chesapeake Ohio	53	46	29	42	45	45
Southern Pacific	56	50	29	45	48	49
Union Pacific	127	114	70	90	45	112
U.S. Steel	54	47	24	40	56	45

most famous rail lines of the country. The Exchange volume on Thursday, May 9, would not be exceeded until 1925. The corner, accidental though it was, remains a legend.

It also frightened public investors, even those who were not involved. *The New York Times* chided the principals in a vivid editorial: "They behaved like cowboys on a spree, mad with rum, and shooting wildly at each other in entire disregard for the safety of the bystanders." Though the outcry died quickly, quieted by the miracle rally, it would be years before the speculative public returned to Wall Street.

The San Francisco Earthquake

In 1901 the Galveston hurricane brought death to 8000 people, nearly 10 times the casualty toll of the San Francisco earthquake of April 18, 1906. But the September hurricane had only limited impact on stock prices. The leveling or burning of a large part of the "American Paris," a port second only to New York in foreign and domestic trade, battered the market.

Even before the full reports of damage began to accumulate, insurance and casualty companies knew they faced astronomical claims. And so the institutions were forced almost immediately to liquidate huge blocks of securities. In Hartford alone, the figure was estimated at over $200 million.

Figure 3-1. The *New York Herald* carried a banner headline announcing the Northern Pacific panic. A joint holding company, Northern Securities, brought a truce, although the Supreme Court forced its dissolution in 1904.

While it is unclear just what part of the San Francisco damage was due to seismic activity and what due to fire, the claims were huge. Bonds and stocks of such institutional favorites as the New York Central, the Pennsylvania, Reading, Union Pacific, and BRT were put under pressure, and the Industrials declined by 11 percent within a three-week period. Selling was encouraged by reason of the speculative excesses of early winter, when the Anaconda "copper mania" had crested.

The earthquake is not ordinarily viewed as a watershed event for the market, but the Dow would be unable to recover its level of early April until August of 1909.

Ike's Heart Attack

Twenty-seven holes of golf in Denver's high altitude did in both President Dwight D. Eisenhower and the market. On Friday, September 23, 1955, the Dow had closed at its highest level in history, 487.45. On Saturday, Ike took to the links at the Cherry Hills Club and late that night suffered a heart attack; he was transferred to Fitzsimons Army Hospital the next day. It was a unique trigger for a market panic.

It will seem curious to modern traders, but Monday's session following the attack was a disaster of record proportions, a genuine triple bogey. The Dow suffered its largest point loss since 1929 and its worst percentage decline since Dunkerque. Volume was the highest since 1933.

Perhaps the market had forgotten how to deal with panic, for the solid advance of the 1950s had only once been interrupted by a crisis—the Korean war—and low inflation and budget deficits had encouraged a dreamlike attitude during the years of gain.

Less than a year earlier, the 1929 high for the Dow had been easily surmounted, and in the post-Labor Day trading of 1955, Dow 500 looked like a "gimme." Unlike many markets which act toppy before the drumroll of panic, the 1955 advance boasted excellent technical underpinnings.

Perhaps it was the shock to the nation's father-image of Ike, or perhaps there were serious doubts about how Vice President Richard Nixon might handle the Presidential duties, if called upon. Regardless, the market turned tail and in just 12 trading days lost 10 percent.

It was a panic of receding stress, and except for the unique trigger it would be already forgotten. One has to search for serious victims. Among them: Anaconda dropped from 81 to 61, and Pacific Western Oil (Getty) fell from 50 to 37. United Airlines, crippled by the worst airline crash in history on October 6, saw its shares knocked down from 46 to 35.

The Silver Panic of 1980

The collapse of great commodity speculations and corners—or almost corners—have always unnerved the stock market. A gold corner in 1869 wreaked enormous damage, and later misadventures in such items as copper, wheat, corn, cotton, and salad oil created financial chaos and a dismal influence on stock prices.

In 1980 it was silver's unique betrayal that battered both commodity and stock speculators. Within a few weeks, silver lost about 80 percent of its value and, it is easy to see now, proved an early indicator for the end of the inflation mania.

Not all of the lawsuits have yet been settled, but the tale of Dallas billionaire Nelson Bunker Hunt's flawed silver manipulation will remain a legend into the next century. The panic of March 1980 produced some amazing bargains in the mining group, which rallied later in the year to a new peak, despite the divergence by metal prices. The incident is discussed in more detail in Chap. 9.

The Kennedy Assassination and Other Non-Panics

Any market decline has the potential of turning a smoke alarm into a fire alarm. Earlier we discussed one panic that didn't jell—Pearl Harbor. In the 50 years since, the most memorable of the panics that didn't quite make it followed the assassination of President John F. Kennedy on Friday, November 22, 1963.

The tragedy in Dallas propelled the market into an immediate selling frenzy, and trading had to be halted at 2:07 p.m. In the final seven minutes before the shutdown, volume ran over 2 million shares. Polaroid lost 16 points before activity was suspended. Control Data, IBM, RCA, Xerox, and several dozen other volatile issues were also shut down. The Dow was already down nearly 3 percent and continued heavy liquidation was forecast for Monday, but the NYSE wisely chose to suspend trading for a day.

The merit of trading shutdowns remains controversial, but it proved of great benefit in 1963. Institutions circled the wagons over the long weekend and by Tuesday's opening, it was immediately apparent that Wall Street's Camelot would continue under the banner of Lyndon Baines Johnson. A buyers' panic swept prices steeply higher, and the Dow's percentage gain was the second best in 24 years. The incipient panic had been stopped, and by early December the average would be at a record high.

The situation was somewhat similar to that following President Garfield's assassination on Saturday, July 2, 1881. Then, the intercession of the weekend plus the national holiday calmed the selling.

In 1962, the fortunate resolution of the Cuban missile crisis saved the market from a downtrend which was beginning to accelerate on high volume. Sixty years earlier, the formation of an overly large banking pool had halted an incipient panic sparked by stressful money conditions and the threat of a German drive for a naval base in the Caribbean. Such frustrated threats of panic can be found in every decade.

No Place to Hide

The causes of panic are easily catalogued, but this knowledge affords little investor protection. We know that war and the threat of war always shake the market, but who knows when the next Saddam will strike? And in 1939, war's paradoxical result was a buyers' panic. Grossly overconfident markets, we learn, are exceptionally vulnerable to violent reversals, but they may remain hyper and overbought for months before giving way to disaster. Crises of unique origin will continue to blindside investors—there is no way to hide from panic.

On the other hand, events that one would think would trigger extreme reaction fail to do so, as was the case with Pearl Harbor. The classic causes of panic are often revived just when they seem forgotten. In the old days, pools and corners were the frequent causes of crisis, but such manipulations were seen as a thing of the past—until the Silver Panic of 1980. Merger mania helped trip the market in 1899 and 1929, among other early years, and it struck again in 1989 when the airline stocks crashed and burned.

It is not the causes, but the workings of panic that remain mysterious. Their psychological complexities will not be solved by a twenty-first-century rationality or new computer strategies.

4
Bear Market Almanac

The causes of panic are easy to identify. A single event triggers shock and fear in a straightforward reaction. Only rarely is a crisis set off by a mysterious implosion. In either case, the affair is quickly over. Panics are quite consistent in their reactions.

Bear markets are more complex. They last longer, but their duration can't be predicted. Some have lasted for years, but many are over within months. Although they do more damage than panics, bear markets are not widely feared. The trigger for a bear sequence is often puzzling, although it is generally rooted in depression or a perception of a depression.

Bull market opportunities command unending investment comment, but bear episodes and their timing are honored by silence, like some troubled family member locked in a back room. They deserve more attention. Consider that since 1890, the stock market, as measured by the leading Dow average, has spent nearly 33 years locked in the bear's embrace. If one adds in the 1923 and 1953 declines, qualified by many analysts as bear episodes, the figure is over 34 years. A centenarian investor has spent something like one-third of his life in a reverse financial gear. Since 1956, there have been nine bear markets, or one every 4.1 years, plus the major panic of 1987.

Averages are notoriously poor tools, but they do suggest that there will be two more down sequences in this decade.

Just in case the average is right, you might wish to acquaint yourself with the bear market file. You'll find that these unstable episodes can ignore recession, spur recession, applaud war, and ignore war. They occasionally blind-side the economy, but at other times they have no impact beyond Wall Street. They sometimes go underground for long periods, as between 1921 and 1929, but they can pop up annually, as in 1937, 1938, and 1939. They make perfect sense in hindsight, but they often lack rationality in being.

Major Declines since 1890

June–December 1890

Our first major decline was triggered by recession, which appeared in June just as the stock market rolled over. Bad crops pressured the "granger" railroads, and the Sherman Silver Purchase Act made the dollar suspect and tightened credit. London selling brought on a climax when the famous merchant bank, Baring Brothers, suspended activity because of "gaucho speculations" in Argentina. A bear campaign against the Northern Pacific added to the pain in November, but the industrials were not slighted. Thomas Edison's company, Edison General Electric, was slapped down from 119 to 65. By the end, the Dow 20-Stock loss was 26 percent.

March 1892–July 1893

The "Great Train Wreck" of 1893 helped to post one-third of the nation's rail mileage on the courthouse wall. The rails' troubles were rooted in their huge expansion debt, spidery branch lines, and the breakdown of the various railroad agreements, such as the "Iowa pool," which had been designed to apportion traffic and support rates. The monopolistic manipulations in the Philadelphia & Reading and other anthracite roads ended in receivership in early 1893, and a recession that started at about the same time added to the carriers' grief.

Foreigners feared a currency crisis because of the Sherman Silver Act, and spurred a run on gold. The collapse of the National Cordage trust in May 1893 led to a panic in the nouveau trust shares and was followed by commercial crisis in June and a brutal bear attack on the rails in July. The episode reached its climax on July 26, when the Erie, a veteran courthouse survivor, entered receivership for the third time. The Mobile & Ohio was driven from an 1892 high of 42 down to 7, and the Union Pacific was a 50–15 loser. Future Dow Jones blue-chips also suffered; General Electric was pounded from 120 to 30, and American

Tobacco fell by two-thirds. Overall, the loss for the Dow 20-Stock average was 43 percent.

September 1895–August 1896

A secular bear trend off the 1890 high wound down in 1896. Successive lows had been made in the crises of late 1890, in 1893, and 1896. The investment-favored New York, New Haven & Hartford slid to 160, which was 90 points beneath its low of 1890. The 1895–1896 ordeal began when London's craze for the "Kaffirs" (South African golds) collapsed and credits were called back from the United States. In December, President Cleveland seemed to threaten war against Britain over the Venezuelan crisis, and a dramatic panic struck. But the war scare died quickly, and the market was quiet until it was aroused again by summer fears about William Jennings Bryan's silver candidacy and renewed attacks on the dollar. Selling was hectic in July, and both General Electric and the National Lead trust lost half their top 1895 values. The Dow 20-Stock average fell 34 percent.

September 1899–September 1900

Rails remained in a bull phase during this bear market for the Industrials; the latter group, however, suffered a hangover from 1899's merger mania. The first hard blow came in December as England's Boer War crisis hit the market with a money panic. Its cause: fear of large withdrawals of U.K. credits and gold to blot up London's "Black Week" losses. In the spring, the iron trade found that overexpansion leads to price cutting, and Colorado Fuel fell to 30 from a high of 64 at the 1899 peak. Brooklyn Rapid Transit, one of the "Flower" favorites of early 1899 and an electric member of the mostly steam Railroad average, was smashed from 137 to 47. U.S. troops were tied down with the Philippine insurrection and the Boxer rebellion in China. The Dow Industrials lost 32 percent.

September 1901–November 1903

Rails and the economy diverged to the up side for exactly a year after the Dow's 1901 high; the economic recession that then began did not end until the summer of 1904. Monetary tension encouraged the collapse of manipulative pools in late 1902, and a heavy slate of antitrust legislation worried the market. Giant shipbuilding and blue-water trusts were trapped in the shoals of public indifference, and "undigestible securities" became a buzz phrase. The failure of such underwriting syndicates gave this bear market the label, Rich Man's Panic.

The U.S. Steel trust, admired (and hated) as the world's largest corporation, pushed the market to an autumn climax by cutting its dividend. Priced at 40 earlier in the year, it slumped to 10. The high-water mark of trustification had passed, and the mightiest industrial names would be dewatered at a cost of billions. American Can, Union Bag, and U.S. Rubber all lost at least 80 percent of their peak values. The Rockefellers' Colorado Fuel & Iron fell from 137 to 25. Many of the great trust names survived in one form or another, but more fanciful amalgamations—in witch hazel, alkali, caskets, bicycles, wallpaper, saws, and so forth—disintegrated.

A pioneer restructuring then worked enormous economies and hardships. U.S. Steel announced that "plants not properly situated when closed...will be dismantled or removed before being reopened." Twenty-five percent of its plants were closed. The number of men employed in the operating department was reduced about 10 percent. Reductions in wages totaled 20 percent. The Dow lost 46 percent.

January 1906–November 1907

Copper mania sparked the early 1906 high, but it was followed by a collapse of metal prices and shares in 1907. Even the Rockefeller-controlled Amalgamated was crushed, from 122 to 42. The "Harriman market" in late 1906 had pushed many rail shares to levels that would not be equaled until the mid-1920s. The worst panic came in March 1907, but tight money worldwide helped lead to depression in May and the commercial crisis of October 1907, known as the Panic of '07. Along the way, commerce was stunned by the perceived antibusiness attitude of President Theodore Roosevelt and a $29 million fine against Standard Oil, a remarkable sum for the day. The year marked a cyclical low for bonds, and such values would not be repeated until 1921. AT&T's $6 preferred sank to 60, and American Tobacco 4s of 1951 were cut from 84 to 54. The leading utility, Brooklyn Union Gas, was crushed from 178 to 80. The Dow fell 49 percent.

November 1909–September 1911

Collapse of the "Hocking bubble" in January 1910 started this slide, but things got serious in early summer when the ICC changed a railroad rate increase into a cut. In July, an ambitious pool aimed at a transcontinental rail system collapsed because of margin problems, and the shares move into stronger and more knowledgeable hands— those of the Harriman bankers. The Rock Island and the Wabash, among other carriers accumulated by the syndicate, were washed out at less than half their January prices. In 1911 the business slump continued, and multiple antitrust suits and steady European selling, because of the crisis in North Africa, dogged the market. An antitrust suit against U.S. Steel was rumored, and its shares fell to 50, down from a high of 95 in 1909. The Dow lost 27 percent.

September 1912–July 1914

Balkan wars and election of the "radical" Woodrow Wilson turned the market down in late 1912 and recession soon followed. Business was slow, and rail confidence was scandalized by flagrant corruption in such lines as the New Haven and the St. Louis & San Francisco. Additionally, the Justice Department forced the Union Pacific to divest its control of rival Southern Pacific, and many investment rails fell below the level of 1907. The New York Central slumped to 77; it had been a $125 stock at the beginning of the century. Balkan wars kept Europe's bourses unsteady and encouraged selling of American stocks. World War I exploded in July 1914, and a tidal wave of European selling forced the NYSE to shutter on July 30. The Exchange would not reopen until mid-December. The official Dow loss was 24 percent (unofficial low prices came in the outdoors, "gutter market," in late October).

November 1916–December 1917

President Wilson's peace ambitions stirred a violent "peace scare" in December 1916, which immediately turned to a war scare that was followed by the U-boat panic and a break with Germany in early February 1917. America entered the war in April. Victory seemed assured, but war chilled the market because it meant new rules, regulations, and taxes for business. The coveted war babies were shunned, replaced by Liberty Bonds. Central Leather was hammered from 123 to 55, and Bethlehem Steel fell to 265 from 700. The rails continued their disastrous secular down trend, amid fears of government takeover. The St. Paul was a 103–35 victim, and the Chicago North Western slipped to its lowest price since 1896. The racy motor stocks were threatened with steel allocations, and Maxwell Motor dropped from 99 to 19. The Dow loss was 40 percent.

November 1919–August 1921

The Federal Reserve Board pricked the oil and commodity inflation boom in November 1919, and the market took a dive. In February, a European currency deflation canceled foreign buying by making American stock prices more expensive. Panic struck again, followed by a tumultuous reflex rally, stoked by many manipulations, including the notorious Stutz corner. But a depression was growing, and public confidence was shocked when Liberty Bonds dropped 10 points because of climbing interest rates. Additional rate increases accelerated deflation and auto showrooms were suddenly empty, with General Motors in severe trouble. Pierce-Arrow Motor fell from 83 to 9, despite its highly regarded car. Inflation favorites of 1919 were crushed as commodity prices collapsed and jobless figures climbed to the highest level since 1898. "Buyers' strikes" tortured retailers, and Associated Dry Goods dropped from 67 to 24. Endicott-Johnson fell nearly 100 points, to 51. The Federal Reserve Board finally relented in the summer of 1921 and the market slowly turned around. The Dow lost 47 percent, the fourth worst drop in history.

September 1929–July 1932

The period following the 1929 crash was, of course, the unchallenged champion. During this period the Dow lost 89 percent.

March 1937–March 1938

An industrial collapse, striking with lightning swiftness, crushed a five-year advance in October 1937. The autumn crash cost the Dow 40 percent, equivalent to a major bear market. America's psyche had barely regained its economic confidence and was shocked by the "Roosevelt depression." Stock traders found that history does repeat, for the two worst bear attacks in modern history came within the same decade. Unemployment increased by 2 million as depression returned; automobile and steel production were particularly hard-hit. Crucible Steel fell from 82 to 21 within the year, and industrial production in general dropped at a faster pace than in the early 1930s. The Rails suffered even more than the Industrial average, falling to their second worst annual loss in history—down 45 percent. The Illinois Central, 38 early in the year, dropped to 8. Southern Pacific had needed five years to steam from 6½ to 65. The return trip to a single digit took only a year. The Santa Fe took a similar bad trip—18 to 95 and back to 22 in 1938. Figure 4-1 shows

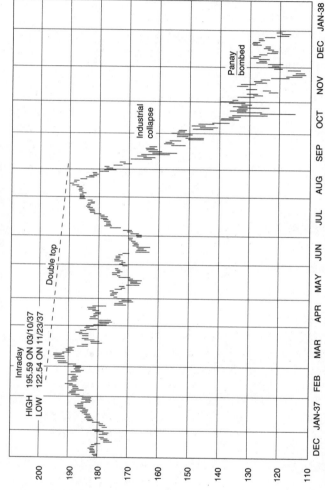

1937: Second Depression of the 1930s Strikes

Figure 4-1. The decline for the Dow Industrials in 1937 was 33 percent, a figure not equalled since. There were multiple reasons for the slump—Japanese aggressions, pricey stocks, and a mature advance, nearly five years of age. But in a rare instance of parallel timing, business prospects and stock prices collapsed simultaneously in the autumn. (© 1993 Knight-Ridder Financial Publishing, 30 South Wacker Drive, Suite 1820, Chicago, Ill. 60606. Reprinted with permission.)

the long top, ending in August, and the violent autumn collapse of 1937. By early 1938, the nation showed signs of revival, but Europe's war scare pushed the Dow to a new low, below 100, in March.

The Japanese sinking of the U.S. gunboat *Panay* in December had helped stifle the reflex rally, and in March 1938, Hitler's Anschluss with Austria pushed the tough one-year decline to a climax. The demand for war goods brought a swift expansion, however, and there was no further business contraction until 1945. During this bear market, however, the Dow lost 49 percent.

November 1938–April 1939

Second thoughts about "Peace in Our Time" reversed 1938's intrayear bull market, which was pushed to climax by the hopeful events of Munich. European liquidation continued to pressure New York, and the market panicked when Hitler marched on Czechoslovakia in March 1939. Again, as in 1937, the steel shares were attacked, with Allegheny-Ludlum and Armco both dropping by about 50 percent. Chrysler was knocked from 88 to 53 in this brief sequence, which is sometimes seen as just one leg of a major 1937–1942 collapse. The five-month loss amounted to 23 percent.

September 1939–April 1942

Giddy buying at the beginning of World War II (September 1, 1939), based on memories of 1915's record advance, focused on the war brides of that earlier era. Bethlehem Steel's heroics were recalled, and the stock was rushed up from near 50 to 100 within days. But the war fever abruptly ended on September 13, and a long decline began. The Dow drifted sideways in a "line" formation until it was blind-sided by Dunkerque in May 1940. Allied war news was all bad for the next two years, but advancing earnings cushioned the decline, and the market only slowly ground lower, even after Pearl Harbor. By that time it was evident that there would be new war babies. Bethlehem slipped below 50, and Sperry (Gyroscope) Corporation, a war "natural" at 52 in 1939, was trading near 22. A low-volume reversal halted the slide just prior to America's ordeals at Corregidor and Bataan. The Dow loss: 40 percent.

May 1946–June 1949

The bear market of 1946–1949 made stocks worth more dead than alive. Many issues sold for less than the cash in the till, for the Cassandras know that a great depression follows every war. Curtiss-Wright's total market valuation at $5 a share was $22 million, but the company had $100 million in cash and no debt. Other cash-rich "steals" included Bigelow-Sanford, Cincinnati Milling, and Douglas Aircraft. Who can afford new carpeting in a depression? Who needs new tooling or airplanes? Consumer confidence was at an extreme low.

Fundamentalists enjoyed a field day as earnings and dividends set records year after year, even as the Dow moved sideways after May 1947. Blue-chips such as Gulf Oil and the Atchison sold for about four times earnings. The Industrials' yield was 7.9 percent at 1949's final low, which was less than two points beneath the panic figure of October 1946. The principal postwar victims were the war babies and high-expectancy stocks, such as the air transports. Trans World Airlines went into a power glide from 79 to 9. In the meantime, a rolling adjustment saw many groups reverse the Dow trend early on. The chemicals and motors made their lows in 1946, the aircrafts and rails in 1947, and the drugs and utilities in 1948. The three-year loss for the Dow was 24 percent.

April 1956–October 1957

Automobile stocks, the market's driving force since the 1920s, turned faint near the end of 1955 and put a brake on the market and economy. Detroit's passenger car production fell 46 percent between 1955 and 1958. Increasing inflation, the Suez war, Russian tanks in Budapest, and a recession added to the strain. A rolling correction to the boom of the early 1950s eased the strain, however, and the Dow in July 1957 was within half a point of the 1956 peak. From there, recessionary pressures and climbing rates chipped away at prices, and the shock of *Sputnik I* finished off the slump under notorious October conditions. The Dow's total loss was a slim 19 percent, but aircraft makers were hard hit, with Boeing falling from 65 to 29. Alcoa, a favorite of the early growth cult, was slashed from 134 to 60.

January–October 1960

Some market students sweep the mini-bear of 1960 under the carpet, but it was a bitter psychological blow to those who believed the hyped "Soaring Sixties" would ignite on New Year's Eve. The slump climaxed a three-year bear trend for aircrafts and oils, and prices fell sharply after Labor Day when the Pennsylvania Railroad was shut down for the first time in its 114-year history. Cyclics were hard-hit;

Goodrich was cut from 90 to 45 and stainless-steel maker Allegheny-Ludlum lost nearly as much in terms of percent. Office equipment companies, meanwhile, signaled their brilliant future by ignoring the mild recession environment. Haloid-Xerox, still an OTC stock, ended 1960 at 74, having more than doubled its closing level of 1959. The total Dow intrayear loss was 17 percent.

December 1961–June 1962

At the end of 1961, bloated price–earnings ratios, the highest since 1929, foreshadowed an end of the 1961 electronic and new-issue frenzy. Prices held until late spring, however, when a confrontation between President Kennedy and the steel industry shattered business confidence. Stocks collapsed in panic; at the psychological low in May, volume reached its highest level since 1929. Big Steel, 109 at its all-time high in 1959, ended at 38. The sequence remains the shortest bear market since World War II, though it was much longer than the major decline of 1987. The six-month loss on the Dow: 27 percent.

February–October 1966

The third short bear episode of the 1960s started from the first-ever Dow 1000 reading (intraday). Vietnam, inflation, and a credit crunch somewhat akin to the "old days" conspired to drive the market steadily lower. Hanoi was bombed for the first time, and the prime rate was raised four times within eight months, finally reaching 6 percent—the highest rate in 45 years. The chairman of the Federal Reserve suggested tax hikes to rein inflation. This bear episode lacked high drama, but many good stocks, including Boeing, Chrysler, Parke Davis, and Fairchild Camera, lost half their value. The year's DJIA loss was the biggest since 1937: 25 percent.

December 1968–May 1970

"Ratcheting interest rates, virulent inflation, and the frustrations of Vietnam fragged the market" in 1968–1970.* Peace hopes fell and banks escalated the prime from 6 to $8\frac{1}{2}$ percent. Synergism, conglomerates, and computer lessors became four-letter words, and puffed-up

---

*John Dennis Brown, *101 Years on Wall Street* (Prentice-Hall, Englewood Cliffs, NJ, 1991), p. 206.

favorites such as Ling-Temco, Levin-Townsend, and Data Processing took 1929-size hits. The historic Pennsylvania and New York Central railroads merged a half-century too late and high-balled toward bankruptcy. In 1970, one J. Ross Perot lost a billion or so on paper as his Electronic Data Systems fell from 164 to 29 within weeks. The sadness of Cambodia and Kent State pushed the sequence to a high-volume finale in late May; overall, the Dow lost 36 percent.

January 1973–December 1974

In the worst smash since the 1930s, the two-tier market of the early 1970s surrendered to radical surgery on price–earnings ratios. McDonald's perfect record of growth, seen as worth 80 times earnings in 1973, continued in 1974, but the stock was by then valued at only 13 times earnings; the shares fell from 77 to 21. IBM dropped from a P–E ratio of 40 to 12 times earnings and wiped out $20 billion of market value. Stock investors, recently introduced to the joys of real estate investment trusts (REITs), learned about the downside of leverage. Chase Manhattan's mortgage pet fell from 70 to 5, leading a parade of such products. Recession and fear overcame reason, and the Industrials were selling at less than six times the record earnings of 1974. Scores of good names were valued at 3 times earnings, and Woolworth, whose dividend record reached back to 1912, was selling at 8 with earnings of $2.14 and a 15 percent yield. (Its earnings would increase dramatically in 1975.)

There were thorns other than recession, to be sure. Watergate, Vice President Spiro Agnew, OPEC, the Arab oil embargo, the Yom Kippur war in the Mideast, and a puny dollar combined to assault confidence. Even President Nixon's resignation in early August 1974 did not stop the bleeding, as consumer confidence fell to its lowest level since 1946. The Dow's low would not come until December, and the overall loss reached 45 percent, the worst since 1937–1938.

September 1976–February 1978

Small investors prospered in the strange bear affair of 1977, while the glamour stocks of 1973 took another whipping. Disney, priced at 82 times earnings in 1972, fell to a 10 multiple in 1974, in a startling 110–16 decline. But money managers demanded that Mickey Mouse and friends return to the stage, and such born-again giddiness pushed Disney back to 60, a P–E of 27. The 1976–1978 downturn dropped it to 32, a 10 times multiple on its ever-increasing earnings. Cheap steel imports hurt the Dow, which was 10 percent steel-related.

Escalating interest rates, indictments against Amex option makers, and a weak dollar struck at confidence; the dollar turned cripple even against the Mexican peso. It was not a clear-cut bear market, for both the Amex and the OTC indices reached new highs during 1977. At the Exchange, 97 stocks gained 50 percent or more during the year, while only 11 lost that much. Possible new taxes, rate escalation, a falling dollar, climbing oil prices, and soaring inflation tortured the blue-chips but mostly ignored the small stocks. Bethlehem posted its first loss since 1938, which helped drive its price from 48 to 18, the lowest level since 1954. Well-regarded Monsanto was victimized by a drop from 100 to 44, but many specialties, such as the cable TV companies, moved against the grain. The Dow loss: 27 percent.

April 1981–August 1982

The progress from inflation to deflation created a terrible economic stew. Deflation, recession, high unemployment, and soaring interest rates made it seem like 1920's collapse. Soybeans fell $3 a bushel even as interest rates climbed; the prime was at $20\frac{1}{2}$ and long Treasuries yielded 15 percent. A classic Dow theory sell signal impelled the market lower in the summer of 1981. Oil and oil service stocks had jump-started the downtrend in the previous November, but recession spread the blame evenly. A quartet of historic Dow leaders—Chrysler, Inco, International Harvester, and Manville—fell to single digits, numbers not seen since 1932. Argentina invaded the Falkland Islands in 1982, and Israel marched on Lebanon. When things quieted down, growing financial scandals in banking (Penn Square) and government bond trading spread. Chase Manhattan fell from 60 to 31.

In July, the Fed eased rates, and by mid-August even Henry Kaufman, Salomon Brothers' "Dr. Gloom," saw lower rates ahead. An institutional buying panic reversed the market. The Dow loss for the sequence was "only" 24 percent, but a blue-chip like Standard of Ohio was a 92–27 deflation victim.

August–October 1987

In August 1987 there were a few traders who thought that the Dow Industrials average might eventually fall 1000 points. But no one thought the damage would come before Halloween.

A lust for stocks had written a dazzling record at the Exchange during the first eight months of the year. Dow 2000 was hurdled on January 8, and 2100 on January 19. The "summer rally" lived up to reputation, and the Dow whistled past milestones from 2300 to 2700. Bears capitulated en masse, and Dow 3500, a famous forecast of Robert Prechter, became consensus. Japan's astronomical price–earnings ratios made American shares appear conservatively valued.

On August 25, the Dow reached a peak at 2722.42, having gained over 25 points in the day's trading. September's traditional nervous venue rattled prices, but in early October the Dow was back to 2641, less than 3 percent below the historic high. By October 13 the Dow had slipped again, but it was still well above the September low. In the meantime, the Tokyo Stock Exchange was celebrating new highs.

Then, striking like a tornado in the night, an unparalleled collapse smashed the world's financial markets, leaving them splintered and crushed, as a trailer park might give way to hurricane forces. In five trading days at New York, the leading average lost 31 percent; the intraday damage amounted to well over 1000 Dow points. On October 19 the Industrials fell by more than 500 points.

Investors were left with a bitter reminder that neither computers, portfolio insurance, nor professional management had solved the riddle of stock market panics.

This major decline had bear market proportions but not bear market endurance. The panic climax spawned a library of complaints, investigations, books, articles, lawsuits, committee reports, and archival records. And the Dow lost 36 percent.

July–October 1990

Iraq's invasion of Kuwait sparked a hybrid decline in 1990. An unusual feature was that it began with panic and ended up more intermediate correction than bear episode. Dow 3000 had a nice ring in July, but that peak (actually 2999.75) was scaled with little enthusiasm. Early August brought the Gulf War and America's hard-nosed response. The panic ended quickly, but $40 crude frightened the world bourses more than Saddam. Tokyo was savaged, with the Nikkei index finally down 48 percent from its year-end high near 39,000.

In America, climbing interest rates, congressional budget clowning, and unemployment pushed the market toward another October low. Rampaging fuel costs and canceled travel plans squeezed the airlines; UAL suffered a big dollar loss, from 165 to 85. High crude prices also hurt chemicals such as Vista, which dove from 43 to 17, while recession-threatened retailers such as The Limited were cut in half; mighty Wal-Mart was hit with a 32 percent loss. The short decline was a true bear market for some stocks, but only a secondary correction for others. Even the Dow's status is debatable; it suffered a short, minimum-type decline, with the average ending at 2365, down 20 percent in three months.

Analyzing the Bear Market Declines

Thus, the market's major declines comprise an atypical melange of relationships, backgrounds, and statistics. Circumstances of depression have been involved in most, but business was booming in 1962 and 1987. Recessions have struck, only to be ignored by the market, as in 1945. The decline of 1939–1942 paid little attention to fast-rising earnings in three of those years.

Primary causes have been varied. Merger mania and new-issue frenzy helped tilt the market downward in 1899, 1902, and 1929, among other years. Deflation wrung out prices in 1920 and 1981. War frightened the market in the early 1940s but was ignored in 1915 and 1916. Great manipulations have often helped set a bear course, and a collapse for industry and commerce, as in 1893 and 1937, has always brought immediate market troubles.

There is no correlation between the length of declines and the damage, as can be seen in Table 4-1. The three-year 1946–1949 sequence erased only 24 percent of the Dow's postwar peak of 212.50. In 1987, the two-month damage was 36 percent. The average duration for major declines has been somewhat over 17 months, but 10 of 25 episodes have lasted between 16 and 25 months. There has usually been plenty of time for a reasoned exit, although three ultrashort declines were over in five months or less; a similar number of sequences were painfully long, lasting over two and a half years.

Excluding the singular crash of 1929–1932, when the Dow went down 89 percent, the average loss in 24 major Dow declines has been 32.5 percent. Add back 1929 and the figure is 34.8 percent. So the Industrials have lost about one-third of their peak value on average. But even good stocks often lose two or three times that amount.

Recessions since the end of World War II have not been as severe as those of earlier days, and the market's major declines since 1950 have also become more user-friendly—shorter and less testing. Ten episodes beginning with the 1956–1957 setback show an average duration of 12.1 months and an average loss of only 25.1 percent. The figures are significantly below the long-term numbers.

It is difficult to assign any bear market benefits, but one can point to several benign affairs. The Kennedy episode, seven months in

Table 4-1. Major Stock Market Declines
Percent Loss and Duration
(Dow Jones Industrial Average)

	Percent loss	Trading sessions		Percent loss	Trading sessions
1929–1932	89	845	1909–1911	27	551
1937–1938	49	317	1961–1962	27	134
1906–1907	49	552	1976–1978	27	362
1919–1921	47	540	1890–1890*	26	155
1901–1903	46	513	1966–1966	25	167
1973–1974	45	481	1912–1914	24	547
1892–1893*	43	418	1981–1982	24	328
1939–1942	40	789	1946–1949	24	857
1916–1917	40	320	1938–1939	23	120
1987–1987	36	38	1990–1990	20	62
1968–1970	36	367	1956–1957	19	389
1895–1896*	34	279	1960–1960	17	205
1899–1900	32	314			

*Dow 20-Stock average.

1961–1962, is one example. There was no recession. Dow earnings not only advanced in 1962, but set a record. The Dow's composite dividend was also a record, and the market would advance for the next three years. Despite such brilliant numbers, the steels proved the treachery of an affection for "yesterday's darlings." During that solid advance, from Dow 536 to 1000 (intraday), neither Bethlehem nor U.S. Steel approached their price levels of early 1962.

George Lindsay grouped bear sequences into basic declines of subnormal, short, and long duration and, additionally, into sideways movements. His "basics" are simple; the sideways movements need too much explanation for this short review. Lindsay measured duration by calendar days, but we prefer to count the number of trading sessions. He did not live to witness the unique, compressed declines of 1987 and 1990, which seem to require an additional classification—ultrashort sequences. Our concern here is the major declines, as listed in Table 4-1 and the Appendix. Lindsay often subdivided these episodes; for example, he viewed the 1929–1932 collapse as a series of three basic declines.

The time patterns of declining markets fit nicely into the following basic moves, identified by beginning date:

Ultralong sequences (789–857 trading sessions): 1929, 1939, 1946 (three)

Long sequences (481–552 sessions): 1901, 1906, 1909, 1912, 1919, 1973 (six)

Medium sequences (314–389): 1899, 1916, 1937, 1956, 1968, 1976, 1981 (seven)

Short sequences (120–167): 1890, 1938, 1961, 1966 (four)

Ultrashort sequences (38–62): 1987, 1990 (two)

The significant feature is the nesting in exclusive time periods. Nearly 240 trading days—not far short of a calendar year—separate the long and ultralong-duration sequences, for example. There are only three oddball numbers excluded from the listings. They were counted in the episodes starting in 1892, 1896, and 1960. The first two seem to be only historical freaks, 418 sessions and 279 sessions, respectively, both awkward fits.

On the record book, the intrayear decline of 1960 (205 days), starting on January 5, also appears as a maverick, being too long for the short grouping. But the *market's* high had come on August 1, 1959, and only the most extraordinary maneuvering allowed the Dow to make a "paper peak" in 1960. Adding on 108 sessions of late 1959 puts the 313-day reconstructed sequence (August 1, 1959–October 25, 1960) at the low end of the medium-duration range. So we have 23 of 25 sequences fitted into neat, broadly separated time bands.

Is It Ever
"Too Late to Sell"?

The true status of the brief 1990 downtrend is not yet clear. If war came, it promised to be brief, and reason said that Saddam would finally bow to the United Nations and withdraw as gracefully as possible. Was it a true bear move—down 20 percent—or just a heavy correction of the advance which had peaked in July, prior to the Kuwait invasion?

Bear markets are generally more easily identified. There were no doubts in 1973–1974 or 1968–1970 about what was going on. The investor's problem is not recognition but a psychological block—fear that it's too late to sell stocks.

Every broker has heard the excuse a hundred times, and every investor has uttered it: "I should have sold last month, now it's too late." The fear of getting out at just the wrong time overcomes fear of a further slump—at least until the pain becomes unbearable, as in May 1970 or September 1974.

Early on, the bearish move is applauded as a much-needed correction and the setback is seen as opportunity. Only rarely has the first bear stage been truly frightening. The psychological problems develop after the first important rally fails. At the time, the investor is tempted to say, "I'll get out on the next rally." And that is just when serious trouble arrives.

Inevitably, prior to that next rally, comes a fall of such nasty proportions that the investor bites his lip and decides to hang on. It is not "too late," but it seems that way. Kidde (Walter) and Co. was a conglomerate favorite of the late 1960s, selling near 70 at the market peak in December 1968. The "spring break" of 1969 dropped the stock to 40, but Kidde held there and then rallied to 50. In June, the sixth prime increase in six months hammered the stock down to 32. Obviously, it was too late to sell, as the stock proved by zipping back to 60, where it seemed too strong to sell. The stubborn owners were proven right. Or were they? By the following July, the stock was at 15.

The bear trend was obvious all along. The investor didn't have to sell Kidde deep in the hole, for there were always rallies, but if he believed the charts and soaring interest rates, he had to recognize the slide for what it was—a bear market. It is never too late to sell on a rally.

Investors will do almost anything except admit a flaw in their personal investment judgment. They brag that they blew $6000 at Las Vegas, but ego makes it tough to sell at 14 the thousand shares of stock they were so proud of at 20, particularly if only a few months have passed.

The final capitulation, as with Kidde in the high teens, comes more from despair than fear. "Abandon all hope" reads the investment sandwich board.

Comparing Bear Markets with the Business Cycle

Panic's myriad causes need an index. Bear markets, on the other hand, develop from the perception that business will worsen, dragging profits and dividends down. Such perceptions, when broadly hyped, are often "wolf" tales. In the late 1970s, virtually every economist was honking his horn and flashing his lights for recession. There was none.

In the early 1990s, a tedious recession apparently dragged on for years, but the market ignored it and rolled to new highs. Perceptions of a business slowdown sometimes prove incorrect despite a collapsing stock indicator. Such was the case in 1962. The market fell sharply during the first half, and despite a strong recovery late in the year, ended lower for the period. In the meantime, the Dow's composite earnings were gaining 17 percent; there was no hint of a recession.

Even when the market and the business cycle are in broad agreement, they are seldom in timing "sync." The market usually leads the business cycle, perceiving trouble long before the unemployment lines lengthen, and reversing to the up side when business is at its worst, as in 1932.

Panics are mysterious, but the precise relation between the market and business conditions is equally baffling. Computer models may accurately forecast the trend of business statistics; they will never translate it into the timing of stock movements.

Dow Movements Precede the Economic Cycle, Both Up and Down

Table 4-2 shows the Dow's timing as compared with the economic cycle in the years since 1948. The average leads the economy both on the way down and on the bounce. But plunging prices don't necessarily mean hard times, as we learned in 1962, 1966, and 1987. Since 1890, stock prices on average have begun to decline about six months in advance of recession, but the range is broad. On several occasions, including 1929, the economy turned before the stock market and the reverse lag extended for more than a year; the Dow peaked in April 1956 and business did not turn down until August 1957.

Table 4-2. The Dow Industrials and Recessions

Stock Prices Anticipate Both Recession and Recovery

Last Dow peak	Recession commences	Dow lead (months)	Dow low	Recession ends	Dow lead (months)
May 1948	Dec. 1948	7	June 1949	Dec. 1949	6
Jan. 1953	July 1953	5	Sept. 1953	May 1954	8
July 1957	Aug. 1957	1	Oct. 1957	Apr. 1958	6
Jan. 1960	Apr. 1960	3	Oct. 1960	Feb. 1961	4
Dec. 1968	Dec. 1969	12	May 1970	Nov. 1970	6
Jan. 1973	Nov. 1973	10	Dec. 1974	Mar. 1975	3
Jan. 1980	Jan. 1980	0	Apr. 1980	July 1980	3
Apr. 1981	July 1981	3	Aug. 1982	Nov. 1982	3
July 1990	July 1990	0	Oct. 1990	Mar. 1991	5

The Dow has always reversed to the up side prior to the business trough, with the exception of 1921 when it lagged by one month. It has been profitable to trust the market and not the business statistics, for the Dow gain in the divergent period has often been substantial. In 1975 the Dow ran up by 26 percent before the economy turned the corner, and in 1982 the gain was 28 percent.

Typically, the business recession of 1907–1908, exacerbated by the stock panics of 1907, did not end until midsummer 1908. Even then, economic recovery was slow. But the market had begun its recovery in November 1907, and it gained a record 87 percent before the economy turned upward. Reviewing the year 1908, the *Commercial & Financial Chronicle* wrote: "In trade and mercantile affairs, the year was one of intense depression."*

Meanwhile, the Dow ignored the sorry state of business and earnings, posting a gain of 47 percent for 1908—an unheralded advance that has not been matched since 1933. In the middle segments of economic contractions the stock market will usually be in step with the business statistics. At the beginning and at the end, the market will lead, anticipating a turn in the tide. Thus three realities emerge:

The business cycle is not a barometer for the stock market, but stock market action—one sector of the leading indicators—is a clue to the economic future.

Big stock market declines have occasionally proven a false signal for the business cycle, as in 1962 and 1966.

Recessions don't always crater the market. In 1923, 1926, and in a rather controversial call in 1953, the Dow suffered only modestly from an economic slowdown. The confusing 1990s saw an "official" recession begin in July 1990, when the Industrials registered an all-time high. Its subsequent slump to an October low was caused by the Iraq crisis and soaring oil costs. In any event, the average recorded another record peak in the following April.

Looking at an "Average" Bear Market

Even a cursory study of bear markets indicates that they are treacherous, back-biting scoundrels. Their *modus operandi* is plagued by incon-

---

*Commercial & Financial Chronicle, January 2, 1909, p. 5.

sistencies. They seem to shout "depression," but one does not always appear. Earnings and dividend growth often continue as prices slide. They can drive a fundamentalist bonkers.

Their unpredictable beginnings can be avoided only by luck. But the ordeal, once sensed, can be cut short. Celibacy is the best method, but a drastic cutback in exposure is the most common protection.

Bear markets appear frequently, if irregularly, and not always to unanimous affirmation. In 1923 and 1953, among other years, some students see mild bear episodes interrupting the long bull markets of those periods. A broad bear market for the high-tech stocks did much damage in 1983–1984, but could not tip the Dow off-balance.

Bear sequences are impossible to identify in the opening stages and often difficult to acknowledge in the middle stages. But the final steep plunge is easily marked and the climax is seldom deceiving, being much more obvious than a bull market peak.

If one is possessed of strong finances at such a juncture, even an inexperienced investor will automatically prosper, for the rewards are always bountiful. The eight leading advances of the past century have recorded an average gain of 237 percent. Ten lesser gainers averaged 69 percent. The worst seven were plus 32 percent. Dominant shares will advance by two to three times the figure for the Dow.

The 1966–1968 bull market was in the "worst seven" category, with the exact average gain, 32 percent. It was an average gain, of average duration, but a strange sequence, dominated by the "go-go" stocks and action at the American Stock Exchange (Amex), whose index advance was six times that of the Industrials. While the Dow dowagers huddled in a corner, the swingers took off in the most sensational gala since 1929. The up-side statistics for trash were extraordinary. University Computing ran from 3 to 186. Mohawk Data was a 4–111 winner. Conglomerates, computer lessors, and franchising scams proliferated. Redman Industries, a mobile-home maker, shot up from 3 to 113. Quality was a relative disappointment. For the first time since the 1930s, the Dow failed to surpass its previous bull high.

This modest market advance, remember, came after a secular move which had started in 1942 and lasted 24 years. And in the shallow corrections of the previous nine years, the longest had lasted barely nine months, so internal technical strength was not as powerful as at most troughs. Which is why it was easier to pump up new names, such as Levin-Townsend, National Student Marketing, Minnie Pearl's Chicken, and Four Seasons Nursing. Even if one missed the sizzlers, quality was rewarding. Chrysler spurted from 30 to 74, and many exploration oils were explosive in their price action. Superior Oil ran from 98 to 235.

Thus, even when bull markets offer lean-to-average pickings, the payoff is big for those who have previously exercised bear market patience, a primary lesson for investors.

Differences between Panics and Bear Markets

Panics are a hardy perennial, able to bloom under both the best and worst of economic circumstances, and at any stage of the market cycle. Bear markets generally lead a recession-bound business cycle, but occasionally work their mischief against the grain of solid commerce and profit.

Investors believe the worst of panic; the mind accepts the possibility that "the end is near." Investors believe the best of bear markets, for almost until the very end, good times are believed to lie just around the corner. Bear markets stand by themselves. Panics flit in and out, sometimes appearing in the strongest of advancing markets but more often accentuating a bear trend.

Definitions and Semantics

Bear markets and panics are sometimes confused, for they both push prices in a southerly direction. But their distinguishing marks are quite different. No matter how soon they end, bear markets are glacial in movement compared with the hurricane forces of financial crisis. The two forces of price destruction are entirely different.

Even the dating of sequences differs. Bear episodes are marked from the bull market peak to the date of the final trough, as measured by the Industrials. The measurement of panic is more subjective. One can state that the 1929–1932 bear market began on September 3, 1929, the day of the legendary peak at Dow 381. But the onset of the autumn panic came at a slightly imprecise day some weeks later and from a much lower level. The start of panic is most often established by internal volatility, a day of extremely high volume, or a violent decline, for example. Occasionally, an ominous news event flags the beginning.

Most panics are surrounded by high drama. As they unfold, they acquire a gunfighter's reputation: Tales of their kills are repeated in boardroom legends. Their notoriety is linked with colorful titles and famous names—the "Cross of Gold," Morgan, *Lusitania*, Dunkerque, Eisenhower, *Sputnik I*. Bear markets, on the other hand, have no personality or stage presence, being sheer drudgery. They are only remembered, as on a tombstone, by the dates of their birth and death: 1929–1932 R.I.P.

Duration and Damage

By definition, panics are short. Bear markets seem endless. We have arbitrarily restricted panic sequences to crashes of about 20 trading days or less. Stubborn slides may slant prices for twice that long, but panic is never sustained. In the early summer of 1969, the Dow fell from 969 to 802, stunned by a record prime rate. Not even the moon landing could halt the selling, which sliced the Dow 17 percent. But 51 trading days is not the stuff of panic.

Even the briefest bear markets test endurance. Three of the shortest occurred in the 1960s, lasting between six and nine months each. We have no explanation for the concentration. The other brief was the post-Munich decline of 1938–1939. Fifteen other major down markets lasted between one and three years, with the average just over 21 months. Crises are measured in days, bear markets in months and years.

The five-day meltdown of 1987 was the most frightening financial experience since the 1930s, but the loss was not substantially greater than the forgotten slump of 1976–1978. Intensity, more than the extent of damage, burns in investors' memories.

Panics often form a segment of bear markets, most frequently near the low of the final down leg. On rare occasions, however, trouble starts right at the top. While individual stocks frequently sketch a church-steeple top, indices roll over more slowly. An exception occurred in November 1919, when the Dow plunged straight off a record high, losing 13 percent before the end of the month, as the Federal Reserve twisted the screws on runaway inflation.

Bear market adventures give investors plenty of time to make decisions. Major declines generally take months to encroach seriously on prices. In 11 major episodes since the 1930s, the average Dow loss at the end of three months was a little over 7 percent. The average loss at the four-month anniversary was just 9 percent, less than the arbitrary panic minimum set for our study.

Panics wreak their damage in days, or even hours. When the UAL buyout folded its wings in 1989, the Transports fell 22 percent in two weeks. It was a time for reflex and not deliberation.

Complexity

Bear markets are deceptive; panics are brutally simple. The stock market, in its longer waves, often lacks credibility. Bull markets climb a wall of worry. Bear markets deceptively ignore record earnings and dividends. In panics, however, perceptions are suddenly changed by accident or incident and a maddening fear, impervious to reason, sweeps over the market. The news is bad and the rumors worse. There is no gray area. Stocks are sacrificed without regard to value, and yet, within days or sometimes hours, the market is cleansed of its fears.

If one excludes the superbear episodes of this century—those erasing more than 40 percent of the Dow's value—bear markets and panics are most sharply differentiated by their duration and psychology and not by the damage done. Nine bear sequences since 1938 have averaged a decline of 25 percent, omitting the historic drops which started in 1939 and 1973. Many panics in the period approached that figure, the damage being recorded in days. And the damage from some panics was worse than that of some of the weaker bear markets. Sudden crisis in 1939, 1940, 1974, and 1987 brought swift losses ranging from 20 to 32 percent. Bear markets, moreover, are invested with historical and economic significance. Panics are mostly lacking in both, but make up for it in drama.

Bear markets ordinarily spread their mischief across the entire country and the economy. Panics have a narrower focus, with Wall Street and a small group of speculators often being the principal victims. The meltdown of 1987 caused major changes in Wall Street and the boutiques of New York City, but there was no recession and no unemployment lines outside the financial community.

Until the advent of the Federal Reserve, "panic" was a grab-bag of commercial crisis, failing businesses, currency shortages, double-digit money rates, and falling stock prices. The Panic of 1907 was the last pure example. The Rich Man's Panic of 1903, really a bear market, was a curious exception to the pattern of commercial crisis.

Psychology

The psychology of panic is instant fear. The psychology of bear episodes is sequential, sliding from high hope to disappointment, to disbelief, to sullenness, and finally to despair and capitulation. Bear markets are easily defined and modeled. Panics? Well, there is not even a consensus definition, except by results. Fortunately, as we noted in the introduction, we have the sly circumlocution of Charles P. Kindleberger, Ford International Professor of Economics at Harvard, to fall back on: "...the genus is like a pretty woman...hard to define, but recognizable when encountered."*

*Charles P. Kindleberger, *Manias, Panics, and Crashes,* rev. ed. (Basic Books, New York, 1989), p. 6.

Panics explode with simple, straightforward drive to the down side, featuring high volume. Bear markets usually develop out of confusing and complex top formations, and the first leg on the down side is seldom seen as dangerous, being generally viewed as a welcome "correction." Only rarely, as in 1973, has the Dow constructed a church-steeple top.

Stretched top formations are the norm. Many last for months, as in 1937 and 1946. The 1903–1906 bull market peaked in January of the latter year, with the Dow at 103.00 and the Rails at 138.36. Twelve months later, the Industrials were selling at over 96 and the Rails near 132. Such lingering tops always create confusing chart patterns.

The movements of the Dow averages lead to the same chart patterns as those seen for individual stocks. In 1899, the Dow worked out a lengthy top over a period of nearly nine months, repeatedly teasing the 76–77 level from April until early December. The chart action appeared as an ascending triangle pattern. The year's high—by a half-point—was reached in September, but the Rails did not confirm the action. When Boer War losses encouraged London's liquidation of American credits and stock, the chart question was resolved by a disastrous December panic, as seen in Fig. 4-2. There had been some warning signals even before the chart failure. The advance was three years old, and volume, often an early indicator, had peaked in January. While merger mania and giant pools continued to promote some heated winners, the death of Ex-Governor Flower in May had cooled public enthusiasm. His manipulated market leaders lost their sponsorship.

The bears, led by James R. Keene, a legendary pool operator, had gained ascendancy even before the December panic. Brooklyn Rapid Transit, 135 in April, was at 85 in November and fell to 61 in the following month. On December 18, the Dow dropped by nearly 9 percent, a record which would stand for 30 years.

The biggest real difference between panics and bear movements is the fact that the psychology of panic stirs selling while the psychology of bear markets spurs buying. Both emotions must be disregarded in favor of a contrary approach. Panics should be bought, almost as soon as they are identified, for crisis melts the risk. Bear markets must be sold as soon as they are identified. Crises demand quick decisions, for the opportunities will be gone almost immediately. Suspected bear sequences require some deliberation: Has a serious downtrend begun, or is it only a deceitful intermediate correction?

Panics are simple and straightforward, like hitting your thumb with a hammer. It's all over before you know it. Bear markets are risky

Figure 4-2. In 1899, a massive ascending triangle, usually a constructive formation, failed when Britain's fortunes in the Boer War turned dismal and panic followed. (The same triangular formation can be seen in a daily graph of the period.)

because they are slow and deceptive. Deliberate downtrends don't attack the psychology of the investor until the slope suddenly increases, or some event, presumed friendly, turns into a Benedict Arnold.

In June 1921, for example, investors applauded an order for railroad wage reductions. But reflection caused despondency. The reduction was not enough. And besides, it would encourage strikes. The market, at its best level in six months, abruptly turned and fell to a bear market low.

Eroding prices in a bear episode are a siren call for bargain hunters, because fundamental ratios are suddenly reasonable, much lower than a few months earlier. Everyone knew that Ling-Temco-Vought had been too high around 160, but at half that price in early 1969, it was intriguing. At 40, halved again, earnings were reportedly improving. At 20, in early 1970, the stock was obviously oversold, but then the dividend was omitted. How about 10? The James Ling saga was over; the stock was driven below 7.

The stock market often fails to make sense, even in retrospect, though the longer declines are usually susceptible to explanation. But both bear markets and panics often leave investors baffled, even with the advantage of hindsight. People are most perplexed by mysterious moves inverse to the business cycle. In 1962, the violent Kennedy panic (part of a seven-month bear market) wrecked the steels and a bunch of the previous year's high fliers, but there was no recession. Ford fell from 58 to 36 during the first six months of the year, but in July the automobile industry posted its greatest monthly sales in history; Ford's earnings would be a record that year. The panic of 1987 was the most frightening in history, but business marched steadily ahead. The panic was not an economic indicator. Neither panics nor bear markets can always be explained by logic.

Volume

Except when the sequences are acting in concert, the volume characteristics of panics and bear markets are entirely different. High volume always accompanies panic. Nearly every important crisis of this century has included a day of record volume for the year, as of the time of crisis. In 1987, volume for five consecutive days chalked figures never before approached at the NYSE; two sessions recorded trade of over 600 million shares.

Figure 4-3 shows the typical acceleration of volume at a selling climax, as seen during the *Sputnik* crisis of 1957, left chart, and during the Cuban missile crisis of 1962, right. The implications of the latter event were tremendous, but a full-fledged panic never developed. On a closing basis, the worst intramonth loss of October was about 5 percent. The slide was a selling climax to the autumn decline, however, and many industrial groups, victimized by war fears, fell beneath the level of June's bear market low. Typical selling climaxes show falling prices and rising volume providing mirror images.

Bear markets proceed with eroding volume, and the final month of decline has historically seen activity at a fraction of the bull peak, most often on a 50 percent decline, or more. Even in the violent war scare climax to the 1937–1938 decline, March volume was only 23 million, compared with 50 million at the crest one year earlier. Not until the 1956–1957 downturn was this volume pattern broken. In the final month, the *Sputnik* panic ballooned trading activity. There have been two anomalies since then.

Bear market *rallies*, however, post astounding volume as frightened short sellers run for cover. Record monthly volume was seen in the

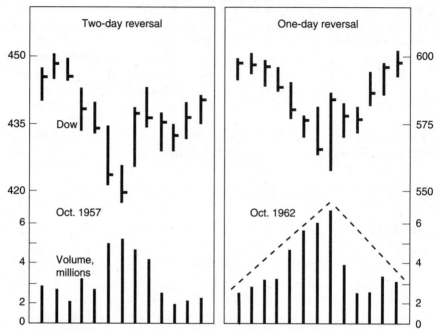

Figure 4-3. Typical selling climaxes end with either a one- or a two-day reversal. Volume ordinarily peaks at the same time, as indicated at the bottom of the figure. The panel on the left shows the two-day reversal which ended the 1957 panic following Russia's *Sputnik I* space victory. The low and low-close came on October 22. On the following day, the market leaped ahead. The right panel displays a classic one-day reversal, recorded during the Cuban missile crisis of 1962. The Dow fell intraday to a low for the sequence, but then reversed on large volume to end sharply higher for the day.

bear rally of October 1973. Similar action and record activity were seen in the surge of October 1969. In April 1930, the climatic month of the blazing rally which followed the 1929 crash, volume was the second largest bull figure in history, and more than in any month of 1929 except for the archival bear figure of October.

There is no accurate gauge of fear, but fright is partially reflected in the statistics of panic's volume, and high-volume reversal days are reliable finales. Figure 4-3 shows peak volume spiking against collapsing prices. Such incidents of panic—not bear market lows—have been responsible for most volume records.

The Northern Pacific corner of 1901 set an activity record which would last 24 years. The crash of 1929 created a day of 16 million shares, a figure which would top the daily volume chart until 1968. Top activity often comes on a key-reversal day, as seen in the right-hand chart in Fig. 4-3, which shows the action during the Cuban missile crisis. Actually, this was not a full-fledged panic, but a selling climax to a stubborn decline which had begun in late summer. Two-day reversals, equally frequent, may experience highest activity on the bottom day but most often it occurs on the second day after the low; in 1970, the biggest trade occurred on the third day of the bottom action. Bear markets, except when given climax acceleration by conditions of crisis, wind down with despair, not fear, and moderate volume reflects that.

The 1900 bear low for the Industrials was made following weeks of skimpy trade and the lowest-volume month between 1898 and 1913. Trade on July 8, 1932, the depression low, amounted to only 720,000 shares. Over 120 days earlier in the year had surpassed that volume figure.

Speed

The destruction of value during a panic is so swift that fright turns many away from opportunity. Bear markets erode and continually seduce investors with what appear to be attractive prices. Inevitably, the passage of a few months erases that flawed vision.

In its 1967–1970 bear episode, Boeing cascaded from 110 to 12. Earnings for the Seattle plane maker were in a frightful dive, dependably lower quarter after quarter; the $1.20 dividend was sliced to 40 cents. The only reason for buying the stock at 55, say, was because of the 50 percent loss. But such discount pricing is terribly appealing, particularly for a well-known name, even when the market's trend is quite evident. One can surmise that the stock's ownership list turned over three or four times on the long downward trek.

In the 1980 panic, on the other hand, Gulf Oil plummeted from 54 to 34 within a few weeks. Such violence is frightening, not seductive. But there was ample reason to chance Gulf. Earnings were rising rapidly and an indicated dividend yield near 7 percent promised to insulate the stock from further severe mischief at the hands of the silver barons.

Panics immediately discount all of the bad news, as perceived at the time. Bear markets only grudgingly accept the rationale for their being, and are much more dangerous. Panics are nearly over before they can be positively identified. Bear sequences may have many miles of bad road ahead.

The only safe time for bear market adventures is when the price cascade steepens into a waterfall. Then panic should be welcomed, for it hastens the end of a dreary process. Postwar bear markets were mercifully terminated by conditions of great stress in 1957, 1960, 1962, and 1970. In that last year, Boeing lost 50 percent of its value in the final two months of the episode. In 1974, the market's low also came under climatic circumstances, although the Dow trough was delayed for two months, to a quieter ending.

Panics' occasional false signals are described in Chap. 8.

Intensity

Intensity, not the extent of loss, is the major distinction between bear markets and panics; their decline statistics are often similar. In March 1938, the Dow fell by 25 percent, struck down first by news of the defalcations of Richard Whitney, President of the NYSE, and then, in a more serious drop, by the Nazi Anschluss with Austria. The 1981–1982 recession, which claimed a 16-month bear market for the Industrials, resulted in a slightly smaller loss. Among more than two dozen bear markets of this century, 12 registered modest losses of between 17 and 30 percent. A dozen panic episodes in the same period caused equal or greater harm to the Dow. Panics' intensity burns in the mind of every investor.

Bear markets lack intensity, save when reinforced by a crisis phase. But intensity is what panics are all about. Intensity might be crudely measured by average percent loss per day. Using such a measure, one of the storied losses occurred in 1933, when the market's celebration of repeal turned into a horrendous hangover. The Dow fell by 19 percent within four days in the marvelously named Whiskey Panic. Brewing and distillery stocks, along with cap and bottle companies, were the principal selling targets. National Distillers was cut from 125 to 65 in the crunch.

On the other hand, a severe bear sequence like that of 1973–1974 lost the Dow 45 percent, but it required 481 trading sessions—an average daily loss of less than 0.1 percent. The intensity of many panics has pushed their average daily loss to several Dow percentage points.

It is one thing to sweat out an 18-month Dow Chemical slump of 50 percent, as happened in 1981–1982. It's another to see the stock decapitated, 109–60, within a couple of weeks, as happened in 1987. It is the intensity of panic which infects the investor with fear.

Attitude toward Fundamentals

Panics pay no attention to fundamentals. Only one panic in the past century developed because of dismal prospects for earnings and dividends; that was in the fall of 1937. And when reason departs during the course of a panic, there is no time to contemplate fundamentals.

Bear markets, on the other hand, are driven by fundamentals—next year's, or the perception thereof. Current statistics, even if they are brilliant, are like yesterday's newspaper. That is why downtrends start so mysteriously; they are born in an atmosphere of strong financials. Since World War II, bear markets have begun in the following years in which the Dow Industrials posted blockbuster earnings: 1946, 1966, 1968, 1973, and 1976.

Earlier in the century, peak earnings were recorded in 1902, 1906, and 1916; bear episodes started in each. Earnings in 1929 set a peacetime record, and we all know what happened then. The investor may be enthralled with current earnings; the market looks over the horizon, and it is next year's perceived fundamentals that motivate it.

In each of the blockbuster years noted—except 1946—the Dow's reversal to a bear trend proved a correct fundamental predictor, for earnings fell in the following year. Typically, the market turned soft in the final trimester of the boom year, becoming suspicious of results for the following season.

The perception of coming bad times, as evidenced by market action, is occasionally flawed, to be sure. Higher earnings failed to stem a bear market in 1910. War fears pressured the market in 1940 and 1941, although earnings gained in both years. Between 1946 and 1949, Dow earnings bulged from $13.63 to $23.54, but the period remains infamous for its depression mindset and stubborn bear trend.

A five-year upswing for earnings which started in 1961 couldn't block the serious downdraft of 1962. And the worst bear market since the 1930s, that of 1973–1974, was accompanied by large earnings gains in each year.

Panic cares not a whit for fundamentals. Historic storms have struck in years of solid financial fundamentals, as in 1901, 1916, 1926, and 1929. FDR's "100 days" in 1933 boomed psychology, the economy, and the market. No sooner did a pause arrive, however, then the Dow was struck down by a classic four-day collapse. Since World War II, panic has never blinked at boom times, striking hard in such years as 1950, 1962, 1978, 1979, 1980, and 1987. In each of these years except 1980, Dow earnings and dividends were at a record level. In the only exception to the pattern, the Dow payout was a record; earnings were only the second best in history. Obviously, the horizons of panic are short, and frightened sellers only want out; they care nothing for fundamentals.

Bear markets are touched off by the perception of a decline in fundamental stock values. Panics are triggered by accidents and incidents, not statistical threats.

5

Serious Money Loves Bad Times

The serious money on Wall Street is made in the aftermath of bear markets. Quick money is made in the chaos of overnight crisis. Occasionally, major declines climax in circumstances of panic, as in 1970 and 1987, and then the parlay of limited risk and reflex opportunity is truly remarkable.

But the public is mostly indifferent at such times. It is the long-continued bull episodes that draw the greatest public participation. Upside fireworks excite the imagination and spur greedy hopes. Precious little money is made at such times, but the bull mania is contagious. In 1929, the public's lust for investment trusts transformed such funds into hot deals and blighted the reputation of professional management for two decades. In 1972, institutions hallucinated: There were not enough growth stocks to go around, or so it was said. And so the Nifty Fifty—growth stocks ranging from Avon to Xerox—were anointed with price–earnings multiples of 50, 60, and 100. Sadly, in both years the end was near and the easy money long gone.

But it is precisely at such times that lambs rush to the marketplace. Lonely senior citizens can obtain a lot of mail by making coupon inquiries to brokerage firms. They will receive a torrent of stock reports and red herrings, along with a Xerox library of charts. They will never be lonely again—as long as the money holds out.

One can almost say that no money is made, or at least banked, in the climatic months of a great bull episode. Serious money is coined by purchases made in bad times, not by chasing the fading rainbows of a mature advance. Such a policy demands discipline, trend observance, and strong-armed timing. Celibacy is a help. Timing may be impossible for institutions whose cash flow forces daily investments, but it is a natural for the individual investor who has the discipline to exit the equity market occasionally.

As dependably as winter follows summer, bear markets will follow bull episodes and inevitable panics will build with shocking speed. The opportunities of such crises will be repeated again and again for those who are prepared.

Making Money without Knowledge

There have been over two dozen bear markets in the past century and nearly four times as many panic episodes, counting only those which slashed at least 10 percent of the Dow's value within a few days. There were three bear markets in the 1960s and a fourth ran into the 1970s, when the gravest economic slump since the 1930s struck in the 1973–1974 market. Another bear episode ended in 1978, and in the last decade a major decline fell between the Silver Panic of 1980 and the Meltdown of 1987.

The great buying opportunities are frequent and well defined. Then is when a great deal of money can be made without great knowledge, for good business will succeed bad business. The Street cliché remains true: Tell me when to buy, not what to buy. Later in the upward cycle, even encyclopedic knowledge will be unable to root out bullish nuggets. Serious market money is made by buying stocks when no one will have them except at distress prices, just as the profits of panic come from buying into an overnight collapse.

Prospering with the Early Birds: Those Big First-Year Gains

Quick stock market gains come in the reflex after panic. Important money is won by recognizing a probable reversal from a bear to a bull trend. Wealth is not gained by prospecting for market laggards years after the advance began, nor by buying a perfect prosperity. The big percentage gains in every market cycle are earned by seizing upon the pricing of fear, early on. Twelve major advances since 1896 have registered gains of 46 percent or more in the first 12 months, although no standalone calendar year since 1933 has achieved an advance of such proportions. In the second years of these sequences, gains have often been in the single-digit range. The early birds prosper at Broad and Wall.

Admittedly, the market is never more excited than in the final six months of a bull market. Rumors fly, manipulations multiply, and the public is irresistibly drawn to the game. How much money can be made in the final quarter? Not much, although this is the very time when volume, excitement, and crowded boardrooms seem to promise the most. The eight super bull markets in history, all of which gained over 100 percent, illustrate the point.

The average gain for the first 12 months was 73 percent. Scratch out the unparalleled advance of 1932–1933, which was 164 percent, and the average is 60 percent.

The average gain in the final 12 months of these record advances amounted to 29 percent, after excluding 1929. We find market tables more meaningful if we omit the nonpareil figures of 1929–1933, radical numbers never seen before or since. That exceptional period is examined separately in Chap. 9.

The World War II market, almost exactly four years in length, displays typical statistics of lurching gains. Table 5-1 shows the largest percentage advance in each 12-month period, as measured from the best previous peak. The final tabulation can be slightly enriched to the May 1946 peak at 212.50, but that figure was only four Dow points above April's best. The final year of this sequence saw victory in both Europe and Japan, and brought most of our combat troops home. Yet the gain fell far short of that of the first 12 months, when Bataan, Stalingrad, and Guadalcanal dominated the news. The advance in the final five months of this victory market was a trifling 10 percent. Buyers who accumulated stocks in mid-1942 were never pressured to sell. The worst decline during the period was only 11 percent, caused by peace worries in late 1943. As such, the period points up a valuable lesson. Despite horrific war news, restrictive government controls, climbing taxes, the aftermath of Pearl Harbor,

Table 5-1. Typical Year-by-Year Bull Market Percentage Gains

April 1942 (wartime low)	To April 1943	To April 1944	To April 1945	To April 1946
Dow 92.92	+ 47%	+ 6%	+ 13%	+ 26%

and the despair of a five-year secular bear market, 1937–1942, the largest 12-month advance of the war began under those circumstances, not in victory's celebration.

Investors Risk Most in High-Prosperity Years

Courageous investors in periods of crisis and panic are generously rewarded. Paradoxically, the highest market risks have accompanied years of high prosperity and confidence—1919, 1929, 1937, 1946, 1972, and 1987—to name a few.

A lagging advance in bullish episodes, as was logged in the April 1943–April 1944 period, usually indicates a roiling group performance rather than a placid market. The Rails average was up more than three times the gain for the DJIA in this war year.

Such sparse gains can be seen as a breathing and survey point in long advances. The 1920s stock boom began in August 1921 and in the third year, ending August 1924, the Dow gain was less than 1 percent. The 1980s excitement began in August 1982, and the gain in the second year, ending in August 1984, was only 3 percent.

Bull sequences lurch raggedly toward maturity, but the most reliable calculation is that the first year will be the best year. Large gains in that period have always been followed by a sharp drop in momentum. Final-year action has been inconsistent. In 1986–1987 the market managed a climatic flying advance. But the last 21 months of the 1970–1973 sequence advanced the Dow only 11 percent.

The important advantage in every major advance is scored in the opening drive. Stocks bought then go worry-free into the lockbox. Stocks bought a year or two later may work out very well but are subject to continued nervous review.

Everyone hopes to buy stocks near bear market troughs. But many are unprepared for the opportunity, either psychologically or financially. Yet the very same investors fearlessly threw money at the market in the preceding bull mania. We shall see how investors can arrive at the moments of opportunity, cash-rich and confident.

6

Indicators of Doom: They Have One Flaw

Technical types are always searching for the Holy Grail of their profession—a perfect market indicator. None has been found. Hindsight has pinpointed some perfect examples, but they fail in real time.

The problem is that even good bearish indicators, our focus here, often ring the alarm months before a market peak. Respected indicators reliably warn of trouble, but they have little value for timing. Like California seismologists, they register increasing stresses, but can't pinpoint when the "big one" will strike.

Speculators are looking for short-selling signals among the indicators of doom, but all investors want is a storm warning. They will then (presumably) switch to a defensive strategy or, even better, an all-cash position.

Such defensive signals can come from sentiment indicators, trend changes, or fundamentals, although the last named is ordinarily too tardy to be of much value. Veteran traders often seem to get a feel that the market is "no good," but such ethereal reckonings cannot be charted.

Joe Granville's well-conceived indicators encouraged him in 1984 to identify 184 parallels with 1929, in *The Warning: The Coming Great Crash in the Stock Market* (Freundich Books, New York, 1985). He was correct: A crash was coming. But first the market would gain about 1600 Dow points.

Nevertheless, technical indicators do flash reliable warning signals. They are not perfect, but when it comes time to exit the market, too early is better than too late. Indicators have only the vaguest value when it comes to panic, however, for they cannot foresee the surprise events which trigger trouble.

Simple Tools Are the Best

Some of the country's most respected technicians—Bob Farrell of Merrill Lynch and Ned Davis of Ned Davis Research, for example—are able to computer-monitor a thousand or more indicators. Obviously, some are more important, or reliable, than others. The best indicators are simplistic and available to every investor. The necessary statistics are available in the leading metropolitan papers and the financial press.

For the average investor, the simplest tool is the best tool because it will be worked regularly. If you prefer armchair research, many chart services offer graphics which display the important technical series.

Esoteric, oversophisticated, and highly mathematical formulations should be mistrusted. It is better to operate on general information than secret indicators. The stock market is not susceptible to arcane crystal balling, or even to scientific insight.

Measuring the Broad
Strength of the
Stock Market

Probably the most popular indicator of overall market performance, aside from the averages, is the advance/decline (A/D) ratio, which measures market breadth. The Dow is not "all," and its bullish action can mask a serious slippage in general strength. The A/D indicator is constructed by taking a cumulative total of the differences of the number of NYSE (or Amex or OTC) issues advancing versus those declining, most generally on a daily basis.

In its simplest formulation, the daily total of declining issues is subtracted from the number of advancing issues (or vice versa on a negative day), and the difference is divided by the total of issues traded. The final figure is then added (or subtracted) to the previous day's total. A running figure is kept and, if desired, a moving average can be constructed. A variety of indicators, including an oscillator, can be derived from the figures.

NYSE A/D Line Lagged at Dow's August High

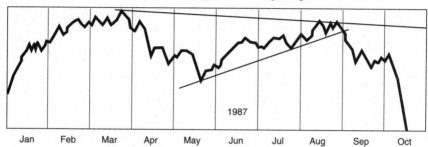

| Jan | Feb | Mar | Apr | May | Jun | Jul | Aug | Sep | Oct |

Figure 6-1. Breadth weakness, as shown by the NYSE advance/decline line, provided an ominous warning in 1987. During the spring, the breadth of the market kept pace with the advance of the Dow, but when the 500-point summer rally exploded, the A/D statistics failed to confirm that strength. At the August peak, they seriously lagged their March high, although the Industrials were 350 points above the best level of the spring.

Down-side divergence between the A/D line and the major average is always a reason for bearish concern, and a *series* of nonconfirmations is a serious warning. In 1987, the A/D plot began to diverge from the Dow in March. It was a valid signal, but anyone who acted on it immediately was premature; the Industrials faltered briefly, but then launched a 500-point summer rally. The poor breadth performance during that period can be seen in Fig. 6-1.

Many other examples of breadth divergence near market tops can be cited, going back to 1929. If they continued, they indicated the probability of a trend reversal—but they didn't say when.

Market breadth figures are generally lacking for the years before 1930, but Col. Leonard P. Ayres at the Cleveland Trust had issued warnings on the narrow advance in 1929. Of 676 stocks studied by the pioneer technicians Robert D. Edwards and John Magee, 262 were in major downtrends before the year 1929, and 181 other issues had already made their bull tops and were "...moving down before the end of the summer."* The year was not quite the screamer it is given credit for. Chrysler had been hammered from 135 to 65 by May, and its best September price, at the market top, was only 74.

Bad advance/decline statistics preceded the Dow top in 1959, 1961, 1972, and 1981, erosion often having started months previous to the market peak. The rallies to a multiple top in 1937, 1946, and 1957 were accompanied by divergence on the part of breadth, warning of a weak

*Robert D. Edwards and John Magee, *Technical Analysis of Stock Trends,* 5th ed. (John Magee, Springfield, Mass., 1967), p. 403.

foundation. In 1959, the Dow was a lone bull late in the year, deserted by breadth, important industrial groups, the S&P, and the Rails. In mid-1972 the market's breadth was consistently bad, and many other indicators forecast trouble in that confusing technical period. Less obvious divergence can be seen at some other peaks, but that may be partly hindsight, for in real time the market and breadth are seldom in perfect sync.

But prolonged divergence leads to serious problems. Figure 6-2 shows the stubborn technical weakness of 1972, when the A/D ratio resisted the rising Dow pattern for months. Despite the divergence, the average reached a record high in early 1973. That peak, however, was violently reversed; there was no second chance to sell near the top.

No indicator is perfect, and the breadth indicator can betray its followers. In late 1986, the market wallowed in the misery of insider trading revelations, "greenmail," and the likes of Ivan Boesky and Dennis Levine. While the Dow reached a record high in December, the A/D chart looked a disaster, having been in a decline since April. The year-

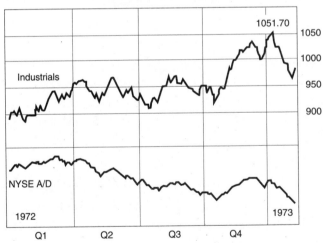

Market Breadth Diverged during 1972

Figure 6-2. Beginning in the spring of 1972, the NYSE A/D ratio warned of trouble ahead. It diverged to the down side in April, when the Dow marked a new high at 969, and performed badly right through the bull market peak of January 1973. The Transports also failed to confirm the strength in the Industrials during this period. Divergence is never bullish, and in 1973, as in 1902, notable divergence was eventually resolved to the down side.

end level was a 12-month low. But a dazzling 263-point Dow jump in January, featuring 13 consecutive Dow gainers, foreclosed on the doubting technicians, and the Dow and A/D figures were back in double harness.

The Dow Theory as a Defensive Tool

Defense is the key to investment survival, and the Dow theory—on the sell side—is a proven defense tool. It is not always perfect, as its many critics point out, but it has served investors remarkably well in every major decline of this century—except that of 1901–1903, when the signal was tardy.

The theory is named for Charles H. Dow, founder of Dow, Jones & Co., but he was looking for a business barometer rather than a market system. Not until some years later did William P. Hamilton, editor of *The Wall Street Journal*, synthesize his thinking into the theory, more or less as we now know it. Robert Rhea, a market analyst, further refined the art. Other market students have added to the thesis, although there is almost always some intellectual splintering about the "true" interpretation. As with every other market indicator, there are defects and occasional failures.

The theory seeks to identify the major trend of the market; it does not attempt to predict the amount of change or duration of the move. The market is seen to be always involved in three simultaneous movements. There is the major trend, which is interrupted irregularly by intermediate movements away from that basic direction. Third, there are smaller, almost random fluctuations, which may be part of an intraday action or may possibly last for a week or so.

We are not concerned in this chapter with the general effectiveness of the bull–bear Dow signals, but only with their workings in warning of a bear market. Did the sell signals occur reliably and within a reasonable period of the top? Did they trigger liquidation soon enough to avoid whipsaw? Primary bear markets since World War II have averaged slightly over 14 months in length, so a good indicator should give timely warning. Table 6-1 shows the often-controversial Dow theory sell signals of the past century, along with their relationship to the previous bull market peak and the total decline which followed.

Secondary interruptions of the bullish sequence usually last from about three weeks to three months and "correct" from one-third to

Table 6-1. Ninety-Year Record of Dow Theory Sell Signals
Percent Loss to Subsequent Major Low

	Sell signal		Subsequent low		
DJIA high	Date	Dow	Date	Dow	Percent lost
Sept. 1899 77.61	Dec. 1899	63.84	Sept. 1900	52.96	17.0
June 1901 78.26	June 1903	59.59	Nov. 1903	53.15	10.8
Apr. 1906 92.44	Apr. 1906	92.44	Nov. 1907	53.00	42.7
Nov. 1909 100.53	May 1910	84.74	July 1910	73.62	13.1
Sept. 1912 94.15	Jan. 1913	71.42	July 1914	71.42	15.9
Nov. 1916 110.15	Aug. 1917	86.12	Dec. 1917	65.95	23.4
Nov. 1919 119.62	Feb. 1920	99.96	Aug. 1921	63.90	36.1
Jan. 1923 99.42	June 1923	90.81	Oct. 1923	85.70	5.6
Sept. 1929 381.17	Oct. 1929	305.85	July 1932	41.22	86.5
Mar. 1937 194.40	Sept. 1937	164.39	Mar. 1938	98.95	39.8
Nov. 1938 158.41	Mar. 1939	131.84	Apr. 1939	121.44	7.9
Sept. 1939 155.92	May 1940	137.63	Apr. 1942	92.92	32.5
May 1946 212.50	Aug. 1946	191.04	May 1947	163.20	14.6
June 1948 193.16	Nov. 1948	173.94	June 1949	163.60	5.9
Jan. 1953 293	Apr. 1953	280	Sept. 1953	256	9.0
Apr. 1956 521	Oct. 1956	469	Oct. 1957	419	10.7
Jan. 1960 685	Mar. 1960	612	Oct. 1960	566	7.5
Dec. 1961 735	Apr. 1962	679	June 1962	536	21.1
Feb. 1966 995	May 1966	900	Oct. 1966	744	8.6
Dec. 1968 985	June 1969	900	May 1970	631	29.9
Jan. 1973 1052	Apr. 1973	921	Dec. 1974	578	37.2
Sept. 1976 1015	Oct. 1977	801	Feb. 1978	742	9.3
Sept. 1978 908	Oct. 1978	742	Signal point was the low		
Apr. 1981 1024	July 1981	959	Aug. 1982	777	19.0
Jan. 1984 1287	Apr. 1984	1131	July 1984	1087	3.9
Aug. 1987 2722	Oct. 1987	2355	Oct. 1987	1739	26.2
June 1992 3413	Oct. 1992	3181	Oct. 1992	3137	1.4

two-thirds of the previous primary movement. The crucial test for the investor is to decide when a correction of the primary trend has turned treacherously into the first leg of a market reversal.

To that purpose, the Dow theory requires a confirmation by both the Dow Industrials and the Dow Transportations—the Rails until 1970—for a change in trend. A reversal to a bear trend, for example, is confirmed when a downward reaction of secondary proportions in an ongoing bull market is followed by a weak rally which fails the high of the previous primary movement. If the market subsequently falls beneath the low of the first reaction, a bear trend is confirmed—but *only* if both the Transportations and the Industrials etch out a similar pattern.

A reversal from a bear trend to a bull trend requires the opposite action, with higher highs and higher lows as the market moves away from its trough.

It seems so simple that we should all surely get rich. But there are those nasty little corollaries and exceptions which were seemingly not learned until they had tripped up the Dow followers. Future false signals will add to the confusion.

Adding Confusing Provisos to the Theory

The Volume Trap. In a bull market, volume should increase when prices rise and erode on price declines. In bear markets, the opposite is true. But what if volume fails to confirm price action? There's the rub. Price is the only conclusive signal for Dow theorists, but volume divergences have seduced some bad calls, with low activity negating apparently valid signals.

New Low? By How Much? The question of penetration causes much debate. First of all, only closing figures for the two averages are used. An intraday slump to a new low, followed by a reversal to a higher close, does not count. Some students claim that any closing penetration makes for a signal. Others opt for a penetration of, say, 2 percent. Certainly, with the Dow in the medium four-digit figures, penetration of the Dow 3500 level by a few points, for example, might be only a cruel deception.

Internecine back-biting between Dow theorists occasionally leads to disparate signals. None were more divergent than during the extended market top of 1956–1957. While most students saw a selling signal in October 1956 at Dow 469, others delayed their call for a year, not anointing the bear sequence until October 1957 at Dow 452.

Timing. There is no required time period for confirmation by the two averages, but it has been demonstrated that a close time pairing usually indicates a very strong move to come, as in 1929. An inordinate delay in confirmation weakens the signal. No market system can be entirely mechanistic, and both buy and sell signals have occasionally been awkward in their timing.

The Dow Theory Is Not Infallible

There have been some very disappointing calls in the past 15 years, as in April 1984. That signal and those of 1978 and 1992 were not consensus declarations by any means, which is just as well for the reputation of the Dow theory.

In 1978, there was no profit to be had, even theoretically. The 1992 sell signal was heralded on page 1 of *Barron's* at Dow 3181, but the average's subsequent fall was barely 1 percent and the index then climbed to a record high within four months.

In 1923 the best possible Dow gain from short selling was only five points, and in 1939 the signal came just six days before the bear sequence ended. The results in 1987 are impressive but somewhat deceiving. The close on Thursday, October 15, triggered a sell at Dow 2355, but the Dow was down 100 points—a first—on the very next day. Meltdown came on Monday, so disciples getting their mail over the weekend risked selling at the worst possible moment.

Table 6-1 shows the potential gain from a Dow theory sell signal to the subsequent low. This is completely theoretical, since a short-selling follower of the theory would only cover his sales at a confirmation point which would automatically be well above the final low. This might even occur *at a higher level than the original selling point,* as happened in 1978 and 1992.

At one time the Dow theory had a broad following. On September 2, 1946, in the post–Labor Day session, spreading publicity about a Dow theory sell signal of the previous week helped push the market sharply lower under panic conditions. An estimated 20 percent of the selling, according to the SEC, came from Dow theorists.

Such fierce allegiance has faded, but the theory remains an important trend indicator. It guarded followers against important losses in the 1973–1974 decline; and it worked splendidly in 1981, as can be seen in Fig. 6-3. The classic summer pattern of 1981 confirmed that the 1978–1981 bull market had ended in April, at point A in the figure. Note that both averages failed at point C to top their April highs and then slumped in July below May's reaction low at point B. That point is extended horizontally. It was, *The Advisor* wrote at the time, an "absolutely beautiful" technical signal, clear-cut and with the two averages "in perfect synchronization."* There was not the usual agonizing confirmation lag.

The Advisor (Houston), July 1981, p. 1.

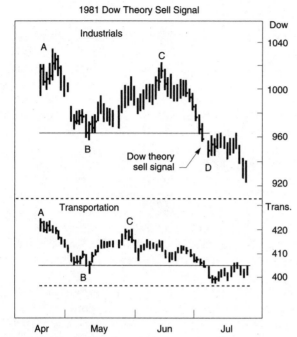

Figure 6-3. The 1981 Dow theory sell signal was straightforward and came less than three months after April's bull market peak, point A on both charts. In early May, both Dow averages fell sharply to low closes of 963.44 for the Industrials and 410.28 for the Transports, indicated by point B on both charts. The subsequent rally to points C ended for the Transports in May and the Dow in June. On July 2, both averages fell below horizontal support lines extended off the low B points. The penetration generated a valid Dow sell signal. Over the next several weeks, both averages rallied back to their former support lines, a typical pullback. (SOURCE: *The Advisor*, July 1981, p. 1.)

We doubt that anyone has ever followed the Dow theory completely and blindly. Even devoted fans seldom use it as more than a tool, since both selling and buying must await a signal. Stock prices in July 1932 were, as it turned out, the greatest bargain in history. But the Dow theory buy signal was not initiated for nearly a year, by which time the average had doubled. Early adventurers were encouraged to hang around by that 1933 trigger, which would not be reversed for more than four years. The theory, which is not often timely, does help confirm decisions already made and, on the sell side, often gives warning of a "turn of the tide" when we are psychologically most unlikely to make such a judgment.

Other Trend Clues

The advance/decline line, the Dow theory, and divergences among the major averages are important and easy enough for any investor to follow. Another simple indicator is the number of new 52-week highs and lows recorded in the daily trading statistics. You can't bet the farm on the high/low numbers, but eroding figures when the Dow is soaring suggest deteriorating enthusiasm. A moving average of the net difference can be constructed, which is of value as the market bottoms; a shrinking number of net lows would indicate a growing resistance to decline. Just following the number of new 52-week highs, a very simple analysis, can be of value.

In 1987, for example, the peak new-high figure was marked in February when the Dow reached 2338, helped by 258 new highs. A market setback was followed by a new Industrial top, 2406, in early April, but there were only 130 new highs. Erosion continued, though there was an indicator rally in late summer. On August 27, with a Dow record at 2722, the Exchange could muster only 135 new highs; the OTC figures had suffered similarly.

The buy-and-hold investor doesn't need to bother, of course. But many "holders" became such only because they ignored the weather warnings. The only requirements for acquiring stock market riches are adequate funds and a confident mental attitude when the bargains are on the table. Switching stocks into cash when the glass starts to fall is the right start.

Other trend determinants are not complex, but they require more time. They are easy enough to interpret graphically, however, and chart services tell the trend story better than a legal pad of statistics.

Trend Lines

Trend lines are a valuable tool. They are simple to use—or overuse—and they give meaningful warnings when they are broken. The implications of a breakthrough of a long, often-tested trend line are ominous. We are referring here to the rupture of an "up" trend line.

There are two problems with trend lines. First, the device is so simple that one hesitates to act upon it. One fears a fakeout and whipsaw. Second, the device is overworked. Many chart observers will lay out a perfect fan of artfully drawn trend lines. Each time one is broken, the boardroom Picasso confides that the next, lower support line is the "important one." It's a game we all have played.

Admittedly, it's difficult to draw the perfect, arbitrary trend line which terminates the bullish adventure. There is no clear demarcation, as one might see upon cresting the Sierra Nevadas. But bull trends *always* turn to bear trends, and the results of holding positions too long are murderous. Draw a trend line and trust it. Figure 6-4 illustrates broken trend lines for the Dow, as they occurred to the up side

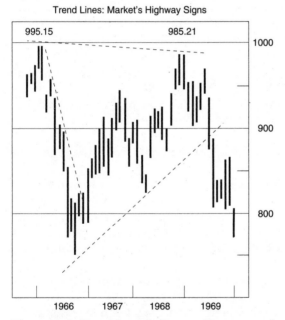

Trend Lines: Market's Highway Signs

Figure 6-4. Trend lines help map the course of the Dow averages. They indicate levels of support and, in breaking, forecast a change in the tide. The intrayear bear market of 1966 was swiftly reversed with a breakthrough of the steep decline line, and a two-year advance followed. In June 1969, the broken "up" trend line convinced doubters that the speculative "go-go" boom had indeed ended. Skeptics had taken earlier warning from the abortive double top, etched just below the Dow 1000 level in February 1966 and December 1968.

in 1966 after an intrayear bear market, and to the down side in 1969. Resistance near the Dow 1000 level, an important psychological barrier until the fall of 1982, is also evident.

While chart formations for stock averages are often more complex than those for individual shares, they produce regular trends, and support and penetration points are reliable. Prices for individual issues are subject to more capricious or manipulative moves which often give confusing or false signals.

Moving Price Averages

Moving price averages (MAs) and combinations thereof are closely monitored by technicians, at least those with computers. Such averages smooth out the wilder fluctuations of the market. A simple 10-day average would total the closing prices of the previous 10 days and divide the figure by 10. On the 11th day, the new closing price would be substituted for the figure of the first day, and the new total would again be divided by 10. A 30-day moving average would be constructed by the same methodology. Nearly every stock charting service displays at least one MA; some have two.

The popular 40-week MA follows the same pattern, except that only weekly closes are used. Several averages of different terms are frequently plotted on the same chart, along with the stock or index being detailed. The longer-term MAs move more deliberately, and their crossover by a shorter average line—bullish on the up side or bearish to the down side—is viewed as an important indicator of a trend change. Exponential averages are also popular. Major works on technical analysis go into full detail on such averages.

Other trend determinants include momentum, or rate-of-change studies, and various price patterns, some of which, like the head-and-shoulders (H&S) formation, have high reliability. Figure 6-5 shows the ominous pattern that developed for the Dow Industrials in the 1916–1917 period.

Many other price patterns, also common to individual stocks, are to be found in the charts of the major averages. They are more reliable in broader translation. A breakdown from a rectangle, a right-angle triangle, or a symmetrical triangle is a danger signal for the cautious. Similarly, trumpet formations and double or, rarely, triple tops speak of coming danger.

Unfortunately, not all price patterns develop in classic fashion. Various irregularities bedevil the investor, but the forms are reliable, even if they are sometimes skewed.

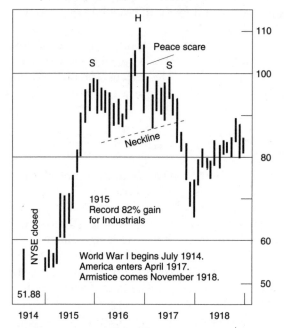

Classic Top Ended War's Bull Market

Figure 6-5. A classic and deliberate head-and-shoulders (H&S) formation topped the bull market of World War I. It remains one of the best H&S examples afforded by the Dow Industrials. America was quartermaster to the warring armies of Europe during the period, and industry's profits surged during the almost three years of nominal neutrality. The torpedoing of the *Sussex,* the "Peace Scare" of December 1916, and the U-boat panic of February 1917 frightened investors but could not collapse the market, which did not crack the "neckline" until the last week of August 1917.

Price controls, higher taxes, and fear of a separate peace by Bolshevik Russia then pushed the market rapidly to a final low at Dow 65.95. That figure was down 40 percent from the high of one year earlier, but still far above the wartime bottom of July 1914, when a headlong selling panic by Europe forced the NYSE to close. When peace finally arrived in November 1918, the event proved to have been discounted and the market eroded.

It's easy to grab profits and sell stocks on a bubble. It's a tough decision to liquidate when the market tilts downward, mostly because of fear that the slump will prove temporary. But selling at such moments is a good insurance policy, and price patterns provide one tool for such decision making. Chart reading is subjective; their artistry and promise lie in the eye of the beholder. Investors will find many excellent books to sharpen their vision.

A slowing momentum or rate of change is an early warning of possible trouble. Often it presages a rollover of an upward trend. It can be easily eyeballed in individual or index charts; the rate of climb slackens, the trend slope flattens. Momentum oscillators help define overbought and oversold issues. Rate of change, or momentum, can be calculated by dividing current price by, say, the price 10 weeks ago. The subsequent entry would be secured by dividing next week's ending price by the price 10 weeks previous. Such continued figures would produce a 10-week oscillator, which is of help in determining overbought and oversold stocks.

Measuring Relative Strength

Often investors get personal messages of trouble when their stocks go dead in the water just when the headlines are celebrating a major market advance. "Everything is going up except my stocks," is the usual complaint, followed by the hopeful opinion that "my turn will come."

A specific way of gauging that feeling is by relative strength (RS). The relative strength of the motor stocks can be measured against the market by dividing an automobile index, such as Barron's or the S&P autos, by the Industrials or any other general average. General Motors' relative strength can be measured against the market, or the auto index, or Chrysler. A declining RS line indicates that the target's performance lags the market. One feels a loss of RS acutely when the Dow makes a new peak and one realizes that a favorite stock is five or seven points below the high of last summer.

Consider a partial retreat from the market when your portfolio's most important holding starts to lose momentum or takes an RS dive.

Setting basic technical safeguards against the brew of overconfidence and the "bear market staggers" requires less time than reading the Sunday sports section. They are simple to construct, a requirement for continued attention and effort. Martin Pring, whose *Technical Analysis Explained* belongs in every investor's library, wrote in the book's epilogue of the importance of simplicity (among other qualities) in judging the market technically. "Because the market operates on common sense, the best approaches to it are basically very simple. If one must resort to complex computer programming and model building, the chances are that the basic techniques have not been mastered and therefore an analytical crutch is required."*

Some Panics Are "More Unforeseen than Others"

The tsunamis of panic cannot be avoided. Many indicators can warn of bear trends, some quite reliably. But panics come with the territory. Hindsight's easy judgments suggest that many panics of the past century should have been foretold. But that is only hindsight. The potential for a reversal in business fortunes is often foreseen, but nowhere is there a forecast for panic. A century of modern stock experience has taught us the dangers of panics, but not how to avoid them.

In 1929 and 1987, as we now know, the market was much too high. In both years, some analysts thought so, but the general view (or greedy hope) was that prices would go higher before serious trouble arrived. A bullish mania always exiles rationality. What in retrospect seem obvious portents of market disaster were not seen that way at the time.

Consider the events of the summer of 1914. Europe was an armed camp, spoiling for war, a fact known to world investors. On June 28, 1914, Austria's Archduke Ferdinand was assassinated at Sarajevo, Serbia. It seems an obvious trigger event, or so we are taught, but there was no financial response. The *Commercial & Financial Chronicle* was impressed by the calm. "The assassination...has impressed not least of all because of the surprisingly small degree of consternation with which the world at large received the news," was its comment on July 4, 1914 (p. 8).

But Austria's ultimatum to Serbia on July 23 sounded military and financial alarms. Selling spread to all the world's bourses. Within days every major exchange in the world suspended activity. The NYSE, the only one still open, became the target for massive continental selling. Overwhelmed by the cables of liquidation, the Exchange voted on Friday morning, July 30, to suspend trading immediately. The decision was perhaps a bit tardy: General Motors had fallen from 94 to 54 during the previous week.

---

*Martin J. Pring, *Technical Analysis Explained* (McGraw-Hill, New York, 1980), p. 248.

The clear vision of hindsight tells us that the probability of turmoil should have been evident since June. It was not. Wrote the President of the NYSE, H. G. S. Noble, one year later:

> It is the nature of panics to be unforeseen, but...some of them can be more unforeseen than others....Up to the final moment of the launching of ultimata...no one thought it possible that all our boasted bonds of civilization were to burst overnight and plunge us back into medieval barbarism. Wall Street was therefore taken unaware....*

A Case for Celibacy

Bear markets always cause more damage than the first estimates suggest, so a defensive strategy is essential. What should one do?

It may sound old-fashioned, but there is a place for occasional celibacy in everybody's life, and there should be prolonged periods of financial celibacy for every investor. The Dow, in January 1966, traded for the first time at over 1000 (intraday) and closed at a record high, 994.20. Fifteen years later, on June 22, 1981, the Dow again closed at that precise figure. During the years between, the Industrials had, in four major advances, gained over 1350 Dow points. A policy of reasoned entry and exit from the market would have been immensely profitable. A buy-and-hold philosophy, as measured by the Dow, had a zero net.

It is fantasy to dream that anyone could have captured both sides of the two-way swings in the 1966–1982 trading market, but an alert investor would have been completely out of the market for prolonged periods—and would have been mentally and financially prepared for some rich advances.

The lesson is that one should accumulate money, not stocks. Summer and winter will not cease. Every individual investor should regularly liquidate his or her account and count the money. Afterward, park the funds in Treasury bills or a money fund. And don't necessarily put it in your broker's fund, however good it may be; buying temptations are too easy to come by if the money can be tapped right in the boardroom.

Segregating your funds encourages recourse to reason in panicky times, when serious risk has evaporated. At such times it is torture for

---

*H. G. S. Noble, *The New York Stock Exchange in the Crisis of 1914* (Country Life Press, New York, 1915), pp. 4–5.

battered investors to initiate stock purchases, even if they have reserves. The secret to objective decision making at such moments is a portfolio of cash and no paper losses.

Fortunately for brokers and market writers, celibacy offers no pleasures to overcome market addiction, and it will not be the wave of the future. But for those with the occasional grace to say "no," dependable profits will be easy.

Gerald Loeb advocated abstinence over 50 years ago: "...the willingness and ability to hold funds uninvested while awaiting real opportunities is a key to success in the battle for investment survival."*

The Alternative to Celibacy: 33 Years at Hard Labor

If celibacy seems a cruel and unusual means of circumventing the bear, consider the alternative. Over the past century, major declines have occupied the market for nearly 400 months—equal to 33 years at hard labor for stubborn bulls. The market addict has spent one-third of a very long life fighting a financial whirlwind.

Obviously, we'd all like to bail out near the top of the market, but a celibacy program doesn't demand such pinpoint timing. When a bear trend becomes painfully obvious, the consensus reaction is that "it's too late to sell." This is not so. Even exiting the market a few months before the final trough will salvage important dollars. The average loss during the final two months of 21 major declines occurring between 1890 and 1978 was 17 percent. The most damaging finale came in 1932, after a down trend that had lasted for 32 months; the Dow average lost 29 percent of its value between May 8 and the bottom on July 8. Injury-prone stocks face a final rout even worse than the Dow. In 1970, Boeing—a former 100-dollar number—had fallen to 24 by the last week of March. It would be smashed to 12 in the final convulsion in May. Avon, 140 in 1973, traded near 50 in early July 1974. By October, the shares were below 19. Avon's dive is seen in Fig. 6-6.

Investors who are not converted to celibacy during the early stages of a bear market will inevitably wish they had taken the vow, however tardily, when faced with the final, treacherous descent. Watch out for that last step.

*Gerald M. Loeb, *The Battle for Investment Survival* (Simon & Schuster, New York, 1965), p. 42.

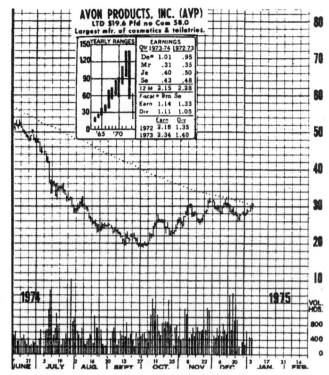

Figure 6-6. Avon suffered a typical late-bear-market collapse in 1974. Its spectacular success in merchandising cosmetics door to door had pushed the stock to 140 in 1973, equal to 60 times earnings. But earnings progress slowed and the market's fury turned against it; Avon melted away to a P–E ratio of 10 in 1974, having lost 86 percent of its value. (SOURCE: Trendline Daily Action Stock Charts. Trendline, a division of Standard & Poor's Corporation, New York.)

Living with Market Corrections

Investors are inured to the occasional corrections which pin back a bull market. Though they are not exactly cheered, such pauses are benign, healthy, and necessary. Secondary, or intermediate, corrections are part of every major advance. We are not speaking here of those jiggles which back the Dow off 5 or 6 percent, but of the intermediate reversals which take the leading average down by about 10 percent and erase between one-third and two-thirds of the previous advance leg. Early in a bull market such slippage is not frightening, and always presents a marvelous buying opportunity. Sudden air pockets in more mature sequences cause nail biting, however.

In the life of every long advance, there comes a time when an apparently innocent correction turns into something neither benign nor healthy—the first leg of a new bear market. The trick is to recognize the terminating action. They don't blow a whistle on the Exchange floor when the defense has to come onto the field.

A survey of 28 important secondary corrections over the past 90 years shows a surprising uniformity in their duration. All were short. The pain of the correction, as measured by the Dow Industrials, ranged from 10 to 19 percent; there seems to be no predictive value in the size of the correction. The Eisenhower panic of 1955 pulled the market down a bare 10 percent, but from there the best gain the Dow could reach in the next year was plus 19 percent. In the spring of 1905, a sudden slump cost the Dow 15 percent in five weeks, but the advance over the next nine months was 44 percent.

The danger signal is not the amount lost in the downdraft, but its duration. Twenty-two bull market corrections surveyed since the 1903–1906 experience lasted an average of just under four weeks. The longest sequence was six weeks. The average meltdown was 12 percent. The worst figure was a 19 percent loss in a one-week binge in 1933.

Suspicions of a trend should develop if the downward correction extends much past six weeks. It's not necessary that the Dow immediately revive to a new high, but it must halt erosion to ease bullish worries.

Hoping Correction Turns to Consolidation

Given a lengthening correction, the best hope is that the slide will turn into nothing worse than a huge consolidation, sometimes seen as a mini-bear. In 1923, 1953, and 1971, the corrections lasted between six and eight months. The first two are seen by some market students as mini-bears, but the loss in the last year was only 13 percent.

The most recent long correction occurred in 1984, when the Dow dragged down for over six months after a January peak. In the meantime, the high-techs and some of the medical high fliers were suffering a genuine bear move after their rocket gains of early 1983. Storage Technology lost 84 percent of its value. In 1992, a mild correction lasted four months, but the Dow loss was less than 9 percent.

Long corrections, not violent corrections, constitute a warning. A severe downdraft is acceptable, but beware a low-volume slump which just won't quit. The worst bear market since the 1930s began in January 1973, but after 15 weeks the Dow was down only 12 percent. There had been no panic incident, and volume was declining. Beware those quiet erosions.

Here are some important differences between corrections and bull market rollovers.

Intermediate corrections are over quickly, usually within six weeks. The initial leg of a rollover market generally drags the Industrials down for three to four months, although sharp, two-month declines are seen occasionally, as happened in the winter of 1916–1917 when war and the German U-boats moved closer to America.

Corrections normally erase one- to two-thirds of the previous advance leg. Larger erasures don't necessarily mean an end to prosperity, but they inevitably cause a stretch-out, as happened after the overkill in the 1978 correction, which took away 74 percent of the spring-summer advance.

Rollovers generally make a second new low within several months. This is not a Dow theory signal, unless it is accompanied by similar action on the part of the Transportations, but it is a warning.

There is no specific timetable for a new bull market high following a correction. Rarely has it come within eight weeks. Delay is disappointing, but not dangerous. In 1968 the lag was nine months. After the correction of 1975, when investors were bugged by New York City's candidacy for Chapter XI, the market needed six months to reclimb the Dow stairs. The extravagant January rally of 1976, which raced the market to new highs, was spurred by widespread bearishness spawned by Dow theory alarms issued just a month earlier.

The first major intermediate usually occurs about one year after the end of the previous bear market, and the monthly rate of advance tends to slow thereafter. George Lindsay observed that when a bull market is going to be short, its deepest secondary reaction occurs during the first year. When a bull market is going to be long, it won't come until the second year.*

---

*George Lindsay's Opinion, May 1983, p. 2.

One strategy for every investor is to exit a bear market when it is identified and conserve funds, looking ahead to the serious money to be made by accumulating stocks in the trough. The ability to distinguish between a secondary movement in a bull market and the first leg of a new bear market is crucial.

A Record Uncorrected Advance

Suspicions run deepest after a lengthy advance. The longest uncorrected move in history lasted just over three years, from July 1984 until August 1987. No reaction cut the Dow as much as 10 percent below a previous peak on a closing basis. But there were some nervous moments in 1986, illustrative of the difficult reaction decisions.

In early September, the DJIA overcame a summer slump and celebrated a record high, only to suffer an outside reversal on the following day. By month-end, the average had fallen by 10 percent, but only intraday. The decline was not devastating, but the action seemed ominous, and had been accompanied by a record one-day drop at Tokyo. Perhaps more important, the bull market was already four years old, and the Dow's gain was nearly 150 percent, the biggest in 30 years. Reaction or reversal? The Ivan Boesky scandal and breadth statistics for the market threatened a trend reversal.

On the other hand, the Transports were buoyant and dividends and earnings were climbing, with a further expansion seen in 1987. It was a difficult decision. The best argument for reaction, as opposed to reversal, seemed to be that the correction, while frightening, was quickly over. The low point of September had been Dow 1755. The November hit which followed Boesky's $100 million fine left the average 60 points above the earlier low. Those arguments, while not compelling, turned out to be correct. The correction was clearly defined in December, when a new high was posted by the Industrials.

On the Warning Track

Only the lucky are able to sell at the market top. Who would have guessed that August 25, 1987, would be a historic peak? Or September 3, 1929? When the market slides a bit, it may appear that the crest has probably been passed. Some of the warning signals—index divergence, a bad A/D line, a sorry bond market—suddenly take on more importance. One looks back and says, "I should've known."

Perhaps one might have suspected, but one never "knows" about the stock market. A Transport-Industrial divergence six or nine months old never said "sell," but it did say "be careful." What is important once a slide begins is to refocus on the negatives previously pushed aside and reach a decision—is this a secondary correction or the beginning of a bear market?

Not all the bearish indicators are in place at every market top, but there are usually at least a pair of suspicious performers. They are like a warning track: it's time to pull up.

Here are some of the suspicious readings at prior market tops.

Rail/Transport Divergence

Until about 1910, the Rails were the more important Dow average. It was the senior average, and railroads were more highly regarded as investments. Their volume and listings far exceeded that of the industrials, and their action was more closely watched than that of the Industrials average, which included among its 12 members a number of shoddy, often-manipulated stocks. Thanks to the Interstate Commerce Commission, a wealth of statistical reports made the railroads easier to analyze than industrial shares. Some in the latter group even refused to provide the NYSE with annual reports.

Nevertheless, a major market trend was already seen as requiring confirmation by both averages; divergence between the two raised suspicions. The Industrials were first calculated in 1896, and the first serious split between the two occurred in 1901–1902, as can be seen in Fig. 6-7. The DJIA went mostly sideways after October 1901, while the carriers gained about 22 percent before both indices succumbed to the Rich Man's Panic of 1903.

As the century went on, the Industrials became the symbol of the nation's economic strength, and it was the Rails that mostly diverged to the down side, leaving a solo advance suspect.

Divergence hoists a warning flag. Thus the railroads turned soft between two and six months before the Dow in 1909, 1919, 1959, 1961, and 1976. In both 1937 and 1957, when the Industrials teased their previous highs, the Rails were down 16 percent from their own peak—a danger sign.

The investor should not be alarmed by minor divergences or short-term splits, but stubborn separations of trend are alarming, though they demand no quick decision. In 1972, the Rails topped in April, nine months ahead of the Dow.

Long-standing divergence, in place before a possible market top, is strong evidence that what first appears to be a market correction is probably the first leg of a new bear episode.

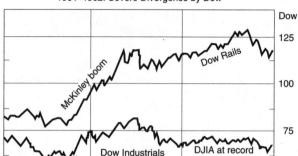

1901–1902: Severe Divergence by Dow

Figure 6-7. Until about 1910, the Dow Rail average was the leading indicator of the market. Between 1896 and 1902 the carriers marked one of their greatest bull advances. The Industrials faltered occasionally, however, most notably in 1901, when they peaked more than a year prior to the Rails' high. At the latter date, they were at a near-record discount to the senior average, barely half the level of the Rails. This ominous divergence was followed by the Rich Man's Panic of 1903, one of the most serious declines of this century.

Bond Average Divergence

The Dow Jones Bond average, along with other credit indicators, raises suspicion when its course diverges downward from the market. First calculated in 1915, the Dow Bond average helped indicate the November 1919 top by turning seriously weak in the summer. In 1929 it turned sloppy in May, and it marked a four-year low in August of that year. And in 1957, when the market arrived at a triple top at Dow 521, the bond index was 11 percent below its level at the time of the first peak, 15 months previously. Equity strength at the end of the 1978–1981 bull market was suspect because of a credit collapse; the Dow bond index had fallen nearly 10 percent within three months.

Utilities Divergence

When both the Utility and bond indices are in gear on the upside, it is relatively easy for the Industrials to advance. Weakness in either is an indication of problems. Dow Jones first calculated a Utilities index in

1929, and in that pivotal year the Utilities remained strong for a few weeks longer than the senior Dow averages, making their final high only in late September. That is not the normal pattern, however, as we will see in the following section on the Utilities barometer.

The two major averages are seldom in lockstep, and alarm need not be taken at the first, trial separation. But nonconfirmations, as with the A/D line, cast serious doubts about the validity of the move. The problem is easy to spot, since most chart series carry the averages in close print proximity. The longer the divergence continues the more menacing are the possible consequences. How long is long? There is no exact answer; the nine-month divergence in 1972–1973 is a modern record. A series of nonconfirmations, or a series of contra-moves, is a more menacing indicator of trouble.

The Utility Barometer

Divergence by the 15-stock Dow Utility average from the course of the Industrials has a good record as an indicator. You can't depend on it for acute timing, however, for its uneasy behavior often sounds an alert only days ahead of market trouble. On the other hand, often it has been only a distant warning; in 1987, the Utility topped in January. Quick sellers left 575 Dow points on the table before the Industrials finally peaked in August. That lead time was not a record, but it was extreme in terms of the large gains for the Industrials after the bearish signal.

More time-sensitive divergence has encouraged investors to lower their expectations on many occasions. In 1981 the Utilities topped in January and were already down by 10 percent when the Industrials hit their April high. The rate-sensitive index gave a six-week warning in 1972, topping in late November, while the Dow advanced through early January. The warning period was about two weeks in 1968 and three weeks in 1961. In the latter instance, the Utility action also confirmed the ominous action of the Railroads, which had topped in October, two months before the Industrials.

A very complex market formation in 1956–1957—actually a triple top—recorded a two-month warning by the Utilities in the summer of 1957. That same time span was recorded in 1937, when the Utilities peaked in January and the Industrials in March. Significant relative weakness enhanced the warning during the summer. The Industrials' strong rally to 190 in August 1937 sketched a double top against a 194 reading five months earlier, but the Utilities lagged 21 percent below their previous peak on that same advance.

A year later, the buyers' panic which followed upon the outbreak of World War II rushed the Dow up to its highest level since the Munich excitement, but the Utilities could not even overcome their best levels of July and August.

Such weak relative action almost always precedes an eventual cave-in by the Industrials. Historically, they have had difficulty in reversing a bad relative trend by the Utilities, for the lesser average is seen as a clue to the course of interest rates, reflecting bond and money market developments. It is uniquely sensitive because its gas and electric company roster has huge debt outstanding and is continually going into the credit market for new or rollover capital. The Utilities barometer is only one of many indicators, of course, and is not a part of the Dow theory.

The longest down-side lead times for the Utility indicator occurred in 1959 and 1965; in both instances, the Utilities peaked 10 months before the Industrials. In neither case did the Industrials achieve dramatic gains after the topping of the Utilities.

On other occasions, however, the Utilities average has acted as a confidence builder, moving higher even when a bear sequence was still hitting the Industrials. Such action is immensely important when the news is otherwise all black, as can be seen in the following bear sequences.

In 1974, the Utility average bottomed on September 13, when the Industrials were at 627. In early October, with the DJIA at a new low of 585, the Utilities were 6 percent over their worst September figure; and at the final Industrial trough in December, at 578, they were 14 percent over that low.

The Kennedy Panic drove the Industrial average to a new low for the 1960s, beneath that of the 1960 bear market. Meanwhile, the Utilities held 13 percent above the trough of that preceding slump.

In the fundamentally confusing postwar years, when record earnings and dividends gained no respect, the Industrials trended downward for a year after an important high in June 1948. In the meantime, the Utilities, which had reached a postwar low in February 1948, traced out a pattern of higher highs and lower lows for the balance of the decade. They couldn't reverse the DJIA single-handedly, but their performance encouraged investors to believe that the credit squeeze of the previous, 1920, postwar period would not be repeated.

Utility strength means that investors see no serious interest-rate problems and indicates an influx of investment money. It is a relevant indicator, possessed of good credentials on both the buy and sell sides of the market. In a constructive mode, it frequently reverses its own downtrend before the DJIA does; and conversely, it has often signaled trouble by its stubborn refusal to follow a DJIA advance.

Measuring Market Psychology: Sentiment Indicators

The stock market, as we have all learned, has no sentiment. It would as soon give its winnings to Ivan Boesky as to an impoverished widow. And it is more likely to bilk the latter.

Investors have a great deal of sentiment for their own stocks, but it's a love–hate relationship. At market extremes that sentiment goes off the gauge: It's either all greed or all fear. Various indicators try to measure such passions, for a contrary opinion will be profitable.

One of the oldest indicators measures the action of odd-lot traders, whose buys and sells are for less than 100 shares. By consensus, they were usually wrong, but such was not always the case. They bought heavily in periods of extreme weakness, but they tended to sell too soon. They were most generally wrong when they grew zealous on the short side of the market. A sizable body of literature, including special market letters, grew around the study of odd-lot statistics.

In the 1920s, small traders often accounted for more than 10 percent of total volume at the Exchange. They were consistent buyers of stock. Typically, they might accumulate three or four odd lots totaling 100 shares and then have a single certificate issued. Or they developed a portfolio of small quality holdings—25 shares of AT&T, 50 shares of General Motors, 50 shares of some local utility, and 40 shares of Standard Jersey. On balance, they probably made money, because they bought and held, and bought more if their favorites declined.

The most important contrary signal from their trade was derived from their short sales, best measured as a percentage of their total sales. High short-sale percentages were bullish, and such extremes were often initiated at retests of market lows, a dangerous move. Options and lower average stock prices have reduced the importance of odd-lot sentiment, although the pattern of heavy net buying swung to consistent liquidation in the mid-1960s. Daily and weekly odd-lot figures are reported in the financial press. Excessive short selling by the public, either in round or odd lots, has always been a good indicator of an approaching market bottom.

Weekly, the NYSE publishes round-lot short sales by members and nonmembers. A short index can be calculated by dividing member figures by total short sales. Members may not know more, but they are presumed to have a better "feel" for the market: When a 10-week moving average of the member short ratio drops to around 65 percent (35 percent of short sales being made by the public), it is a bullish reading. A member sales level near 85 percent would indicate a comfortable floor feeling for the short side of the market. Numbers from 70 to 80 are seen as neutral. A shorter time span for the moving average would broaden the range for extremes.

Similarly, insider transactions (which must be reported to the SEC) are seen as a sentiment indicator, at least in broad terms, and are valuable in aiding trough identification. But such figures are of little short-term help, for the SEC has been lax in enforcing timely filings. Several investment services specialize in summarizing such transactions.

Investment letter sentiment is another popular indicator. While interpretation of the letters' true meaning is subjective, one-sided consensus—either bullish or bearish—is usually incorrect, and contrary market action can be expected. If the advisor consensus is 75 percent bullish, the indicator points toward trouble. If it is only 25 percent bullish, the contrarians say "buy." *Investors Intelligence,* of Larchmont, New York, has been compiling and interpreting these statistics for years.

In early 1993, *Investors' Business Daily* added daily graphics for some of the psychological indicators, easing the chore for technical types. Each indicator is charted once a week, starting on Mondays with the put–call ratio. Other graphs, on a regular weekly schedule, include NYSE short interest ratio, percent of investment advisers bullish, percent bearish, and odd-lot short sales.

Learning about Margin Debt

A lot of individuals in 1929 and 1987, and on many occasions in between, learned a great deal about margin leverage in a few weeks, or even days. It was not the fault of the brokerage houses—or not entirely, anyway. Brokerage firms do encourage margin accounts, to be sure, for they earn a tremendous amount of interest income off the debit balances. Merrill Lynch's interest income has recently been running over $5 billion a year. And, since $10,000 invested in a 50 percent margin account will buy $20,000 worth of securities, a lazy broker can find an easy way to double his or her commission income.

Margin trading is not complex. Margin is the amount paid by the investor using credit to buy securities, the balance being advanced by the broker. The client, under present Federal Reserve regulations, can borrow 50 percent of the value of a margin purchase. This creates a debit balance, against which interest is charged. Interest is accrued monthly, so it is a high-income loan for the creditor. Margin trading is not new. Around the turn of the century, when there were no regulations, "good" stocks could often be margined for five points ($500). Naturally, the margin clerk kept an eagle eye on such ventures.

Wild-eyed critics of the Street's 1929 performance have blamed the Crash on unregulated margins, some as low as 10 percent, but such were actually rare. Margins of 25 to 40 percent were more common, but that was not enough when a stock like Case Threshing Machine could be crushed from 467 to 130 within a few weeks. Other performances were worse, and there were an estimated 600,000 margin accounts.

Partly as a result of that disaster, the Securities & Exchange Act of 1934 gave the Federal Reserve the power to regulate initial margins. Since then, minimum beginning requirements have ranged between 40 and 100 percent. On occasion, volatile stocks have been penalized with a requirement above the norm.

Trend of Debt Is the Key

For a century, market analysts have studied the level of brokers' loans and margin debt for a clue to market action. The trend, not the absolute level of such debt, has been the key. Paradoxically, climbing margin debt is bullish, for it indicates a rising flow of funds into stocks. Falling margin debt is bearish, for it indicates negative flow. Other statistics from the NYSE roughly measure the quality of the debt. Accounts whose equity has fallen below 40 percent of market value are viewed as vulnerable, for although the NYSE requires a minimum maintenance of 25 percent, individual firms mostly have minimums of 30 or higher. In the early fall of 1974, nearly six of 10 margin accounts at the Exchange had equity of less than 40 percent, and forced liquidation pounded prices.

The percentage drop in total margin debt is of only crude assistance in forecasting market lows. Modern figures are released monthly and are not directly compatible with those of the past; margin history is composed of a variety of statistical series used as a rough indicator of customer debt. Regardless of the series, a rule of thumb has been that debt should be reduced by 30 to 50 percent to put margin accounts back on a firm footing. This was never accomplished more swiftly than in the 1929 bloodbath, when "loans to brokers" (the money was then mostly reloaned to retail clients), as reported by the Fed, fell from $6.8 billion to $3.3 billion within about two months. This unprecedented liquidation encouraged the spring rally, but then the debt figure again reversed to the down side and thereafter declined steadily until the summer of 1932, when it stood at one-twentieth of the 1929 top.

An increase in margin debt serves as reliable confirmation of a bear market low, usually coming one to two months after the price trough. It seldom signals a reversal in advance. We can find only three instances in the past 75 years where debt started to climb prior to the Dow's reaching its low point. The last two occasions were in 1949 and 1960; in each of those years, debt started to gain three months before prices did.

There is at least one notable exception to every Wall Street rule, of course, and margin debt befuddled the experts in the 1976–1978 downtrend, rising by over one-third. That "bear market" was itself bizarre, as it ended the two-tier social structure previously enforced by institutional buying. The big-name stocks and averages declined, but the Amex and OTC indices advanced, on aggressive margin buying of secondary issues.

A decline in margin or broker debt is usually mirrored by a bear market or crash loss for the Dow. Some of the close pairings are seen in Table 6-2. Note the large figures in 1929–1932 and the small decline of 1960. Since 1935, the NYSE has compiled customer margin debt on a monthly basis. Prior to that time, the Fed figures for brokers' loans can be seen as a proxy for customer credit.

The rise of margin debt in 1993 to a record high, approaching $50 billion, was seen as a warning by some. But rising margin debt is a

Table 6-2. Pairings of Dow Loss and Stock Market Credit

Bear market	Dow loss (percent)	Credit decline (percent)
1919–1921	47	55
1929 crash	48	53
1929–1932	89	96
1937–1938	49	51
1939–1942	40	34
1960–1960	17	12
1968–1970	36	43
1973–1974	45	51
1981–1982	24	27

SOURCES: Federal Reserve Board, New York Stock Exchange.

positive indicator, showing an inflow of funds to stocks, and in 1993 it had been increasing irregularly for several years. Trouble comes when margin debt starts to unravel. Again, those figures are available only on a monthly basis.

Changes in Margin Requirements Have No Predictive Value

It should be noted that changes in margin requirements are of no value as a near-term timing technique. The first change by the Federal Reserve of the original (1934) requirement of 45 percent was an increase to a 55 percent minimum in February 1936; the Dow climbed for another 13 months. The last change was a cut from 65 to 50 percent in January 1974; the Dow low came 11 months later. When the initial requirement was hiked from 75 to 100 percent—a real shocker—in January 1946, the Dow's peak still lay four months ahead.

Changing Rate Prospects Influence Markets

Neither high and increasing interest rates nor low and falling rates can reverse markets by themselves. In the last half of 1980, 19 increases in the prime coincided with a 14 percent gain in the Industrials. But, aside from the "dirty thirties," when few wished to borrow money, the prospect of easier credit has been a major influence in blunting bear drives. This was particularly true in the days of commercial crisis prior to the establishment of the Federal Reserve. It often seems that a bull market can live with any level of interest rates, but—regardless of the 1980 experience—the prospect for change is stressful.

When interest rates crumble, market psychology improves; and if a bear market is involved, equity lows can be expected within a few months.

Bond market reversals traditionally precede bear market lows. Bonds turned dramatically higher on June 1, 1932, and stocks were only a few weeks behind. It is wise to await some confirmation from other indicators, however, for bonds, like stocks, enjoy deceptive bear market rallies. Expert opinion is not that much help. Leading economists regularly stub their collective toes. In early July 1982, *The Wall Street Journal* surveyed 14 leading economists with regard to the rate outlook for the last half of the year. Most expected that the prime rate, then 16½ percent, would still be at 15 percent or higher at year-end.

Alan Greenspan forecast 16 percent; hopefully, he has a better crystal
ball at the Federal Reserve, which he now heads. By mid-October there
had been seven cuts in the bank rate, and the 1982 year-end figure
would be 11½ percent. Thanks to the dramatic reversal of rates, the
Industrials spurted to a 34 percent gain in the last half of the year.

Changes in interest rates affect stock movements because they
impact on corporate profits and alter relationships between competing
financial assets. Near the turn of the century, when call money often
reached 60, 80, or even 100 percent or more, such increases immediately influenced stock trading in margin accounts, but such murderous
rates have disappeared, along with the call money desk, which was on
the floor of the NYSE.

"Two Tumbles and
a Jump" Theory

Easing interest rates will not turn a stock tide by themselves. The
deflation of 1920–1921 overwhelmed stocks, although bonds had generally bottomed a year prior to 1921's summer reversal for equities. A
tardy reduction in the discount rate finally got the message across and
helped prod stocks into a turn. On May 5, 1921, the rate was down to
6½ percent, and four more reductions occurred before Thanksgiving.
The last two were a double bonus for Norman G. Fosback's "two tum-
bles and a jump" theory, which holds that when the Federal Reserve
eases in two successive steps by decreasing one of its basic policy vari-
ables (discount rate, margin, or reserve requirements), conditions are
favorable for a jump in stock prices. In December 1990, a pair of reductions sparked a large advance, despite war circumstances in the
Middle East.

Many indicators have been researched looking for the secret to
changing interest rates, for around cyclical market troughs, debt markets reverse their primary trends ahead of equities. None is perfect,
but all are of some help. In the credit crunches of the past 30 years, the
bear's withdrawal has been assisted and usually signaled, if imperfectly, by a reduction in short-term rates. Other debt instruments are also
popular as indicators—commercial paper, utility bonds, T-bonds, corporate bonds, Federal funds—along with the prime and discount rate
and the spreads between various instruments.

Bond market reversals have preceded five out of six of the last Dow
bull markets; the exception was the advance that began March 1, 1978.
Treasury yields had turned to the down side earlier that winter, but it

was only a short-term affair, reversed in May. The strong stock–bond divergence led to an ugly market decline in October.

While the stock market can reverse without bond market cooperation, such action is to be viewed with skepticism. Reversals in debt instruments are among the most believable and reliable of market barometers, and provide great fundamental strength following credit-crunch crises.

A 10 Percent Rule?

There is no captain with a bullhorn to order investors to the lifeboats when the investment ship hits an iceberg. When do you run for the lifeboat station? Unfortunately, there is no perfect timing rule.

In the 1984–1987 period, a perfect formula was to hold on until the Dow suffered a 10 percent correction. None occurred until October 1987, and the strategy would have let the investor escape at Dow 2450 on October 14. Just in time, for the average was at 1739 three days later. But in the even grander bull markets of 1921–1929 and 1932–1937, such a rule would have pushed the investor out early and often. In the former, the Dow endured 10 percent corrections six times before the big crash, including a pair in 1926.

Price patterns, the Dow theory, various indicators, and seat-of-the-pants flying have been used, with varying degrees of success, as a means to encourage exit in a dangerous-looking market. None are perfect, but if they occasionally fail, the cost must be regarded as an insurance policy against total wipe-out. Failure at a second top after weeks or months of lagging performance is a good indicator of coming weakness. If no significant yardage is gained in the second assault, the market will swiftly unravel. These failed second efforts come about two to six months after the original top.

In 1981, after an April Dow peak at 1024, a June rally pushed the market to 1012 but then failed, and the market dived nearly 200 points. The 1976 bull market high of September, Dow 1015, was threatened by a December rally to 1005, but after that frustration the Industrials would not return to the 1976 peak for over four years.

A sharp rally in May 1969 carried the Industrials within 16 points of the 1968 bull peak, but enthusiasm then melted and the Dow fell 17 percent within about two months. In each case, rally volume was poor, typical of doomed efforts and double tops. During the period of suspicious action, good news is disregarded and former leaders lose relative strength.

Monitoring Rallies for Warning Signals

Second efforts must be closely monitored. There are three clear warning signals of a suspect advance—eroding volume, a bad A/D ratio, and clear divergence among the important averages, or a combination thereof.

In August 1937, the Dow, which had been at 166 in June, rushed back up to 190. It was a stout rally and left the average only four points below the March high. The economy was strong, and excellent earnings were anticipated in the third quarter. Dow 200 seemed the next target. But despite the Industrials' strong performance, storm flags were flying. The Rails, at their best August level, were 16 percent below the March figure; clearly they were not about to give confirmation. The Utilities were off nearly as much. The A/D line remained in a clear downtrend.

And volume was badly out of sync. At the time of the March high, every trading session since January 4, including Saturdays, had boasted volume in excess of 1 million shares; there had been 10 days of trade over 3 million. At the August peak, volume had exceeded a million shares only once since mid-June.

It was a clear case of a failing rally. But even if the Dow had been able to nick a temporary new high, logic would have indicated a bull trap. Stocks needed to be sold. The formation remains the classic, but similar action was seen in 1902, 1946, and 1976.

Flagging technicals have buried bullish hopes time after time under outwardly promising circumstances. There is no banner hoisted for such watershed events, but the scripts are quite consistent. Just as new highs seem imminent, the Dow, hobbled by poor technicals, suddenly balks and then falls sharply lower. The result is widely recognized as a "failure," and price action and volume quicken to the down side.

It should be noted that there is no time-span uniformity in the consolidation which occupies the market between an important peak and the next serious assault on that height. But if the attack fails, expect the Dow to remain under attack for about 15 weeks as the second leg of the bear sequence unfolds. Figure 6-8 shows the dramatic waterfall as it developed in 1937.

Sometimes, the two market peaks are so level that they form a classic double top, but usually the second is skewed to the down side. The most deceitful of all market moves occurs when the Dow overcomes poor technicals at such a crucial testing point and accomplishes a shaky new high. All too often, the strength is narrow, based on the action of a handful of stocks, and a brief bullish hysteria is followed

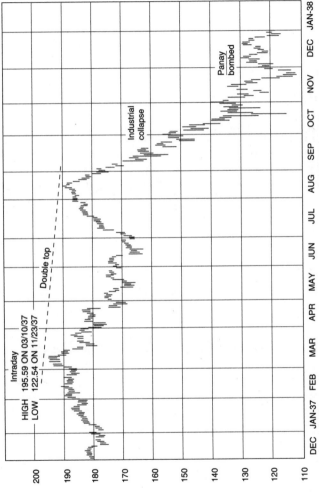

Figure 6-8. Bull markets seldom surrender without a prolonged battle. Often, the change in the tide is not recognized until a serious effort to surpass a previous peak suddenly fails. One of the Dow's most perilous descents, that of 1937–1938, took five months to rev up on the down side. Its course was clearly signaled only after the steep summer rally was reversed about four points short of the March peak, leaving an ominous double top in place. Bullish hopes were finally smashed during Labor Day week, when the Dow gapped downward and then, on large volume, plunged beneath the summer low. The market tumbled into a cascade of panics, aggravated by London weakness. (© 1993 Knight-Ridder Financial Publishing, 30 South Wacker Drive, Suite 1820, Chicago, Ill. 60606. Reprinted with permission.)

161

by swift remorse and a disastrous reversal. Such action is often labeled a "bull trap." Such costly deceptions occurred in November 1919, in February 1934, and in January 1960. Nearly a century ago, after the Flower Panic of May 1899, the Dow regained its footing and eked out a new high in September by less than half a point. It was on low volume, and serious trouble lay ahead for the manipulated market.

The most recent experience was in April 1981, when the Dow popped up to a peak just 1 percent above that of January. The bellwether Utilities were already in serious decline, and the Industrials would quickly follow.

A Few Warnings about Indicators

In the past 25 years, a mania for indicators has focused on everything from the height of women's skirts to Super Bowl winners. The alchemists' attempt to wrest gold from lead was a simpler task.

Every indicator is perfect in hindsight. Yet there can be no perfect indicator, or we'd all be rich. An overpopular indicator will quickly self-destruct, because it draws too big a crowd. The investor should avoid, in particular, those secret, arcane, and proprietary methods that promise "big $$$$$$$" to new subscribers.

A few warnings:

Every indicator has its limitations. None is completely automatic, for the market's response to even identical physical circumstances is never predictable.

An indicator must weigh the balance between extreme sensitivity and laggard response. Too sensitive means false signals and market whipsaw. Slow reaction works fine in a long-trending market, but tardy signals lose all value in short-legged markets. In the 1960s, three bear markets were each over and done between seven and 10 months. The 1990 Iraq decline lasted only three months.

Indicators which work best in timing market lows seldom perform well near tops, and vice versa.

Indicators can't effectively predict the duration or extent of market moves.

Every market system and every indicator will have its failures, always at the most awkward time. They all have defects.

Computers enable market technicians to perform within seconds thousands of calculations which would have formerly taken days or weeks. It is not proven that the quantity of such work has improved the quality.

Don't forget: You are trading stocks, not indicators. Just when all the indicators lock on, your stock may get caught peddling carcinogens; it happened to Johns-Manville. Individual stocks don't give a whoop for market indicators.

There are thousands of indicators. Which ones do you believe, and when? Do you go with the majority, a plurality, an average, last year's MVP, or some odd-ball contrarian? The most valuable indicators require your judgment. Computers are designed to crunch numbers, not to guarantee you early retirement.

Indicators are just that. They don't prove that the market is weak or strong, or that it is headed up or down. If your brother-in-law is *always* wrong about the market, his mindset is an indicator, but you can't take it to the bank. Indicators are an aid to forecast, a warning, a signal of better times ahead, or, not infrequently, a puzzling disappointment. They don't always point to the exact, true path, but they are better than having no road signs at all.

7
Thriving
on Panic

Panics guarantee reliable profits for contrarians. Buyers, not sellers, thrive. But the rewards of bargain prices vary greatly. Sometimes the benefits are of bull market proportions, as in 1929–1930. At other times the crisis event is followed by a stubborn convalescence. Harry Truman's upset Presidential victory in 1948 caused a mild panic, but the three-month rally which followed lifted the Dow only 6 percent above its November trough.

Often the finale of panic signals a reversal of the major trend and the beginning of a major advance. In December 1974, skeptics who doubted that Western civilization was about to end profited immodestly as the Dow soared by 36 percent over the next three months; a quality rebounder like Disney raced up from 17 to 47. But that was only the beginning. The Dow advanced until the autumn of 1976, and other segments of the market continued the bull run into the late spring of 1977.

But strong rallies don't guarantee a new bull market. The courageous buyers of October 1929 gained marvelous profits in the record-breaking rally which followed, but the bullish game was up for good by the following April.

Selling into a panic is financial suicide, for the event is usually a *fait accompli* by the time the investor recognizes it. There will always be a rally following panic, and those who do nothing but wait out the storm will at least have the opportunity to bail out on a rebound.

Those of stout heart who seize the opportunities of panic will thrive brilliantly, if not uniformly, from each crisis. The reflex from panic is not connected directly to the violence of the preceding events. Here are some of the differences.

Rallies after bull market panics recover more ground, more quickly, than rallies after bear market panics. But such recoveries are not automatic big winners. In 1978, 1979, and 1989, the three-month rebound was a Dow gain of less than 10 percent.

The most remarkable rallies follow panics which are part of the final climax of a bear sequence. The contrarian buyer captures the best of all pricing—a bear market expiring under panic conditions, as in May 1970.

The worst panics, regardless of cause, don't automatically create the most profitable three-month reflexes. The 1987 meltdown slashed the Dow by 33 percent in five trading days, but the rebound—a gain of 18 percent in the next three months—was modest considering the violent downdraft and the fact that the secular bull market which had begun in 1974 (or 1982, depending on one's viewpoint) would continue. The advance barely surpassed that of the 1980 Silver Panic, which followed a panic loss of only 11 percent.

On average, panics in bear markets do more damage than those in bull markets, but because of the psychological shock in bull panics, the legends of crisis are mostly attached to such latter episodes. Thus the Northern Pacific corner, the *Lusitania* collapse, the Nickel Plate panic of 1926, Ike's heart attack, the "Saturday Night Massacre," and the Silver Panic of 1980 all occurred in bull markets.

The triggers of panic make no distinction between bull and bear markets. They can strike at any time during the market, or business, cycle, but the damage and the reflex response vary in a rather logical fashion.

The surprising fact about panics is that the damage differential between bear and bull episodes is rather minimal. Since 1890, bear market panics have struck down the Dow for an average loss of 14 percent, as compared with a decline of only 12 percent in crises that hit the market during a bull episode.

Bear market convulsions occurring at the end of a long slide magnify the difference slightly, but their main statistical distinction lies in the magnitude of the reversal pattern from the trough. We will survey this special facet of panics separately.

Contrarians will flourish from the aftermath of all panics, but the rewards are greater and, obviously, longer-lived when the major trend of the market is higher. Nevertheless, reflex gains are larger than one would suspect in the aftermath of bear market crises.

Measuring the Dow's Panic Reflexes

The lure of quick and gaudy profits, far larger for individual stocks than for the Dow, is what lures both speculators and investors to chance the many "Black Fridays," and even Saturdays, which dot the market's archives. Those who thrive on the reflex from panic find that good-trading stocks will return two or three times the amount of the Industrials' gain. In 1929–1930, the biggest bear market rally in history rushed the Dow up 48 percent; Standard Oil and Deere made new highs. RKO's advance was 317 percent.

In the Appendix, 90 financial panics of the past century are capsuled. They can be cataloged in many ways, but in this chapter they are surveyed for the magnitude of reaction in the periods ending one, three, and six months after the trough. Additionally, the results are measured separately for bear market crises as opposed to the collapses that occurred during bullish sequences. A third division measures the rebounds that have followed the special convulsions which have climaxed a major bearish episode.

Table 7-1 shows the average figures for the three categories, as gauged by the leading Dow Jones average. The reflex gains measure the largest rebound recorded at any time in the various time intervals. In the figures for "all panics," no individual crisis matches the rebound averages perfectly, but the 1962 crash, which ended in June, comes close. Its figures show rebound gains of 11.6, 14.9, and 22.0 percent. The looming Cuban missile confrontation pinched the rally's enthusiasm in September, making the three-month figure a laggard to the average of all panics, but otherwise the numbers are a close fit.

Typically, Chrysler—a dependable rebounder since the 1920s—made the average figures meaningless. The auto maker, 39 in June, reached 57 in September and 75 near year-end.

Table 7-1. Reflex Gains from Panic Lows

Leading Dow Average

	One month (percent)	Three months (percent)	Six months (percent)
All panics	11.5	16.2	21.9
Bear market panics	9.6	11.1	14.2
Bull market panics	11.9	14.0	29.3
Bear market climaxes	18.2	25.5	33.6

Recouping in Bear Markets

Frightening as they are, panic conditions in bear markets produce reliable reflexes. The adverse conditions which set up such opportunities are something we would all like to avoid, but they inevitably blindside us. The investor's best reaction is to make additional purchases, unnatural as this seems. There will be company. Fire-sale prices will pull hoarded funds from under the mattress.

The days of crisis may not mark the final low of the bear trend, but they will offer good trading turns. There was a lot of bad road still to travel in September 1946, when the postwar panic struck. After a double bottom in October, a strong rally developed which lasted until the following February, but the Dow's final low did not come until 1949. And at that point it fell to less than two points beneath the earlier trough.

The 1946 crash was one of those rare occasions when the most logical buying candidates, the auto stocks, performed as expected. The unprecedented demand for new cars—there had been none produced since 1942, because of the war—had been temporarily ignored. Chrysler fell to 38, down from an earlier high at 71. It had sold for more in every year from 1935 until 1940. Those who braved the storm and bought Chrysler under 40 did well. The stock sold for 67 in the following year. Earnings, barely $3 per share in 1946, increased to over $15 in 1949.

The attenuation of the Dow from 1946 through June 1949 was exceptional. The common response to a sudden bear market crisis is a decent rally, followed by new Dow lows within a few months, though the U-boat panic of February 1917 hung on a bit longer than most. That market held until July, ignoring April's declaration of war. Leading stocks added some remarkable gains. Baldwin Locomotive and Allis Chalmers were both up by half, and Crucible Steel ran from 50 to 90.

Struggling against the Major Trend

Sustained rallies such as those in 1917 work against the odds. Bear market panics are not as vigorously recovered as the average of all panics. They suffer particularly at the six-month milepost, since they are working against the major trend. The only time that such pressure is relieved is when the bear episode ends during the interim. A gain of 17 percent has been about the maximum at the three-month interval (excluding the volatile 1930s), but a single-digit advance has been most common, recorded in more than half the studies. The 90-day interval often sees the peak rally level.

Following the 1973 panic, which ended in December, the Industrials marked their recovery high in the third month, March 1974, and then slid lower until December. The three-month and six-month peaks were at the same level, a common occurrence in ongoing bear sequences.

The summary for bear market recoveries shows just how weak the advance is between the second and third time series. Excluded from the summary are those mercurial recoveries which occur when panic exacerbates the climax of a bear episode, as in December 1974. They are computed in the last row in Table 7-1.

The best performance of the past 50 years under continuing bear market circumstances was in 1940, when the six-month gain after Dunkerque was 21 percent, a good mark under any circumstances.

The reflex from the 1929 crash remains the best of all bear market rallies, but it required an extraordinary air pocket to set it up. Other advances have been much more restrained. Except under the most exceptional circumstances, a Dow rebound of 17 percent has been a common top mark. Such a figure was first recorded after the Venezuelan incident of 1895.

The average loss from bear market panics—just under 14 percent—has been a bit more than the reflex gain. Losses of 20 percent or more have been rare, excluding the excitements of 1929–1932. The shadow of war caused the two worst smashes, in December's "Black Week" of 1899 and during Dunkerque.

During bear markets, one can thrive on panic bargains, but it is a defensive battle. But what are the alternatives? Liquidation—which always seems to come right at the bottom—destroys both psyche and purse. Standing pat stirs "what if" regrets when the inevitable rally develops.

Panics during Bull Markets

As one might suspect, it is relatively easier to thrive in the aftermath of bull market panics. The bounce is higher and faster. In nearly every instance surveyed, the percentage gain after a bull crisis exceeded the preceding loss. One of the rare exceptions occurred in 1978, when tight money plunged the Dow by 12 percent; the revival which followed pushed the Dow up only 9 percent.

Leaving out the miracle figures of the first half of 1933, the six-month reflex from nearly three dozen bull panics has amounted to 29 percent, about double the rebound from bear troubles. The best gains in the three-month period following the trough have often been sensational—between 25 and 30 percent—although the largest rebounds occurred before World War II. The last really large advance was in 1935, a 25 percent jump after the troubles caused when Hitler rejected the Versailles Treaty.

Not only do bull market panics recover strongly, but the preceding damage is typically less than those of bear episodes. Such downdrafts are less threatening than those of bear sequences, but seem to carry equal shock value. Bull market portfolios can be routed overnight as easily as those of bear markets. Psychologically, the declines are often more damaging, for they frequently tip the market just when it appears to have no possible room for weakness. December 1928 saw such a break. And the Whiskey Panic of 1933, which destroyed the "wet" stocks, was of the fiercest intensity, although the market had just completed a record advance and there was great hope and confidence in the new FDR administration.

Since World War II, however, the largest panic decline occurring in a bull market has been only 12 percent; many bear market crises have exceeded that figure, with the autumn collapse of 1973 reaching 20 percent. The major decline of 1987 wrote its own ticket and rules, of course, down by nearly one-third within days. But its peculiar credentials of time and damage mark it as one of a kind.

Most investors know the major trends of the market, and should thrive in the aftermath of bull panics. Such opportunities must be seized, for the investor will be quickly enriched. In nearly two-thirds of all such incidents, the Dow has recovered within three months to a level higher than the prepanic figure. The last occurrence followed the sharp slump of October 1989; by January, the Industrials were at an all-time high. Unfortunately, UAL and the rest of the airline group, whose merger mania had sparked the collapse, were still in trauma.

Reliable Rebounding from Bull Market Panics

The reflex from a bear market crisis is occasionally dicey, but panic buyers during major uptrends have reliably grown wealthy. In the years before 1955, the rebounds were often sensational, with six-month gains approaching or exceeding 50 percent—as in September 1898, 1908, and 1915. The unique advances from two crises in early 1933 averaged 100 percent, but there were very special circumstances. A four-digit Dow would seem to argue against a repeat of such figures.

Small risk is attached to adventures in bull market panics, since cyclic reversals rarely develop from crisis at the top. No such action has occurred since 1919.

The grandest recovery figures from a bull market panic during the 1890s were posted in 1898, after the incident at Fashoda. In the aftermath of the peace treaty with Spain, a bullish mania for giant amalgamations developed, and the Dow far outpaced the Rails, gaining by 45 percent to April 1899. It was a time of feverish public activity in the marketplace.

Pools and manipulations abounded, and none were more successful than those in the "Flower stocks," bulled by ex-Governor Roswell Flower. New York Air Brake skipped up from 89 to 204 during the six months, and the politicians' stock, the BRT, was elevated from 57 to 137. Railroad expansion, slow since 1893, offered little opportunity, but Wall Street found riches in the promotion of industrial trusts, which were shamelessly watered. *The New York Times* complained on October 5 that "manipulation has reached the point of scandal."

Outside the 1930s, only one postrally advance has outdone the one following the Spanish-American War. In the six months after the sinking of the *Lusitania*, the Dow climbed 62 percent. It was an easy rebound, for the war-boom year remains the absolute best in the long history of the Dow averages. The gain was 82 percent. In the torrid 1980s, the best year was 1986, when the advance was only 23 percent. The summary figures following bull market crises are not wildly better than those of bear sequences, except for the large average advance in the second three-month period, which doubled the 90-day figure, as seen in Table 7-1.

Just why the reflex figures were superior in the years before World War II is not entirely clear. But the best one-month bull market bounce since 1955 was an 8 percent runup in April 1980. In 1950 and the 60 years preceding, there were 19 double-digit recoveries. Few were stronger than that of December 1928, after a warning from the Treasury to speculators plunged the Dow by 13 percent within seven trading sessions. Its Saturday climax came on a record half-day volume, 3,750,000 shares. Radio Corporation was crushed from over 400 to 293, and the Dow, having briefly kissed the 300 level, ended its fall at 257. The advance to January's best level was 24 percent. Modern-day figures lack that drama, which saw RCA near 550 by March.

There was no panic of note in the following bull sequences: 1958–1960, 1960–1961, 1962–1966, 1966–1968, 1970–1973, 1974–1976, and 1982–1987. Between 1984 and 1987, the Dow advanced for a record period without a single correction of as much as 10 percent. The closest call followed a high in early September 1986; the Industrials immediately fell by 10 percent, but only intraday. Following that minor rout, which was accompanied by a record drop in Tokyo, the six-month recovery was 500 Dow points.

Investors still thrive from bull market adversities. There just haven't been that many serious opportunities in recent decades. The poorest modern recovery was in 1990—which was a slump sometimes viewed as a bear market of extremely short duration. The worst bull decline was a raid engineered by Thomas Lawson in 1904, but it was for less than 15 percent. Do not expect "going out of business" prices in bull panics. The average loss, excluding 1932–1933, has been under 11 percent.

Counting the Biggest
Payoffs from Panic

Bull market crises provide reliable contrarian profits. But the most spectacular reflexes come when a bear sequence ends in a seeming doomsday panic. Grasping the nettle at such perilous moments has led to big payoffs. Even the impatient have thrived.

There is no way to positively identify such double climaxes in real time. Frequently, an earlier crisis during the bear episode has caused more damage than the finale. The loss in the 1973 panic far exceeded that of any action in the autumn of 1974.

The rewards come immediately, for when panic unloads on a long-continued bear trend, the next market move will be a rocket reversal. The trough will be left far behind in the first month following the crisis. As seen in Table 7-1, the average first-month gain is 18 percent, and the 90-day average advance shows the Dow up by one-quarter.

The springboard for such rewards is the oversold condition which results when the double-dip statistics liquidate the last weak holder. The biggest rebounds have followed the cruelest bear markets—1974, 1938, and 1932, for example.

An exception occurred after the modest bear episode of 1895–1896. The summer panic of the latter year was sparked by fears for the dollar, fomented by William Jennings Bryan's Presidential campaign and the Silverites. When those threats were seen to peak in August, hopes revived for a GOP victory, and the Dow raced up by 44 percent by election day. While the preceding bear market had not been severe, the late summer panic, which began just after Bryan's stirring "Cross of Gold" oratory, cost the Industrial average one-fifth of its value, about double the minimum panic standard. Other 20 percent haircuts which were followed by extraordinary gains occurred in 1938 and 1939.

But reliable gains have come even when major declines ended quietly. Panics with small damage numbers but rewarding reflexes were recorded in September–October 1903 and November–December 1917. The figures for 1914, at the beginning of World War I, were modest enough, but only because the NYSE suspended activity in order to halt the wave of selling from Europe. The exceptional advance following the 1974 low was not signaled by a wild crash. The climatic damage had been exceeded twice earlier that autumn and once in 1973.

The most dependable profit centers have been won in the climax of record bear market declines or extreme pricing following more normal sequences. It is difficult to find an exact relationship. The major decline of 1987 led to substantial reflex profits, but they were modest in comparison with the damage suffered, being less than those compiled after the 1968–1970 decline at the three- and six-month intervals.

Panic conditions can deceive, as in September 1974, when buying commitments proved premature. But it is usually more a test of nerves than resources, as in 1962. On the worst day of 1974's final crisis, in December, there were only 459 new lows, compared with 616 on October 4, the day the "market" scored its low.

Bear market panics usually produce *immediate* gains superior to those of bull sequences. Figure 7-1 details the Dow's biggest daily gains of this century. Only the largest advance in a particular year is shown; for example, although the biggest gain of 1932 occurred on September 21, on three other days that year the Industrials advanced by over 9 percent. Only two of the record days, in 1901 and 1939, appeared under clear-cut bull market conditions.

"Freezing at the Stick"

It is the nature of panic to overwhelm reason, and irrational fears often cause the investor to "freeze at the stick." Every tiny tremor, every minor correction in a bull market is seized upon by alarmists and professional doomsayers.

In the autumn of 1978, a number of rather conservative investment letter publishers were taken by a plague of bearish recklessness. "Killer waves" and "Dow 400" were popular pronouncements. A similar malady had encouraged bearish conversions in the fall of 1975, when the prospect of Chapter XI for New York City excited a great burst of fear east of the Hudson. Those of bullish convictions must capitalize on such recurrent tremors and corrections, and not sit on their purses.

Panic does not strike down bull markets from the very top, but rather puts the "terminated" stamp on them some months past the peak. Investors must not be gun-shy of panic during bull episodes. Twelve panics interrupted the 1932–1937 advance, so there were plen-

PANIC'S REFLEX FIREWORKS

Of the nine largest daily Dow advances in this century (see table below), eight came in the immediate aftermath of panic. The exception, in 1939, was caused by a buying panic that followed the outbreak of World War II. Traders recalled the huge market gains of the first World War and scrambled to buy the war babies of that era, like the steels, along with the newer aviation issues. Up-side volume in that post–Labor Day session would not be matched until 1961.

The largest daily advance in history came in 1933, after the Exchange had been closed for nine days due to the banking crisis and moratorium. Economic hopes were excited by FDR's new programs, and all three of the Dow averages gapped sharply higher.

Date	Gain	Catalyst
Mar. 15, 1933	15.3	NYSE re-opens
Oct. 6, 1931	14.9	Sterling crisis ends
Oct. 30, 1929	12.3	"Crash" rebound
Sept. 21, 1932	11.4	Bargain hunt
Oct. 21, 1987	10.1	Meltdown reflex
Sept. 5, 1939	7.3	World War II
Mar. 15, 1907	6.7	Short sellers cover
May 10, 1901	6.4	Rail war resolved
Oct. 20, 1937	6.1	Panic takes breather

Figure 7-1. The stock market is full of paradoxes. Perhaps none is more surprising than the record that shows that the most spectacular daily market gains have sprung out of the debris of panic.

ty of opportunities for strong-minded bulls, as well as for those who had missed the turn of the tide in July 1932. When the end to that great advance, the second largest in Dow history, occurred, it was off a top formation which had stretched for five months, not an overnight stroke of bad news.

One of the biggest of all postpanic advances occurred after the slump of May 1929. Chrysler had fallen to 65, having taken a terrible beating since its January top at 135. General Motors was an 86–66 loser in the May turmoil, as both the Industrials and the Rails were knocked down to new lows for the year. It was a bear trap, however, and buyers who took advantage of the bargain pricing enjoyed one of the grandest "summer rallies" in history; the Dow gained 30 percent.

Other sensational advances following bull market panics occurred in the fall of 1898, in 1908, in 1915, in 1928, and frequently in the roller coaster action which began in the second half of 1932 and lasted until mid-1934.

It should not be inferred that panics present the only opportunities for contrary buying; they are just so swiftly bountiful. In addition to the many panic sequences of 1921–1929, there were eight occasions when the Dow "adjusted" downward between 6 and 9 percent and three longish corrections of between 11 and 13 percent, plus the controversial "bear market" of 1923, when the average fell 19 percent. There were 97 months involved from August 1921 through August 1929, and the Dow closed lower in 36 of them. There were a multitude of corrections in that longest and biggest of all bull markets.

Investors must not allow a hyper imagination to choke off the recurrent opportunities of crisis.

Statistical Overkill

Like *Gray's Anatomy*, the anatomy of a stock market panic is vividly illustrated. The statistics of the market sketch an accurate portrayal. In periods of great stress, they become so bearish that there is room only for improvement. Among such technical readings are the daily advance/decline figures, the high/low figures, advance/decline volume, and the put/call ratio, to name a few.

Statistics for advancing stocks versus declining stocks at the NYSE have an excellent record for both trend and climax. A 1:10 ratio, with only one gainer for every 10 declining issues, has been a reliable buying signal in normal declines, though bear market low figures are often more moderate. Panics stretch the ratio almost beyond belief, emphasizing the oversold condition and underlining the buying opportunities.

Panics create statistical overkill. The most damaging advance/decline figure we have noted occurred in the Dunkerque panic, when there were 14 advances and 930 declines at the Exchange, a 1:66 ratio. Meltdown 1987 produced a 1:38 figure. The news of Eisenhower's heart attack stirred huge liquidations, and the first day recorded only 36 gainers against 1157 losers, 1:32. In September 1946, the postvictory collapse posted a 1:29 ratio on its worst day.

Bear market finales have been much more modest. In 1932 there were 114 advancing stocks and 218 decliners on the final day of the 1929–1932 sequence. The ratio on December 6, 1974, was 1:5. In February 1978 the last day's reading was 1:3; and in 1982 it was less than 1:2. In all of these sequences, however, there had earlier been bitter days approaching a 1:10 down-side ratio; they had signaled "rally" but not reversal.

The worst statistical numbers frequently come on the day preceding the panic climax, since the final day is often one of momentum reversal, with the A/D ratio improving dramatically late in the day.

High volume also helps sketch panic and is a dependable signal of an impending reversal to the upside. There are typically two or three days of enormous relative volume at the climax. Accidents and incidents, however, change the timing of this market characteristic; such triggers excite peak activity as the market first tilts into crisis. In 1898, the *Maine* tragedy rushed the market lower on average daily volume of 440,000 shares. A few weeks later, the threat of war drove the Dow to a new low, but volume fell 40 percent below the earlier level.

A half-century later, in November 1948, Harry Truman's upset Presidential victory was followed by next-day volume of 3.2 million shares, but activity then trailed lower until it was only 1.2 million at the end of the decline. Ike's Denver heart attack also spurred typical repercussions for a news-incited panic.

The Eisenhower Panic: Biggest Volume in 22 Years

It seems a bit overdone now, but on the first day's trading following the news of President Eisenhower's heart attack in Denver, NYSE volume was the highest since 1933—nearly 8 million shares. In a reversal of the usual panic form, that figure was halved on the last day of the crisis. The intraday loss on the initial day of shock was 9 percent, while the number on the last day of decline was less than 1 percent.

Similar action occurred in 1979, when, on a Saturday night, the Federal Reserve Board took steps to tighten credit. The Dow—which had been at the year's high—collapsed in the following week. Volume raced to over 80 million shares, 10 times the panic level a quarter-century earlier, on October 10. Activity then slowed dramatically, though the Dow continued to slide until November 7, when it marked its low for the year. Volume often fell below 30 million shares.

Figure 7-2 shows the front-end volume load which is so often created when shocking news triggers panic. Activity peaks almost immediately after the news break and then tapers off even though prices continue to decline.

But statistical overkill more commonly appears at the finale of panic. October 19, 1987, was the most frightening day in stock market history. An avalanche dropped the Dow 504 points; the percentage loss of 23 percent was equal to the total for 1929's two worst days. At the Exchange,

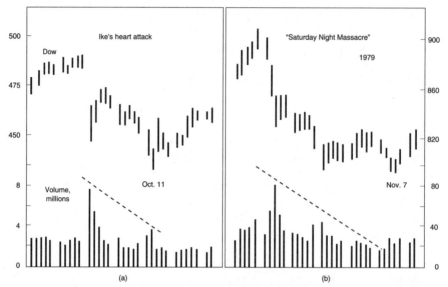

Figure 7-2. Panics triggered by news events spur volume peaks within a few days of the first shock. Activity figures at the final price trough are always much lower. (a) The action following news of President Eisenhower's heart attack on Saturday, September 23, 1955, illustrates the pattern. The Dow had just closed at a record level. Monday's panic selling, encouraged by a huge opening gap, counted the largest volume at the NYSE since 1933. The sequence low, however, did not come until October 11. (b) When the FRB tightened credit unexpectedly in 1979, the market was immediately convulsed by record down-side volume. Panic conditions ended within several weeks, but the Dow continued to decline until early November. It had fallen from the year's high to the year's low within about a month.

there were only 52 advancing stocks as compared with 1973 declines, a 1:38 ratio. Declining volume was 534 times that of advancing volume.

Frantic sellers became the risk takers, burying their hopes beneath the black statistics. Buyers invested in stocks at a fraction of the levels seen a few days earlier, prices which guaranteed—at the very worst— a material rally. All 30 issues in the Dow Industrials fell sharply; Eastman Kodak was down 30 percent for the day. Stock index futures in Chicago were in chaos, stunned by a two-year move compressed into an hour or so.

Brilliant fundamentals got no respect. Microsoft revealed that third-quarter revenues and earnings had exploded, but the stock, 65 on Friday, fell to 45. It slipped to 42 on Tuesday.

Burlington Northern, whose parent companies were so ardently pursued by Harriman and Morgan in 1901, had been 84 early in

October. It closed at 70 on Friday, October 16. By Tuesday morning the shares were at 35. It was statistical overkill, obviously. Was there risk? Certainly. But the investment value far outweighed any further temporary risk. With the market down nearly 1000 points, the initial assault was certainly almost over. As it turned out, it had ended for most stocks. Burlington closed at 52 that Tuesday evening.

Doomsday statistics mark the end, not the beginning, of financial apocalypse.

Unfortunately, it is not possible to quantify "overkill" precisely, but you'll know it has come when the evening newscaster intones "Wall Street's worst day in years."

Bargain Prices Don't Last

The bargain-basement prices seen in every panic are not open-ended. Buying selections must be made quickly; there will seldom be more than a half-dozen days of low pricing, as measured by the Dow.

We are talking here of fire-sale figures, where the Dow trades within 1 or 2 percent of its absolute low. Table 7-2 shows the number of trading sessions in which the intraday bottom hugged the panic low. On occasion, as in the worst example, 1940, the opportunities have been more numerous than might be wished. It is the fervent desire of risk buyers that the averages quickly levitate after a period of panic; a prolonged sideways movement invites further distress liquidation.

Table 7-2 counts only those low days immediately before the trough, or occurring within two weeks after. Thus the 1980 figure indicates only three sessions of low pricing following the trough; actually, the

Table 7-2. Duration of Panic Prices
Intraday Dow Ranges within 1½ Percent of Absolute Low

Low date	Prior to Dow low	On/after Dow low	Total	Low date	Prior to Dow low	On/after Dow low	Total
Nov. 1929	0	1	1	Oct. 1960	2	6	8
July 1932	1	3	4	June 1962	2	6	8
Mar. 1938	1	1	2	May 1970	1	2	3
Apr. 1939	0	3	3	Dec. 1974	1	6	7
May 1940	3	12	14	Oct. 1978	1	7	8
Sept. 1946	3	4	7	Oct. 1979	1	12	13
July 1950	1	4	5	Mar. 1980	3	4	7
Oct. 1955	1	6	7	Oct. 1987	0	2	2

Dow recorded a new low—by less than a half-point—about a month later, adding several days of cheap Dow pricing. But many of March's worst victims supported well above their lows. Dome Mines, at 48 in March, held near 56 in late April.

In 1940, the May bottom near Dow 114 was attacked day after day, for a total of 14 additional sessions within the next three weeks: The Dunkerque defeat was seen to doom Paris. Not until mid-June could the market pull decisively away from the low. That lengthy bottom supported a 13 percent gain for the Dow over the next three months, despite the war's unending bad news.

Such a consolidation at a panic low is unique. Those who would thrive from panic's bargains seldom have more than a half-dozen days of grace. The shortest turnarounds came in 1970 and 1987. The former was a classic, because there was no secondary test of the disaster area. In 1987 there were several December days when the Industrials were within 3 percent of October's worst levels.

Fortunately, the investor doesn't have to pinpoint the Dow low to pick up bargains. Group lows will be spread across the calendar. In 1970, most of the aircrafts scored their lows in July, and the farm and office equipments delayed until August, by which time consumer stocks such as Whirlpool and Sears had already gained nearly one-third.

Despite occasional whirlwind reversals by the Dow, most large-cap stocks spend a few days near their lows. Figure 7-3 shows *Trendline's* 1970 chart of Ford Motor Company; the automaker spent the better part of six days in an extraordinarily tight range, 39–40. Buyers who missed out had a good opportunity six weeks later, when the shares fell sharply below 42.

During the volatile 1930s, panic reversals were dependably swift. There were few opportunities for second guessing, and frequently there were only one or two companion days at the panic low. No performance can compare with 1929, however. The final day of panic was a solo performance. No intraday range of that year, before or after, approached the Dow 199 low of November 13, and the speculative rewards from that date are striking. United Aircraft, having plummeted from 162 to 31, would more than triple by April of 1930.

The swift turn of 1929 was truly unique, but investors usually enjoy a bit more time than Table 7-1 indicates, since low ranges falling beyond the two-week cutoff point were not counted. In 1979 the ordeal of low prices continued for about a month, and in 1946 a complex bottom formation returned the Dow to the area of the panic low during 19 sessions, stretching into December.

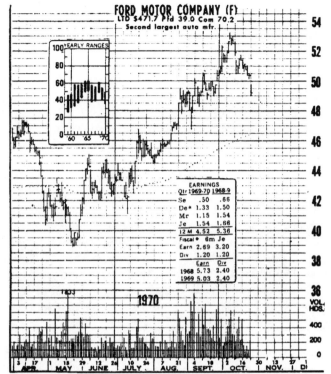

Figure 7-3. There was an extended tight buying range for
Ford Motor Company in 1970. The compactness of the chart
bottom indicates that a large buying program, probably
attracted by the $2.40 dividend and projected earnings of near-
ly $5, was in effect just below 40. (source: Trendline Daily
Action Stock Charts. Trendline, a division of Standard & Poor's
Corporation, New York.)

Why Take the Risk?

Panic? Why take the risk? Some people obviously do, for there is
always huge volume at panic lows. But most of that comes from professionals and institutions. The average investor shies away from a crisis market. "Too much risk" is the excuse.

Yet riskless investment is an oxymoron. Remember those Southern
Bell Telephone bonds your Dad bought back in the 1950s when Ike
balanced the budget and the dollar ruled the world? The inflation rate
was zero, and Pop was happy to get the "riskless" bonds at par. By
Jimmy Carter's last year in office, inflation had cut the value of those
Triple-A, 3 percent bonds to $310.

Inflation is just another of the risk devils waiting to strike at your investments. Sometimes, to be sure, inflation has been seen as a boon to stock prices, but not in recent decades.

Defense is the secret of investment survival, but risk is the secret of investment profit. And profits must be prospected vigorously, to offset the constant attrition from accidents, incidents, and the occasional poor judgment which plagues us all. Some risk must be accepted.

Panic contrarians are seen as foolhardy, but consider this: By the time panic is fully defined, the risk has mostly passed. In the meantime, the final spasm has identified itself with enormous volume and a phonebook of new lows. You know the crisis is already over when "Stock Market Panic" is the lead headline and the first item on the evening news is a report from Wall Street. The crisis is announced, defined, and explained. Experts are quoted and comments are sought from the White House and the Federal Reserve Board.

What is the risk at such times? The market was awash with risk a month earlier, but no one mentioned it. There was plenty of risk a week ago. But now? Another day, possibly two days. And then the reversal will come so dramatically that it grabs the news spotlight. Unfortunately, your broker was so busy cleaning up margin calls that he failed to call you.

And suddenly, the stock you've been coveting for months turns on a dime and leaps from 60 to 70 within a week. Panic does not erase risk, but shrinks it to the point where even a prudent man can handle it.

Discounting the Bad News

In the autumn of 1973, in the middle of what would be the most severe bear market since the 1930s, an avalanche of bad news drove the Dow down by over 200 Dow points, more than 20 percent, with panic conditions prevailing during the last several weeks. The news was the blackest since the war days of 1940. Inflation, a currency crisis, and the Agnew scandal had chipped at confidence for months, and then the Yom Kippur war spurred an Arab oil embargo and the first of many energy crises.

The Watergate torment worsened. Archibald Cox, the independent prosecutor, was fired. Six "break-in" artists were sentenced. The Nixon tapes were found to have been erased. Gasoline lines and shortages shocked the nation, and the President asked for a 50-mph speed limit and Sunday closings for service stations. There were demands for his impeachment, and not just from surly motorists. A Constitutional crisis seemed at hand. Worse yet for the market, the mystique of the high-PE growth stocks was suddenly stripped away. New England Nuclear, at a record high of 65 in the last week of October, imploded to 38 before Thanksgiving. National Semiconductor was knocked from 108 to 48.

But by early December, all of the problems, as then understood, were discounted. Oil fears moderated, and the energy-sensitive Transports jumped by 21 percent within four weeks. UAL, 17 at the December low, flew to 30. U.S. Steel advanced by nearly one-third.

Consider another example. In February 1917, Germany announced that a new policy of unrestricted U-boat warfare, even against neutrals, would begin immediately. It seemed that America would inevitably be drawn into the Great War, and the Dow collapsed, suffering its worst one-day ordeal between 1907 and 1929. But the panic ended within another day, and the average rose by 13 percent by mid-March, having discounted not only the winds of war, but the actual outbreak of hostilities, which came in April.

The violence of panic guarantees that the bad news which triggers a crash will be immediately discounted. Risk, for the time being, is effectively removed.

Not for Everyone

Despite the proven richness of opportunity, financial brinksmanship is not for everyone. Those who are already overburdened with stocks cannot take the chance. If the purchases are not an overnight success, they will pose such a financial strain that the entire portfolio may be sacrificed.

Margin distress automatically eliminates many speculators, who find that they must sell, not buy, at cheap prices. In September 1929, such players were in debt to the tune of $8.5 billion, some on margins of no more than 10 percent. On such equity, the customer could barely stand a bump, let alone a crash. Fifty percent of all margin debt was liquidated within the next two months.

Margin buying fuels bull markets, but when panic strikes, the speculator is buried by melting equity, forced either to back up the play or liquidate. On 50 percent margin, equity can disappear in a hurry. A chap who bought 400 shares of Black & Decker at 25 in early October 1987 needed to put up only $5000 against the cost of $10,000. When the stock closed at 14 later in the month, his equity was only $600. Most brokerage firms have maintenance requirements of at least 30 percent, so the speculator had a margin call for nearly $1100. Survival, not new adventures, was the only game left.

Addicted bargain hunters adjust well to basement shopping. They have a built-in skepticism about market pricing and always have a stash ready for a rainy day. They glory in the opportunity. "If they're going to give stocks away, I think I'll take some," remarked a veteran player in May 1970. This is the course a reasonable person should pursue.

But panics are psychological, not economic, events, and the intelligent investor needs to prepare mentally for the inevitable doomsdays. It helps to have a few quality stocks in mind which would be irresistible if they were whacked for 25 or 30 points within a few days.

Don't bug your broker with orders a mile from the market. Panic may not come for a year. The problem then will be that prices fall so low that they frighten. But that's the time to buy "at the market." The window of opportunity may be open only an hour, or a half-day. Without some previous consideration of desirable values it's hard to get a focus on opportunity.

What the Very Rich Do

The big profits resulting from panic go to those investors with wealth and vision who seize upon distressed property in perilous times. Deep pockets spur the courage to act and the patience to hold for a return to value.

In the stressful autumn days of 1907, when he was working night and day to patch up the Street's banking crisis, J. P. Morgan found the time to acquire massive new holdings in U.S. Steel, which he had himself created. Morgan's pool gained a reported $25 million as the stock, near a low of 22 in 1907, rose to 95 by 1909, attended by great excitement and volume. Activity in 1909 was double that of 1907, and earnings rose to $10.50 from the 1908 figure of $4.05. Presumably, insider confidence encouraged the patience to hold.

A generation later, J. Paul Getty took advantage of depression pricing to bag up a parcel of crude-rich oil companies, including Tide Water Associated, the ninth largest oil company in the country. His first heavy buying in the stock came in the panic days of March 1932, following the suicides of the "match king," Ivan Krueger, and of George Eastman. Getty funneled his orders through the Los Angeles office of E. F. Hutton and bought his first stock at $2.50. By the end of April he owned 41,000 shares. Pacific Western, Mission, and Skelly holdings were also accumulated. After Pacific Western made a fabulous strike in the Kuwait Neutral Zone, the incestuous corporate family was consolidated into Getty Oil. The pennywise Getty, who insisted that visitors use the pay telephone in his Sutton Place mansion near London, welcomed panic pricing for asset collection. "I buy when other people are selling," was a favorite bromide of his.

John D. Rockefeller held the same simplistic view. His counsel to the Standard Oil of New Jersey executive committee, offered over a century ago, capsules the contrarian philosophy. Any panic in crude pricing was not a reason for anxiety, but an opportunity to buy:

> Hope if crude oil goes down again...our executive committee will not allow any amount of statistics or information...to prevent their buying....We must try and not lose our nerve when the market gets to the bottom as some people almost always do.*

Warren Buffett, a legend who has collected rich market rewards for Berkshire Hathaway, is best known as a value investor, but he made an important panic coup 30 years ago when he bought thousands of shares of American Express in the aftermath of the de Angelis salad oil scandal. One of the travel company's warehouse subsidiaries was seen to have a costly exposure to claims arising from the empty cottonseed and soybean oil tanks. Buffett penciled American Express as a bargain, with or without the claim liability, and bought heavily in the crash, as the stock fell to 35, down from a high at 63 the previous year. For the talented Omaha observer, the solo panic spelled opportunity.

The courageous investor should be willing to chance Tiffany wares at Wal-Mart pricing. Panic sweeps both good and bad stocks into the gutter, and it doesn't take a Wall Street diploma to pick out the gems. In October 1987, Dow Chemical, which had closed at 88 on Friday, October 16, was clubbed down to 59 on Monday; it would rebound to 93 before year-end.

Gutsy speculators also benefit. They are always ready to go against the grain and never hesitate to steal bargains on bad market days. They often have near-perfect timing—much better than that of average investors—but long journeys bore them and they will inevitably be gone long before the likes of Morgan, Rockefeller, Getty, and Buffett cash their tickets.

---

*Daniel Yergen, *The Prize: The Epic Quest for Oil, Money, and Power* (Simon & Schuster, New York, 1991), p. 46.

1987: How It All Came Out

"This time, it's different." That's the time-honored excuse for inaction in crisis. And Monday, October 19, 1987, did seem different. It was computerized violence—a loss of 500 Dow points on a volume of 600 million shares. Such nightmarish figures had never been dreamed of before.

But it wasn't different, and the ritual of panic was played out with all its usual trappings. A couple of billion dollars in margin calls helped crush the market, and when distress liquidation peaked around noon on Tuesday, the Dow Industrials were 900 points below their October peak. That nearly four-digit figure was unique, but the percentages stayed in place. By Wednesday's close, the average had bounced for a 17 percent gain and many losses had been cut in half. Baltimore Gas & Electric, driven down from 33½ to 22¼ within three days, raced back to 32 by the week's end. But BGE was an exception. The panic of 1987 is remembered for its meltdown and not its rebound.

Arriving with Unnecessary Baggage

No one ever encounters panic while in a state of perfect financial grace. There is always some untidy baggage strewn around—the stocks already owned when the trouble started. Let's see how it might have come out in 1987. Assume that in a burst of unfortunate timing, an investor bought a portfolio of four quality stocks at October's absolute highs. The holdings might have looked like the example shown in Table 7-3. All were A rated or better.

Table 7-3. Quality Portfolio Takes 1987 Meltdown Hit
100 Shares of Each Stock

	Value at October high	Value at October low	Percent loss	Top value to October 1988	Percent gain
Gerber Products	$ 5,200	$ 2,300	56	$ 6,200	170
Hewlett-Packard	7,400	3,600	51	6,500	81
Johnson & Johnson	10,000	5,500	45	8,800	60
RJR Nabisco	6,900	3,500	49	8,800	151
Total	$29,500	$14,900	49	$30,300	103

Nobody bought all of those four stocks at the absolute highs, where 100 shares of each would have cost a total of $29,500, but various pilgrims did scratch their names on each price peak. Everyone who owned them suffered cruelly as the meltdown took the paper value of the four-stock portfolio down to $14,900 several weeks later. It was the most spectacular collapse since 1929.

A Mercurial Increase in the Value of Money

Assume that our tardy and unfortunate investor had divided a $60,000 investment fund into two almost equal portions, using one-half (actually $29,500) to buy stocks and holding the balance of $30,500 in cash equivalents.

The reciprocal of the paper loss was that the value of the cash reserve enjoyed a mercurial increase. Money was growing at its fastest rate since 1929—in terms of stocks. A sum of $5200, worth only 100 shares of Gerber Products in early October, would buy 232 shares of the babyfood maker at the lows of late October. The value of money invested in Hewlett-Packard or RJR Nabisco, each A+ rated, increased by about 100 percent within the month. The collapse of Hewlett-Packard can be seen in Fig. 7-4.

But the bonus could be earned only if the $30,000 was spent on stocks. A coveted $30,000 auto was still the same price, and the mortgage broker still demanded $30,000 as the down payment on a resort condo. The two-for-one bonus was only at the bourse. The only way to spend the incremental value was to dive into the stock market.

Yet there were many in 1987 who enjoyed no money enhancement, having already committed all of their investment funds, because of greed or euphoria.

Table 7-4 illustrates strategies that could have gotten 1987 investors in serious trouble or, more fortunately, enabled them to thrive on the crisis.

A margin investor who used the $60,000 pool to buy 400 shares of each stock, a market value of $118,000, was quickly wiped out. A cash-account buyer who invested fully bought 200 shares of each issue, spent $59,000, and was effectively frozen out of any further action.

Those investors who committed only half their funds at the peak displayed equally bad timing, but better planning. Their cash cache allowed them to take advantage of the sacrifice prices of late October. A reasonable move at that time would have been to increase holdings in the established portfolio. A sum of $14,900 would have doubled the position, and still left $15,600 in the investment pool.

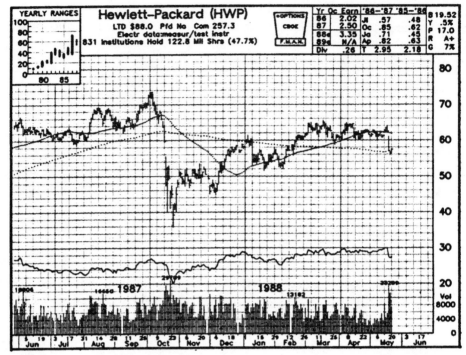

Figure 7-4. The 1987 meltdown granted no quarter. A quality stock like Hewlett-Packard, 74 in early October, was slammed down to 36, abetted by a very large gap. But the furious and dramatic loss discounted every possible problem for the A+ rated stock, and the shares recovered to over 60 by early January. (SOURCE: Trendline Daily Action Stock Charts. Trendline, a division of Standard & Poor's Corporation, New York.)

Adding Some New Stocks to the Portfolio

But what are reserves for, aside from emergencies? A more courageous approach would have doubled the original holdings and added some low-cost diversification. For $15,000, seven high-visibility names could have been added. The bad timing of early October, when $30,000 was recklessly committed, could be offset by spending an equal sum under conditions of crisis.

The new stocks, an across-the-board selection, were commonplace names and cost only $15,000. The list was made up of 100 shares each of Fannie Mae, selling at 27; H & R Block, 20; Gillette, 18; Albertson's, 20, and Deere & Co., 23. Two hundred shares of Bethlehem Steel, 10,

Table 7-4. Surviving the Big Hits of October 1987
How a Select $60,000 Investment Pool Might Have Fared

Beginning strategy	Cost at October high (Table 7-3)	Cash remaining	Panic response	Cash remaining	Top portfolio/cash values within: 3 months	6 months	1 year
Margin account							
Buy 400 shares of each stock*	$118,000	$(58,000)	Nothing; "wiped out" after commissions	0	0	0	0
Cash account							
Buy 200 shares of each stock	59,000	1,000	Nothing; only odd-lot money left	$ 1,000	$48,800	$51,200	$61,600
Buy 100 shares of each stock	29,500	30,500	Freezes, does nothing	30,500	54,400	55,600	60,800
Buy 100 shares of each stock	29,500	30,500	Doubles up; added cost is $14,900	15,600	63,400	65,800	76,200
Buy 100 shares of each stock	29,500	30,500	Doubles up; adds new stocks† for $15,000	600	68,700	79,200	93,300

*Stocks: Gerber Products, Hewlett-Packard, Johnson & Johnson, RJR Nabisco (Table 7-3).
† New stocks listed and priced in text.

and Phillips Petroleum, 11, were also added. It was a broad-based list with financial, service, consumer, retail, energy, and cyclic issues represented.

Five of the selections were of excellent quality, only Deere and Bethlehem having poor ratings. Both of them, however, had long histories of top rebounding ability.

Was there risk in becoming 100 percent invested? To be sure. But rather less than when the Dow was 1000 points higher. We will see that some stocks, such as AMR, slumped to modest new lows in the late autumn. On the other hand, if an A+ rated stock such as RJR Nabisco, with a dividend record stretching back to 1900, was severely overvalued at 69 in early October, surely it was undervalued a few days later at 35.

The prospects for further immediate market damage were small. At the very worst, there would be a rebound of significant proportions. In the right stocks, at the right time, even the most conservative investors must commit their reserves.

The portfolio additions of late October added quality balance to the holdings plus a pair of typical low-priced issues—Bethlehem and Phillips Pete. Such "cheap shots" boast a sizzling record in post-panic action.

Obviously, the new portfolio, based on the low-priced bargains of late October, was superior in its cost basis and diversification to the old one. All of the new stocks were "old" stocks to every investor. Their average loss from the October peak had been 48 percent. There were no high-tech, biotech, or other high-flying fancies included. We are sure that every reader has owned some of the inexpensive old names at one time or another, and they would not disappoint in 1988.

Of the original portfolio, two issues, Gerber and RJR, exceeded their October peak during the 1988 year. All of the new selections ran to record highs in 1988. Money's huge gains against stock prices added huge leverage to the broader portfolio. Few issues rebounded faster than the surprising veteran, Deere & Co. By March 1988 it had doubled its October low. Perhaps someone knew something. Its October low held above 1987's previous worst figure in a display of relative strength.

Diversification's merits were proven in both portfolios. What seer would have picked Gillette for the largest gain of the next 12 months—up 172 percent? Or foreseen the spectacular RJR Nabisco buyout?

The four stocks in the original portfolio were there because they are quality issues, known to everyone. The package lost about 50 percent of its value in a couple of weeks. Many issues of lesser quality or more speculative flavor fell by much larger amounts. Amdahl dropped from

50 to 19, Owens-Corning from 24 to 9, and Vista Chemical from 54 to 20, all within the month. It was the worst bloodbath since 1929, but during the brief turmoil, the value of money in terms of stocks soared.

The second group of stocks was chosen for rebounding ability and wide diversification, which is exactly what a canny investor should have opted for. Buying lower-priced stocks allowed a broad sweep for the $15,000 of investment cash still remaining.

Panics thus offer reliable reflex opportunities, and the 1987 logic applies to lesser crises, many of which have offered superior returns. Money will grow in value during every crisis, but only to the extent that it is converted into equities. The ability and willingness to employ those enriched funds will enable the investor to thrive from panic.

Those who must sell or who are frightened into selling are the ones who enhance the value of money, as they sacrifice stocks at whatever price they bring, regardless of value, ratings, and fundamentals.

The trader who was 100 percent committed at the October highs could not move. One who was 80 percent invested was severely handicapped. He had only $12,000 in additional funds to employ and was already looking at a paper loss of nearly $15,000. To really thrive on panic, substantial reserve funds are absolutely necessary.

Buying during Panics Is Rational

Panics are irrational, but buying during panics is quite rational, and is a sensible market strategy.

Buyers will thrive for both fundamental and technical reasons. Panic automatically improves fundamentals as high P–E ratios melt away and dividend yields are enhanced by lower prices. Value is offered at a decent and often cheap price. In August 1987 the Dow's peak was 2722, where it sold at a near-record level, 22 times its trailing earnings. At October's low close, 1739, the multiple was a reasonable 12.6 times.

Risk had been diminished, not enhanced, by panic. Johnson & Johnson's P–E multiple fell from 21 to a commonplace 11. At the trough, RJR Nabisco was priced at only 7× its estimated earnings of $5. Gerber's yield was near 6 percent.

In 1980, McDermott was tripped from 36 in February to a panic low of 19 in the following month. At the March price, the oil boom made the driller fundamentally cheap. Its P–E ratio had shrunk within a few weeks from the high teens to about 10 times its estimated earnings.

Panic buyers would be quickly rewarded, as the shares bounced by 50 percent before the Fourth of July. They would peak at 47 in November.

Technical as well as fundamental values are vastly improved by the collapse of prices. Buyers thrive because anxious sellers and desperate sellers have been liquidated. The books are cleared. There will remain a few stubborn holders who want to liquidate on any worthwhile rally, but their number is limited at levels near the panic low. No important selling will show up until those who had snared the bargains of crisis decide that, on a short-term basis, they have done well enough. In the case of Gerber Products, there was really no selling until the stock had gained 10–12 points, which took all of two days. For Burlington Northern, pounded from 82 to 36 within the month, there would be no organized selling until the stock reached 56, a matter of only a few days.

Psychologically, panics satisfy the shopper's urge for a bargain. Everyone likes to buy stocks on a correction, and buyers at least don't have to worry about "getting in at the top." Such concern is eradicated in panics; from the valley of prices the previous peaks are easily sighted.

Prices Too Cheap: Is There a Deeper Meaning?

Sometimes the problem is that prices seem too cheap. If Upjohn, an A+ rated stock in a top-ranked industry, can fall from 46 to 23 within days, as it did in 1987, the suspicion arises that there may be a deeper meaning which eludes us all. Fear takes over. Is the end, indeed, near? To be sure, even from the depths of panic, an individual stock may slip lower, but generally the loss is not material. At least, one who hazarded panic did not get "bagged" at the top.

Some shares, like those of AMR (American Airlines), did make a new low following 1987's climatic selling. Having fallen from 58 to 30, the stock rallied to 37 but then drifted to a final bottom at 27 in December. The low-volume decline was not ominous and the stock immediately reversed, bouncing to 38 before the end of the year.

A corollary benefit of panic is that lower prices encourage diversification. While the investor can always purchase multiple odd lots of high-priced stocks, most prefer, say, two 100-share lots of a $25 stock to 50 shares of a $100 number. That is one reason corporate management uses stock splits and dividends to keep the share price at a reasonable level. The enhancement of money's value makes diversification easier.

More important is the fact that panic pricing sometimes leaves the new owners with real "keepers," stocks whose low prices may never again be tested. A number of such treasures were uncovered in 1970's crisis. Allied Chemical, Baxter Laboratories, and Continental Oil were among the issues which would stand up to inflation, an energy crisis, a major bear market, depression, and 20 percent interest rates over the next decade and never threaten the lows of 1970. Such selections are not ABC simple, to be sure, but those who challenge the bear attacks inevitably wind up with some lockbox keepers.

The Lessons of 1987

The principal lessons and opportunities of panic, as typified in the 1987 meltdown, are simple.

Financial storms strike with frightening speed. Many stocks will lose more than half their value within days. There is no warning of such violent downdrafts.

Protective strategies are mostly useless. Anointment by institutional ownership means nothing. Scores of stocks which were more than two-thirds owned by institutions lost half their value within days. Texas Instruments was one of them, diving from 80 to 36.

Defensive-type issues do not insure against an overnight smash. Pacific Gas, A rated and paying $1.98, fell to 15 in October, where its yield was 12.8 percent. It had lost nearly half its year's top value.

Stocks already hurt may be hurt a lot more. An early 1987 favorite, The Gap, was already down from 78 to 39 by early October. The bloodbath did not slow; the shares were pounded to 16 within the month.

Quality selection offers no protection. Margin traders who relied on A+ ratings were sacrificed when issues such as Hewlett-Packard, Upjohn, and Borden lost half their value within days. The leveraged speculator was wiped out. The first margin call is never the last.

An aggressive, in-your-face attack against panic will reap rich rewards in a short period. The worse the panic, the quicker will be the rewards.

Any investor reaction is better than liquidation. Buy or hold; do not sell.

Diversify when buying in a panic. Stock leadership usually changes after a panic. Diversification improves the chances of catching a reflex bonanza. The worst victims of panics will often rally best.

Viacom suffered disaster in October, falling from 29 to 10. It tripled by July. The widely touted recovery stocks in 1988 were outperformed by such overlooked groups as apparel retailers, casinos, textiles, coals, and airlines. Foods did well. Poultry raising is not generally a magnet for imaginative investors, but Holly Farm's chicken operations helped it post a 106 percent gain while "everyone's" favorite computer choice, Compaq, gained only 8 percent.

"Doubling up" in quality is not life threatening under conditions of panic pricing.

Is 1987 a Fair Example?

The 1987 meltdown was one of exceptional fury, the worst since 1929. But in every panic the value of money rises more rapidly than we imagine, and 1987 was not the richest "dig" for proving up panic bonanzas. While its numbers are convenient, they are not Guiness records.

Each financial crisis reveals rich ore for those with rainy-day funds. The first crisis capsuled in the Appendix was in 1890, when the market lost about 12 percent in 11 trading days—not a "killer wave" by any means. But bear raiders smashed the North American Company from 35 to 7 and Oregon Improvement from 35 to 11. They were the worst victims. Edison General Electric lost one-third of its value. Within the next three months the 20-Stock average enjoyed only a labored rally, but the most prominent losers were up over 150 percent and Edison General jumped from 65 to 111. Few 1987 recovery numbers match these figures.

The down-side statistics in 1987 will remain archival records. The revival figure into 1988 was only average. The gain in the next 12 months was surpassed after the lows of 1980, 1982, and 1984, to name three occasions within the same decade.

At the three-month reading, the 1987 postpanic advance was 18 percent, compared with plus 16 for all panics surveyed in the past century. The six-month milestone showed a gain of 20 percent, several percentage points *less* than the average of all panics.

Statistics for the gains shown are not unfairly biased to the thesis of thriving on panic. The monthly postings are most pertinent to the aftermath of panic, since the circumstances of crisis are mostly buried by other developments after a year. The one-year rebound, however, amounted to only 26 percent.

Thriving with GE, GM, and USS

The events of 1987 were, perhaps, an extreme example. But what would have been the historical rewards of panic if one had bought and rebought the same small group of stocks in every crisis? What stocks might have been selected?

Three veteran issues, popular for more than 75 years, illustrate the reliable profits of contrary action. They are General Electric, U.S. Steel, and General Motors. They have been among the most public of all stocks.

The three are fairly selected because all have been household names to investors for generations, being the giants of their respective industries. It required no special research to seek them out under crisis conditions. Their postpanic results, shown in Table 7-5, have been tabulated from a cross section of 12 major incidents, some of which occurred during bull markets and some during bear episodes. The study omits the easy and sensational winners—those panics which terminated bear sequences, as in 1970, 1938, and 1914, among others. The unique

Table 7-5. Reflex Rewards of a Consistent Panic Portfolio
Three Market Leaders* Compared with the Dow

	1 month (%)	3 months (%)	6 months (%)	12 months (%)
Average percent gain following panic low				
Average: Leaders	21	28	42	57
DJIA	12	17	21	28
Best rebound percentage through 6 months				
1915: Leaders	20	55	131	141
DJIA	19	36	51	53
1929: Leaders	34	40	63	16
DJIA	33	37	48	(5)
Rebound results in 1980s				
1980: Leaders	10	17	37	69
DJIA	8	17	28	34
1987: Leaders	29	38	45	41
DJIA	13	18	21	23

*Equal dollar amounts of General Electric, General Motors, and U.S. Steel.

episodes of 1920 and the early 1930s are also omitted; they presented very special circumstances and are reviewed in Chap. 10.

The recovery figures for the dozen panics have been averaged to show the reflex reward from the panic low to the highest price level one month, three months, six months, and one year later. Maximum gains were higher than the numbers shown, since price peaks for the three stocks were not on a close pattern. Gains at the 12-month intervals often lagged the six-month figures, it will be noted.

The first panic surveyed occurred in 1915 and was sparked by the *Lusitania* tragedy. It was the first serious episode in which reaction by all three leaders could be fairly calculated; the war crisis of July 1914 was eliminated because it coincided with the climax of the 1912–1914 bear market. The last study was for 1987. Despite the high drama of that 1000-point collapse, the rebound statistics were unremarkable and do not unfairly weigh the bullish argument. Over the next 12 months, the Dow's best gain was 26 percent, considerably less than was afforded after the Silver Panic of 1980.

The 1915 crisis provided the largest postpanic rewards, and the 1973 affair, midway through both the Watergate and market crises, posted the most disappointing figures. The 1974 bear market trough came exactly one year after the panic's climax, so one who bought and held stocks came up a loser. The Dow's loss was 22 percent. Even the interim rally figures were slim, but U.S. Steel proved the value of even a three-stock diversification. Big Steel was 35½ at its *worst* price in December 1974, as compared with a panic low of 26¾ one year earlier. It had gained some fundamental revenge on the glamours, which suffered 1929-type losses.

The 1946 autumn panic also produced disappointing figures, for 1947 was part of the long postwar slump, which lasted until 1949. In the 1946 aftermath, however, crowded showrooms helped General Motors to a strong advance; it ran from 48 to 66 between September and February 1947.

Biggest potential gains for the portfolio during a one-year period came following the panics of 1915, 1926, 1929, and 1980; all were over 50 percent.

8
Adversity's
Silver Lining

Panics offer easy profits for courageous contrarians. Bear market troughs offer a silver lining of serious profit. Forget about options, commodities, collectibles, and the precious metals. Stocks bought anywhere near the trough of a bear sequence are fortune builders. And we are not talking about some exotic which no one had heard of until it was up 500 percent. The profit record for good, old All-American household names is fabulous. The kind of stocks which you would buy for the kids, or the church's trust fund.

First of all, these are not once-in-a-lifetime opportunities. There were three serious bear climaxes in the 1970s and an equal number in the 1960s. A pair of serious panics struck the market in the 1980s, along with the recession slump of 1981–1982 and the mini-bear of 1984.

There is only one secret to such wealth-building opportunities. No guru is needed, just cash in hand.

It also helps to have patience. It takes alacrity to seize the opportunities of panic, but bear markets are exploited by patience—patience both before and after the trough. The hardest wait is for a bear trend to expend itself. Since 1950, the average decline has lasted about 21 months. A great part of that term was spent in confusing movements—sideways action, irregular declines, and occasional sharp rallies.

In the 1981–1982 sequence, one rally occupied three months, frustrating both bears and bargain hunters. Of 13 down months, eight were for less than 15 Dow points and five of those lost only six points or less. It was a wearing experience for stubborn longs, and tried the patience of those who had believed the bear market signal of July 1981 and moved into cash.

In 1931, the worst year in Exchange history, the Dow lost 53 percent. But during that same period, four of every 10 sessions was an up day and five months ended on the plus side. June enjoyed the largest monthly gain ever seen at the time, up 17 percent. Even in the worst of times, the market doesn't go straight down for long.

Bear markets drag on and on. Finally, everyone who bought and held becomes a victim, including the most conservative investors, for quality is no defense. Scores of blue-chip names—Montgomery Ward, Southern Pacific, Otis Elevator—lost 95 percent of their value between 1929 and 1932. In 1973–1974, Polaroid fell by over 90 percent, and Disney was not far behind.

Bargain hunters who purchased Polaroid at 75, down from its 150 peak, were mangled as the shares continued south to 14. Serious money is made by identifying the probability of a market low, not by buying apparent bear market bargains.

Aggressive bear market strategies, such as short selling, will frustrate investors and will prove inappropriate and costly, as we shall see.

Three Ways You Will Not Get Rich

Few investors will make any money on the short side of the market, and none will get rich. Bear market strategies in options and contracyclical investments also show lean profits for the average investor.

Short Selling

Theoretically, a trader can make as much money on the short side of the market as on the long side. It does seem easy. In the first place, the market goes down faster than it advances. It took 14 years for the Dow to climb from 577 to 1045 between late 1958 and 1973. It took only 23 months for the reverse to happen. Second, there are no interest charges on a short account. Until the crash of 1937, which was widely blamed on short sellers, there was not even a regulated margin requirement— just a good-faith deposit. Today, short sales require the same margin as a purchase.

While some legendary speculators of the past—James R. Keene, Jesse Livermore, and "Sell 'em All" Ben Smith—made and lost millions on the short side, they were Street players with uncanny trading ability. We all know several people who attained real wealth in the stock market. Who among them gained it on the short side of the market?

Admittedly, the rewards of short selling can be quick. Panic sequences create sensational gains overnight. On the other hand, one learns that the short seller must pay any stock or cash dividend which may be declared. The buyer doesn't care or even know if his ownership was accommodated by a short, but he is due any dividend declarations, and the short must pay. The seller is not only short the stock, but all benefits declared to those who own the shares.

Owners of stock in cash accounts never have to sell, but short sellers are sometimes "squeezed" and must repurchase their speculative commitments when the borrowed shares are recalled and a new lender cannot be located. Such circumstance may occur under stressful conditions, as in the case of the Northern Pacific corner, or the Stutz Motor Car corner of 1920, when the shares were forced up from par to 700 within a few weeks.

And there is the problem of mathematical infinity. A buyer of stock can lose only the full purchase price. A short seller's liability is unlimited. Shares sold short at 10 could go to 100 or 1000; a $1000 bet could mushroom into a $100,000 bet.

The most serious "short" problem for average traders, however, is the fact that they may find themselves strangely disturbed by their position. We buy homes, cars, real estate, stocks, bonds, in the natural order of things. Selling short is different. We are not accustomed to the mental state of wanting something to go down in value, nor of selling something that we don't own, or of first selling what we don't own and then buying it back. It seems vaguely unethical, or even illegal— as it has often been.

Many commodity traders are comfortable only in a short position, but they are professionals and love to fade the wirehouse orders. At the same time, they have no problem with mercurial changes of opinion. Floor traders on the Exchanges and security dealers have a similar outlook. Individual short sellers of securities are prone to be too nervous. They might ride a long position in General Motors down 10 or 15 points, but a three-point loss on the short sale of some hot software stock will set them to kicking the dog.

Short selling has always endured a bad press, and never more so than during the early 1930s. The public howl against the short sellers was overwhelming, and Washington could not ignore the uproar. In May 1931, short sellers were, for the first time in history, required to be logged and counted. There were plenty, but the numbers were far shy of the rumor.

After England left the gold standard in September 1931, short selling was briefly prohibited by the Exchange. The astonishing rally later that autumn was spurred by short covering, for which no thanks were ever tendered. The Dow raced up 36 percent in just five weeks and bullish hopes stirred, but it was only another bear market rally and the Dow returned to its evil ways, recording a new low in December.

If you insist on a short account, you'll first have to sign a margin agreement. And then your broker must ascertain from the home office that the stock you want to sell short can be borrowed. Incidentally, you'll find plenty of statistical aids to play with. Many market indicators are based on short selling, and the financial press carries the daily odd-lot short figures, and weekly numbers of round-lot selling, both by the public and by member groups, specialists, floor traders, and others. The NYSE releases the total short position, by individual stock, on a monthly basis. Similar figures are available from the Amex and NASDAQ.

Many historical ratios on short selling have been rendered useless by the popularity of options and futures indices, which are often used to offset equity shorts. If you must try, stick with the big-cap issues and don't short a stock just because it has run up more than you think is decent. Take a shot at a cripple—a former hot stock which has lost power and turned into a glider.

There are some individuals who operate almost entirely on the short side of the market, but they seem to be "naturals." Most traders will come out better in a bear market by liquidating and parking the funds while awaiting the important bull opportunities.

Playing Options

Speculative types with a bearish attitude can also work out various strategies using option contracts. The present form of exchange-traded option contracts has been around for 20 years, and their mandatory prospectus is Ned's First Reader to most investors. Each contract is for 100 shares; a call is an option to buy, and a put is an option to sell. Both are good for a specified time, and if they are "out of the money" at that expiration time, they expire without value. There are also options on indices—the Standard & Poor's 400, the Amex, Value Line, and so forth.

Newspapers hate options, as they must devote pages of fine type to their transcript. All type, no advertising. Computers adore options.

There are scores of Nintendo games with which to play with values, expiration timing, and other risk strategies. Brokers love them too, because those arcane game plans always involve some combination of options on a multiplicity of contracts, all richly commissioned.

Puts and calls are an apparently low-cost play on a possible bear trend. One problem is that they are generally low priced, a seductive lure to action. A three-month, out-of-the-money put might be only $287.50. But, as with a cheap stock, no one—particularly the broker—wants to bother with a one-lot order. So, buy five or 10. It's only $2875, plus commission. But the clock is running on the purchase; it is a wasting asset. If the stock is stable, the value downticks every days. Before you know it, the lot is worth only $875. Would you have ridden a $29 stock down to $9?

Most players will "roll over" into a longer expiration date. But normal fluctuations are perfectly discounted in the option pricing. After several rollovers, it will take an overnight meltdown to get the option account back to even.

Don't take our word for it. Give options a go. But sooner or later you will need help. The phone number for Options Anonymous is in most yellow pages.

Baiting the Bear

Many traders will do anything reasonable except divorce the market. During hard times, they often attempt an end run, seeking some magic stock that will just kill the bears. Homestake was once such an issue. As the depression of the 1930s deepened, it became apparent that the veteran gold miner had the best of two worlds—falling costs and a guaranteed selling price of $20.67 an ounce for gold. By 1933 Homestake was selling near 400, having quadrupled its 1929 high. It paid well, and was the highest-priced stock at the Exchange. President Roosevelt's inflation program gave a further boost when he ratcheted the price of gold to $35. Homestake rose to 465 and reached 680 in 1936. A special dividend in 1935 boosted the payout to $70.

The gold mining industry was quite special, of course. There are always little pockets of bear market strength, but they are tough to stake out. In July 1932, *The New York Times* was able to find 15 stocks that had advanced in that terrible year. Most were really "penny" issues. But Real Silk Hosiery had made a solid advance; the firm, rumor had it, had developed a no-run hose. The rumor was not true, but that was unimportant.

The golds advanced again in 1973–1974; it was a lonely but profitable trail. Homestake, which had closed at 24 in 1972, ended 1973 at 71. In 1974, the only other group that showed solid strength was the sugars, buoyed by buyouts and buyout rumors. But who but an insider would have chosen a stock like Great Western United, a beet sugar farmer? Ignoring the major trend, it spurted from 4 to 24, propelled by a tender offer from the Hunt brothers of Dallas. During the year 1318 common stocks declined and only 140 advanced—of which 61 gained less than 10 percent. In the meantime, nearly 300 stocks lost more than 50 percent of their value, led by the REITS and mortgage companies. Great American Mortgage fell from 30 to 2, and Cousins Mortgage from 20 to about 1.

Locating an against-the-grain stock in a major downtrend requires a lot of luck and faith. Such unique winners are often small, niche issues, but the Washington Post, Southland Corporation, Consolidated Edison (along with many other utilities), and General Foods were among widely followed issues that ignored the recession market of 1981–1982.

What contrary heroes might have appeared if the "bear market" of 1987 had not ended so abruptly is impossible to know. A few issues had countered the initial slump and were able to make new highs in mid-October, only days before the violent climax. Not surprisingly, many of those stocks reached record highs in the summer of 1988, even though the Dow was battling to hold above 2000. Among the uniques were MCI, Nike, and Wrigley.

But baiting the bear is a game for insiders, professionals, and, in the past, gold buffs. Other strategies, designed to profit directly from a falling market, either through short sales or option operations, are equally inappropriate for the investor, and will prove costly.

Boardroom speculators, always eager to seize upon a possible quick turn, may do a bit better, but both groups will generally fare better in CDs during rough times.

Estimating the Size and Duration of Major Declines

After a bear market gets under way, it is possible to estimate the size of the decline or duration, but such is only an educated guess based on experience and technical indicators.

There is no connection between the dimensions of a bear episode and that of the previous bull advance. What with laws of action and reaction, this is difficult to believe, and engineering types have wasted a great deal of computer time trying to prove otherwise. All that can definitely be said is that the biggest, longest advance in history, 1921–1929, was followed by the biggest, longest decline in modern history.

Cycles refuse to fit a tidy pattern. Exclusive of the 1921–1929/ 1932–1937 numbers, comparable to a pair of 100-year flood plains, the average bull market has gained 125 percent in a span of 789 trading days. That has been followed by an average decline of 33 percent lasting for 413 days. Such a drop means considerably more pain for individual stocks, however. Trough to peak to trough, those 1202 trading sessions equaled four years in the days of Saturday trading. Nowadays, there are about 251 sessions a year, equal to a periodicity of 4.8 years.

All this just helps prove that average figures are of little trading help. The 1906–1907 and 1937–1938 smashes both lost 49 percent, but the former lasted for 552 trading sessions and the latter only 317. Three hundred eighty-nine sessions in 1956–1957 pared the Dow only 19 percent, but a shorter decline, 367 days in 1968–1970, hurt the average twice as much.

Such inconsistencies will not slow the number crunchers' enthusiasm. Fortunately, the books can be partly cooked to taste; some of the dates are slightly subjective. The roller-coaster periods of 1890–1896 and 1937–1942 can be viewed as extended bear markets rather than a series of bear–bull sequences. But how does one treat the Iraq crisis decline of August–October 1990? It had a minor bear market drop, 20 percent, but it lacks the credential of duration. Its inclusion in average length tables would seem to require a change in the definition of a bear market. The 1987 experience also created some pesky statistics. The collapse was too short for a bear market, but a thousand-point drop in the leading average has to be accommodated. We'll cast it as one of the major declines but omit its 38-day time span from the duration average; it was basically a five-day panic. Like the events following 1929, it is so exceptional that it tends to warp the picture of typical movements. Scholars will argue about its true meaning for decades.

Searching for Bottom Clues

Market bottoms are easier to identify than market tops. Clues to a bear market reversal seem easier to read, or at least receive more attention, though that may only reflect the consensus desire for better times.

Contrary to popular opinion, heavy volume does not ordinarily accompany bear market troughs. Only when panic commands the climax, as in 1970 and 1957, does monthly activity set records. One or two high-volume days near the low may provide a weak clue, but sustained high volume is generally lacking. Such deceptive activity has often come several months before the final low, as in 1917, 1921, and more recently in 1966, but it's a pretty vague indicator.

Activity at the cycle low will be far less than at the bull market peak and is occasionally near the low point for the entire decline, as was the case at the troughs of 1932 and 1942. Only when panic accompanies a bear trough will volume be heavy; then it is often at a record level. At such times, a high-volume key reversal is seen as a reliable clue of the ordeal's end.

After a perceived low, huge volume will generally flood into the market within a few weeks, adding a lot of argument to the bull case. This is more of a confirmation than a clue, however, and there was one notable exception. It took months in 1949 for confidence to return after the bear market low of June. Traders had become skeptical of rallies, having been burned too often during the three-year consolidation. Volume did not confirm the low until after Labor Day.

More normal was the action in January 1975. One month after the bear trough, record trade pushed the Dow to its largest monthly gain since June 1938, and helped flash a successful Dow theory buy signal. In 1982, easily remembered, volume broke all daily and weekly records immediately after the reversal, a tremendously convincing indicator.

Frenetic activity accompanied by large price losses in a bear market suggest an imminent low, but this is quite exceptional. Low-volume endings are more common. A high-volume advance after an apparent low is typical of reversal and provides a dependable confirmation of a low.

What we all want are sure clues to market reversal. Charts can help. Double bottoms are a reliable chart formation, as detailed earlier. Two of the biggest advances in history, beginning in 1921 and 1982, sprang out of such a chart picture. But there are many other, less esoteric clues.

Look for Quality Resistance

Quality resistance to the market's down trend is a bottom indicator. Market leaders cannot ignore a collapse, but when they refuse to join the rout, view collapsing prices as opportunity. In 1974, United Aircraft bottomed in July and Sohio and Squibb in August. General Electric, General Foods, American Brands, and American Can, among other closely watched stocks, recorded their lows in September, whereas the Dow's low came in December.

The record of bullish resistance in 1982 was even more impressive. Despite the depression, Wal-Mart and General Mills made their yearly lows in January. Ford and General Motors never threatened their February troughs during the summer weakness. And diverse names such as American Home Products, American Broadcasting, American Cyanamid, and General Dynamics were at their lows in March—not August. Such were the clues of quality resistance to the eroding Dow average.

Major bear markets have, more often than not, been associated with climbing interest rates or fears of a credit crunch. A reversal toward lower rates points toward a constructive change in the market. The bond market turned sharply to the up side five weeks prior to the Dow's depression low in 1932. More recently, the Federal Reserve lowered the discount rate in July 1982 and in the same month the Dow bond index made its low. The Industrials reversed to the up side one month later.

The Dow Utility average, also sensitive to rates, often signals the potential for market relief by refusing further declines. In the late 1940s, the Utilities made their postwar low in February 1948 with the Dow at 165.65. After a strong rally, the Industrials again turned weak and recorded a new low in June 1949 at 161.60. In the meantime, the Utilities had shown stubborn relative strength in the shakeout which occurred after the election of November 1948, encouraging investors to seize the great bargains of the period. In June, they held far above their 1948 low. In the major bear market that started in 1973, the Utilities made their low on September 13, 1974, and helped investors face up to the continued autumn weakness in the Industrials.

Clues from the "Real Market"

The leading Dow averages are nearly a century old. In 1900 they presented a realistic picture of market action. At that time there were only about 100 common stocks traded actively at the NYSE, most of which were railroads. The Dow Jones Railroad average of 20 issues gave perfect recognition to the group. The Industrial average—only 12 stocks—adequately represented the giant trusts—General Electric, National Lead, Federal Steel, and so on—which dominated American commerce.

The Dow Industrials remain the most widely watched of the world's market indices, but no one claims that the 30 stocks (since 1928) present an adequate picture of "market" action. There are over 2000 issues listed at the NYSE, hundreds more at the Amex, and about 5000 OTC stocks. Upon occasion the action of a broader index, usually the

Standard & Poor's 400 or 500, is seen to reflect more accurately the
action of the "real market."

While divergence between major averages is never bullish, a stubborn buoyancy by the S&P when the Industrials are sinking is regarded
as a clue to better times. Even relative strength can be a clue to a turn.

A famous early divergence occurred in 1932 when the S&P, like the
bond market, made its low on June 1. The Dow dragged lower until
July 8, but bullish action then developed at a record pace.

In 1949, the S&P signaled encouragement when that index held
above its 1948 low, despite erosion by the leading average. During the
Korean crisis, the S&P's slump was contained above its 1949 closing
level while the Industrials were hammered beneath their ending figure. A remarkable summer rally followed.

The market's trough in 1974, as measured by the S&P, came in
October, two months before that of the DJIA. Such outright divergence
remains rare, but relative strength on the part of the broader average
can often be seen as a clue to reversal.

In all of the examples mentioned so far, we have been talking about
clues which can alert investors to the possibility of an impending
trend change. The indicators should at least forestall reckless selling
and encourage renewed attention to the buy side of the market. They
are not blind signals, however. A rush into equities in early June 1932
would have been a mistake. A stock like Macy fell from 25 to 17 during June. And despite the "market's" relative strength in the autumn
of 1974, highly regarded Eastman Kodak slumped from 78 to 58 in the
sell-off from October's rally peak to early December.

General Motors' bellwether reputation, proven once again in
February 1982, would not have helped the believer who, convinced
that he had heard the bullish call, opted for a stock like Houston
Natural Gas at 40 in April. It would trade below 25 in August. Chase
Manhattan fell from 59 to 32 in the same period, even while General
Motors held steady.

Bottom clues and indicators point the finger of suspicion at ongoing
bear markets. They don't solve the problem.

How Can You Tell When the Bear Market Is Over?

Bear market despair inevitably translates into bullish statistics. As the
market falls, fundamental values are enhanced. Fat P–E ratios melt
away. Dividend yields are enriched. Inflated prices lose their premium
to book. Sometimes the market even gets down to bedrock values.

The statistics of bedrock value have been proven time and time again. A Dow yield of about 6 percent and an earnings multiplier of 10 or lower have established some of the great buying opportunities. Bear market reversals often come from a less attractive base, but average investors are more likely to push their chips forward when they can buy such cheap fundamentals. Quality individual stocks will be found with more attractive numbers than the averages. In 1982, A-rated stocks such as American Brands, American Express, Coca-Cola, General Mills, and Exxon could be bought for yields between 7 and 12 percent and at single-digit multiples.

Changing sentiments and a rush of new money is what changes the course of bear sequences, but bargain fundamentals encourage such changes. Sentiment is difficult to measure precisely, but investors may find the scorecard of bear market lows in Table 8-1 to be helpful. Absolute bargains—a 6 percent yield and a single-digit P–E ratio— aren't available at every market trough, but they show up often enough to prove that they are not just a statistical quirk. Seven bear markets developed such an attractive statistical parlay, and three were

Table 8-1. Scorecard: Major Market Lows

Bear market low	DJIA	Earnings ($)	P–E ratio	Dividend ($)	Yield (%)	Best Dow level in next 6 months (% gain)
Dec. 1917	66	20.36	3.3	8.03	12.2	21
Aug. 1921	64	(def)	—	3.87	6.0	28
Nov. 1929	199	19.94	10.0	12.75	6.4	49
July 1932	41	(def)	—	4.62	11.2	95
Mar. 1938	99	6.01	16.5	4.98	5.0	47
Apr. 1939	121	9.11	13.2	6.11	5.0	29
Apr. 1942	93	9.22	10.1	6.40	6.9	24
June 1949	162	23.54	6.9	12.79	7.9	24
Oct. 1957	420	36.08	11.6	21.61	4.8	9
Oct. 1960	566	32.21	17.6	21.36	3.8	25
June 1962	536	36.43	14.7	23.30	4.3	22
Oct. 1966	744	57.68	12.9	31.89	4.3	21
May 1970	631	51.02	12.4	31.53	5.0	24
Dec. 1974	578	99.04	5.8	37.72	6.5	52
Feb. 1978	742	112.79	6.6	48.52	6.5	35
Aug. 1982	777	79.90*	9.7	54.14	7.0	44
Oct. 1987	1739	133.05	13.1	71.20	4.1	21
Oct. 1990	2365	172.05	13.7	103.70	4.4	27

*Trailing.

posted between 1974 and 1982. We have added the figures for the 1929 crash to the table because of their historical interest. Stocks were temporarily fundamental bargains, as the rebound column shows.

Here are a few clues to watch for at bear market lows.

Weekly reversals may signal the end. Violent, one-day key reversals—a new low for the move followed by a big-volume reversal to a higher daily close—are typical of panic endings but are less common at bear market closures. Weekly reversals, however, have given a dozen reliable signals. The last was in the second week of August 1982. Monthly reversals are less decisive.

The final bear convulsion will usually be part of a two- or three-day attack during which the Dow drops sharply on the final day, or on the next-to-last day. A loss of 2 and 3 percent on the worst day can be expected. More severe figures will occur when panic overwhelms the exodus. Such double hits are not that common, however, having occurred only eight times since 1890. When they do occur, they create havoc. In 1893, the fall on the final day was 7 percent—the biggest last-day loss of any bear market in the past century. Panic has produced many larger declines, of course; they just didn't ring down the curtain on a bear market.

High volume will ordinarily mark the passing of the bear sequence, and high volume plus a severe loss is an indicator that the end is, indeed, near. Confusion arises when volume and price diverge. A classic example occurred on July 8, 1932, the final day of history's worst bear market, when volume was only 720,000 shares. Nearly 125 sessions earlier in the year had counted trade over that figure. What to make of it? The previous day had seen the Dow down 5 percent, but the low activity confused traders, and it was not until the last week of July that big volume—1.5 to 2.7 million shares—proved up the bull case.

Extremes of loss are a more reliable indicator than volume. In late 1942, the Dow wound down to its wartime low. Volume for the month was the lowest since February 1915, despite a bit of exciting good news—Jimmy Doolittle's air raid on Tokyo. And NYSE volume on the final down day was only 313,000 shares, half the volume registered on the century's opening trade day, January 2, 1900. Price change, not activity, signaled the possible bear low. The Dow had lost nearly 10 percent in the previous three weeks, and the Utilities were at an all-time low, 10.58, one-third below the worst 1932 figure. The lack of volume on the final day, however, made it a confusing trough. Bataan and Correigidor were already doomed, but still the Dow edged back over 100 within a month, despite a trade slower even than in April.

Bear markets end when the last bull has capitulated and when price discounts all the bad news known or perceived. There is no magic formula for picking the bottom, but such are much easier to pinpoint than market tops. And, fortunately, they provide a decent amount of time for consideration and action.

Long bear markets have always been followed by big bull markets, usually long ones. Short bear markets, those of less than a year, don't generate enough liquidation to spark big advances.

Violent endings to bear markets are friendly for reflex profits. The biggest six-month bounces from cyclic lows came in the aftermath of the hard cases of 1974, 1938, 1932, 1914, 1907, and 1896. The modern big winner was an exception, as it followed the subdued climax of 1982. The Dow jumped by 44 percent within six months.

Fundamentals lure buyers near market troughs. But faith alone has reaped giant rewards when the outlook appeared most grim. The largest advances in history came after the bear lows of 1921 and 1932, the only years in which the Industrials posted red ink. Should such an event happen again, or threaten to happen, the market will again be a rich lode; the horrific earnings news will have been fully discounted.

A similar discounting function can be observed when an earnings slide threatens the Dow. The average doesn't wait to throw up its hands late in the autumn of the bad calendar year. The year's low will normally discount the bad news by late spring. Record postwar earnings declines for the Industrials came in 1958 and 1975, but in each case the average recorded its bear low in the fall of the previous year. When everyone begins fussing about "lousy earnings," the low is long past.

Consecutive-day moves are confusing, but not meaningful. Long strings of declining days may seem to signal overkill and an important bottom, but the only such instance which has accompanied a major low was in September–October 1974, when 11 Dow straight declines did mark the end of the market's bear sequence. In the fall of 1967, the Rails fell for 12 days, rallied for one session, and then declined for 12 more days. It was just a secondary correction.

The longest string of consecutive loss days for the Industrials occurred in July–August 1941, when the market dropped for 14 straight days. But the average continued its decline until April of the following year.

Incidentally, bull markets don't peak in a consecutive up-day frenzy. Many apprehensive investors foresaw the end of an era in January 1987, when the Industrials rushed up for 209 points in a whirlwind advance that lasted for 13 straight days. The average actually gained another 600 points by August.

Buying Time Is Ample at Bear Market Lows

Panics seldom grant more than a few days of extreme opportunity. Bear market troughs offer ample buying time. Sometimes, as in 1978, there were more quality buying days than one might have wished for. At that time, stocks could have been bought within 5 percent of the Dow low for a month and a half—33 trading sessions, including the trough.

A 5 percent premium to a bear market low is a quality purchase. Even 10 percent is excellent. In 1974, General Motors' low was 29, and the stock could have been bought within 10 percent of that price, before and after, for nearly a month. When the shares sold at 79 several years later, it made no difference whether the investor had caught the exact low day.

Investors also benefit from the fact that many blue-chip stocks will retest their lows even when the Dow has made a convincing turn. There will be many laggard treasures, as we shall see later in this chapter.

Two-thirds of the bear market lows of this century have recorded at least 11 days—more than two trading weeks—when the Dow's range was within 5 percent of its trough. Several of the reversals occupied nearly a calendar month.

There have been seven major turns in which the investor had only two to six days of luxury pricing, as measured by the average. But in every case except two, the bargain shopping lasted over two weeks if the low ranges prior to the final low were counted. The hurry-up turn in 1982 saw only three days of cheap Dow pricing, including the low session. But two-score days earlier in the summer had carried ranges within 5 percent of the important August low.

The epic reversals occurred in 1938 and 1970. Even including prior low days, there were only four and five sessions, respectively, when the Industrials ranged within 5 percent of the sequence lows. In the 1932 instance, there remained plenty of cheap stocks about, even after the Industrials had gained over 15 percent. Chrysler, $5\frac{3}{4}$ on July 8, was at $6\frac{1}{2}$ two weeks later; it would sell at 21 within six weeks. General Electric was up from $9\frac{1}{8}$ to $10\frac{1}{4}$; it quickly ran to 23. The early runaway gains had been mostly among the railroads. They still had ardent followers, and the Rail advance in July—an amazing 65 percent—was more than twice that of the Industrials.

Bargain days—those sessions when the Dow traded within 5 percent of the extreme low—have been distributed as follows. Before 1929, intraday ranges are generally unavailable and closing levels are used. Additionally, 1914 is omitted because of the NYSE closing.

Two to six quality days: 1917, 1921, 1932, 1938, 1962, 1970, and 1982 (7)

Eleven to 15 days: 1907, 1942, 1939, 1960, 1966, and 1987 (6)

Sixteen to 20 days: 1900, 1903, 1949, and 1974 (4)

More than 20 days: 1911, 1957, 1978, and 1990 (4)

In every case, other quality days (as it turned out) preceded the low, and many people purchased what turned out to be cheap stocks. Leading stocks and groups will often record their lows before the major average. These datings measure only those days of opportunity on and after the low.

No one can positively identify a bear market low in real time, but the market does give a reasonable time for reflection and recognition. And there are always those laggard blue-chips to be snatched up, even after the Dow has made a visible reversal.

More about Bear Market Reversals

Bear market reverses necessarily break down-trend lines within a few weeks or months following the absolute low; such action is dependable, if not always believable. The 1973–1974 bear market was the worst since the 1930s, hitting the Industrials for a loss of 45 percent. When it wound down in the fourth quarter of 1974, there were plenty of technical signs to encourage buyers. Contrarians could believe because consumer sentiment was at the worst level since World War II. Many market hopes had been crushed when stock prices crumbled immediately after President Nixon resigned. The investment malaise was so overwhelming that it seemed to anticipate an end to Western Civilization.

In October, the S&P and the Dow Transports recorded their market lows, the Utilities having bottomed in mid-September. But the Dow held off until December, when it recorded a classic double bottom against the worst October figure. In the meantime, a promising *invert-*

ed head-and-shoulders formation had been aborted by the November smash. The Dow's December low was a lonely and unimpressive one, and technical readings were much improved from October.

At the first of January, the Federal Reserve lowered the discount rate, and in the resultant excitement the Dow cracked through an important down-trend line. Within several weeks both averages soared above their November rally peaks, generating a Dow theory buy signal. It was quite timely and helped spur some exorbitant first-half gains, with the Dow advancing to 879, up more than 50 percent from the December low. Many analysts, however, were claiming that the market was in a vigorous but dangerous bear market rally, with Dow 400 seen as the final low. They stubbornly refused to believe that the broken trend line was meaningful. That classic, and rewarding, trend-line smash is shown in Fig. 8-1.

In 1930–1932, the steep descent pattern lined up along the multiple rally highs and was clearly broken at midsummer near the Dow 50 level. After that the average quickly ran up 60 percent.

Figure 8-1. In 1974–1975, the bear market reversed after a classic double bottom in December 1974. At the end of 1974, consumer confidence was at the lowest level since World War II, but the market had already discounted that, along with the recession. In January 1975, the bearish trend line was cracked and a Dow theory buy signal helped the average to its best monthly gain since 1938.

The bear market which ended in 1982 witnessed a high-volume surge through the 16-month bear-market trend line within days after the bottom Dow figure. It developed so quickly that by then the Dow was about 50 points off its low point—a ton of points at the time. Skeptics might have doubted except for the overwhelming up-side volume.

Quality buying days are ordinarily distributed generously on both sides of the trough. But the conservative investor who demands hard evidence of a final bottom might delay a decision for a month or two. The penalty for a more cautious approach has not been too severe. Buying the leading Dow average exactly one month after the bear low would have meant paying a premium of 9.5 percent over the low values, as measured in 24 important reversals since 1890. A two-month wait would have been more costly, a 14.6 premium. Three months' insurance was generally higher, but in 10 instances a cycle was apparently working against the advance, for the Dow had fallen below the high seen at the two-month anniversary.

The sizzling one- and two-month gains of 1932—plus 64.3 and plus 88 percent—have been omitted from the average figures, which would have been 11.7 and 17.6 if they had been included.

The 1970 bear market climax is the best postwar fit to the averages. The Dow's May low was 631. One month later, the Dow closed at 688 (plus 9 percent), and two months later it was at 730 (plus 15.7). The bull peak was at 1052, so the potential sequence gain for the late-July buyer was sliced by one-third, as measured by the average.

Fundamentals are of little value in predicting market bottoms. We know what figures are attractive, but the ranges have been extraordinarily wide. Some markets turn on frightening fundamentals, having already discounted financial disaster. Other markets, as in 1949, have ignored rich figures. And hesitant fundamentalists were left at the post in 1960 and 1970 when the bear campaigns failed to turn up attractive numbers. In the former year the Dow at its low sold at 17.5 times earnings. In 1970, even after a violent downturn, the yield on the average was only 3.4 percent.

Shocking news, and a final convulsion, not fundamental values, have most often turned the market, flushing out the last weak margin account. This happened in 1970, following the Kent State tragedy and the news of U.S. troops in Cambodia. *Sputnik I* provided the catalyst in 1957. In 1939 it was the invasion of Czechoslovakia, and in 1938 it was Hitler's Anschluss with Austria. Each event culminated in panic.

In 1903, the world's largest corporation, U.S. Steel, which had been on a $4 dividend basis since its founding in 1901, cut its payout, and in the aftermath the Rich Man's Panic was ended. Steel's shares had already fallen from 40 to 10 during the year. When the dividend was entirely eliminated early in 1904, there was no market reaction. The Erie bankruptcy in 1893 and the Baring Crisis of 1890 both climaxed bear sequences.

Getting a Second Buying Chance: Double Bottoms

Although panic-inspiring accidents and incidents frequently mark the end of falling prices, such action doesn't mean that there won't be some second thoughts. Or that the troubles will not return in some different guise, as was the case with Hitler's aggressions in Central Europe.

Which is just as well for the conservative investor, who is likely to find a less stressful second opportunity to buy stocks. The Dow seldom makes a perfect double bottom, but it rarely turns on a dime; there is usually a low-risk second chance. But not in 1932, when the most exceptional rebound in history occurred; the average doubled within just two months, rushing up from 40.56 to 80.36, intraday. There was only the slightest pullback.

Double bottoms are conspicuous in the light of hindsight, but when they actually occur, they are nerve-wracking. Will the old low hold? Does a small percentage penetration of that first low destroy hope? It is only when the rally point of a "W"-looking bottom is exceeded that one can breathe safely again. There have been so many classic Dow turns from that formation that the investor compulsively looks for a repeat.

A double bottom is formed when the average (or a stock) declines to a certain level on large volume, rallies on lesser trade, and then falls again to about the level of the initial low, on diminishing activity. In the perfect sequence, an upturn from that level attracts large-scale volume as the index moves above the first rally peak. For the Dow, the time between the two lows has most often been about two months, although a six-week period, or even something closer—as in 1890's three-week interim—does not destroy the reliability.

Robert Edwards and John Magee described the formation thus: "...the second bottom is usually conspicuously dull and is apt to be quite rounded...the rally up from the second bottom shows an increase in turnover and volume should pick up to a marked degree as the...height between the two bottoms is surpassed."* Such successful action brings previously hesitant sideliners storming into the market.

*Robert D. Edwards and John Magee, *Technical Analysis of Stock Trends,* 5th ed. (John Magee, Springfield, Mass., 1967), p. 134.

Important double bottoms were witnessed in 1987, 1982, 1974, 1911, 1903, and 1890, among other, less perfect reversals. Not all went exactly by the script, however. On a number of occasions the second down leg fell slightly below the initial trough; we have arbitrarily used a 3 percent deviation, plus or minus, as successful test of the low. In October 1974 the Dow bottom was 585, and following a November rally to 675, the average fell to a modest new low of 578 in early December. It was obviously a moment for caution, but the fact that other leading averages held above the October figure encouraged chance taking. In any event, late January saw the Dow gap above the best November figure on record volume.

Lagging Mavericks
Can Be a Gold Mine

Even when the Dow refuses investors a second chance, there will always be lagging mavericks, issues marching to their own drummer and recording lows weeks after the market bottoms. This does not mean that they are of secondary quality.

In 1970 the Dow whistled up nearly 100 points following the May reversal, but then churned for weeks on rotating lows. During July the list included California Standard, Rohm & Haas, Scott Paper, and Dun & Bradstreet. In August the Dow, at its worst level, was 12 percent above the May trough. At the same time, scores of quality stocks—Disney, Avon, Xerox, American Home Products, Merck, and Alcoa among them—were making new lows. It was not an indication of future relative weakness. They would be among the strongest of the "Nifty Fifty," the P–E elite which led the market until 1973.

In 1987, a secondary test of the low occurred in early December. Despite the brilliant rally after the October low, tax selling had pushed many good names below their earlier trough.

All it took was a little faith to pick up such All-Americans as American Airlines (AMR), American Brands, American Express, American General, American Greeting Card, American Standard, and American Stores, to list a few of the "A" bargains.

Many of those laggards, as in 1970, turned into market leaders. Digital Equipment, which didn't make a bear market low until January 1975, one month after the Dow, raced from 46 to 141 during that year. Xerox's low came at about the same time, and it managed a 46–88 advance by midsummer. Stocks of proven quality must not be ignored solely because they are modestly out of phase with the market. The careful shopper will find out-of-sync bargains.

Bear Market Reversals
Lack Predictive Value

It would be helpful if one could establish some predictive value from the nature and volume of bear market reversals, but the search has proved frustrating. The high excitement and record volume of 1970 led to a mediocre bull market, one which gained only half as much as that which followed the subdued turn of 1942. Nor does the damage of the bear episode seem to have relevance to the bull market which follows.

Furthermore, there is no consistency in the length of major declines. One can't predict a bear market end by either its depth or duration. In 1981–1982, a recession and continued interest rate fears depressed the market for 16 months, with the Dow dropping 24 percent. A bear market lasting less than one-third as long, in 1938–1939, created a similar loss.

Major bear markets have a consistency of loss, but not of time span. Eight of them have taken the Dow down between 40 and 49 percent, a close nesting of losses, as seen in Table 8-2. The 1929 crash was for 48 percent. Minor bear markets have cost the Industrials between 20 and 37 percent. We should say "about" 20. That figure is the rule-of-thumb minimum for bear markets, but the 1956–1957 occurrence and the 1960 intrayear decline, both slightly less than 20, are usually included in bear summaries. The latter is marginal, but a number of good names, such as United Aircraft, Goodrich, and Bucyrus-Erie, saw their price cut in half.

You can't tell when a bear market is over by the extent of loss. When the Dow falls by about 25 percent, the move is often over or nearly over, as was the case in eight sequences since 1890. But such a figure may be just the beginning, as in 1973. One interesting note on Table 8-2 is the fact that of the eight major declines, only one has occurred since World War II. Perhaps, like our recessions, the bear has become less menacing.

Or so it seemed until 1987.

Table 8-2. Major Bear Markets*
Leading Dow Average

Years	Loss (%)	Duration	Years	Loss (%)	Duration
1937–1938	49	12 m + 22 d	1973–1974	45	22 m + 26 d
1906–1907	49	21 m + 28 d	1892–1893	43	16 m + 24 d
1919–1921	47	21 m + 22 d	1939–1942	40	31 m + 17 d
1901–1903	46	28 m + 24 d	1916–1917	40	12 m + 29 d

*The unique 1929–1932 episode—down 89% in 36 months, 6 days—is omitted.

Lagging Dow Theory Signals

Most technical studies are superior to the Dow theory in detecting a bear market reversal. Serious money never waits on a Dow signal; it moves into the market long before such a formal revaluation. Serious money likes to buy in periods of extreme adversity, and Dow theory buy signals, by their construction, are at least two levels pricier than the values at the bear trough.

An examination of 21 bear market reversals (as measured by the theory) in the period since 1900 shows that the Dow had advanced by at least 20 percent in 12 of them before a buy signal was confirmed. That is an insensitive indicator, particularly when one counts the fact that many full-fledged bull sequences since World War II have gained less than 50 percent.

After the 1932 depression low, the Dow doubled—from 41 to 84—before the theory gave an official seal of approval. Following the post-war low of June 1949, it required 16 months for confirmation of an uptrend, and the average had already spurted by 41 percent. The average lag from bear trough to Dow theory buy signal has been slightly over five months. The average advance recorded before the signal was 25 percent, but "only" 21 percent if one excludes the extraordinary figure for 1932–1933.

Table 8-3 shows some of the Dow theory's tardy calls. In every case, an investor with even minimal trading instincts would have already made commitments. In 1970 the Dow gain before the buying signal was 30 percent. Champion Homes, a small-cap mobile-home favorite, was already up fourfold from its low at 8 when the signal was executed. Fortunately for theory disciples, the stock kept on running, peaking two years later at an unadjusted price of 260.

A more common price action, however, is for the largest gains to come early on, which handicaps lagging indicators. The popular off-shore

Table 8-3. Bear Market Lows and Dow Theory Buy Signals

Tardy Calls by the Dow Theory

Bear market low	Dow theory buy signal
July 1932	May 1933
Apr. 1942	Feb. 1943
June 1949	Oct. 1950
May 1970	Dec. 1970
Feb. 1978	Aug. 1978

driller, Reading & Bates, had run from 10 to 32 in the same 1970 period. But for the Tulsa service company, the bull market was mostly over by the time the theory's green light was flashed; its sequence peak would be 36. And even for many of the glitzy "Nifty Fifty" stocks, the 1970 gain from the May low would equal or exceed the percentage advance of the following two years to the bull market high in January 1973.

For the investor who follows the Dow theory religiously, there is a one-in-three chance that the bull bugle will not sound until after the market has already advanced by at least 30 percent. That is the bad news. The good news is that buying signals have seldom whipsawed disciples, and the many long-continued trends have encouraged investors to hold their positions for important gains.

The theory rode the bull trend from 1924 until late October 1929, and from May 1933 through August 1937. Similar multiyear patterns were marked in the years of World War II and, by those students who did not interpret the 1984 weakness as a selling signal, from 1982 to 1987.

Despite its tardy arrival, the bull signal of 1933 was most effective. The following four-year advance posted the Dow up by 95 percent to the August selling signal; the gain to the March peak was 110 percent. The total 1932–1937 gain was a gaudy 497 percent, however. Anybody chancing the market in the summer of 1932 scored gains fourfold more than those possible simply by following the theory.

The record for buy signals has been more effective than those on the sell side. One of the most timely calls was in January 1975, when a consensus buying signal was issued only a few weeks after the December low. It was triggered by the avalanche of institutional buying which had already pushed into the market, rallying the Dow above its November peak. When it came time to sell, however, a bullish 1976–1977 divergence by the Transports delayed theorists' liquidation until October 1977, by which time the Dow was at 801, a sorry selling level compared with the 1014 peak of the previous year.

Investors must remember that they are trading stocks and not the Dow theory, but should stay tuned to its signals for the occasional timely buying signal—and, more important, for the encouragement to practice patience in long-trending bull markets.

Insider Profits Bested

The average investor probably owns eight or 10 stocks, accumulated over the years. They have been bought for a variety of reasons: a broker's pitch, an "inside tip" from a golfing buddy, an investment letter recommendation, or possibly some personal selection, made after a little kitchen-table research.

The most profitable holdings, regardless of origin, will be those shares chanced after a bear market has apparently reversed. The profits may not be sensational, but they will bloom worry-free over the years, for there is never the nervous compulsion to grab profits, the shares having been bought under such bargain circumstances.

Holdings purchased later in the market cycle can also do well. Mergers, earnings increases, dividend hikes, rate cuts—they all add spice and profit for traders. But those profits dim beside the opportunities offered around bear lows.

A great deal of money was made in the merger boom of the 1980s, some of it honestly. A great deal of money was also lost in the merger rumor mill and in failed deals, as happened when UAL's buyout ticket was canceled in 1989. In 1984, three giant oil mergers were consummated. Merger rumors had flown all year, and some shrewd speculators made a short-term killing. But how much of a killing? Plenty of points, to be sure, but the percentage gains paled beside what investors had already picked up by buying the oil shares within, say, 10 percent of the 1982 lows.

In 1984, Texaco stole Getty Oil away from Pennzoil, Chevron took over Gulf, and Mobil grabbed the great oil finder, Superior. How much money could you have made if, at the end of December 1983, you had been tipped that the three energy giants would be bought out? Plenty. But not as much as an investor who bought 100 shares of each in 1982 and, with rare bad luck, sold out just before the merger year began. Note in the following comparison that we give the oil "insiders" the 1984 high price and buy the investor's stock well above the 1982 low.

One hundred shares of Getty, Gulf, and Superior Oil would have cost $9500 in 1982, if bought 10 percent above the year's low, not a difficult chore. If sold at the closing prices of 1983, an unfortunate decision, the gross proceeds would have been $17,900, a profit of 88 percent.

An inside tip might have encouraged a trader to buy the same three-stock package at the end of 1983; the results would have been splendid, for the companies were merged out for a total value of $25,300 in 1984. Insider merger gain: 41 percent less than half the "honest" profits. Serious money is made by patiently waiting for something that looks like the cycle low, not from chasing insider tips, even when they turn out to be true.

Dependably, two or three bear episodes darken every decade. Lightening up or taking a celibacy pledge at the first sign of serious

trouble is the investor's insurance step. Then comes the final act—the
time to reinvest. The timing isn't as reliable as the appearance of the
fat lady at the opera.

Fundamental values and comparisons help, as seen in Table 8-1, but
they vary tremendously; only about one-third of the major declines of
the past 100 years have developed the superbullish, high-yield, low-PE
ratios which spell great value. The duration of the down trend offers no
help. Excluding the longevity freaks, major declines have lasted from
two to 31 months, and there is no correlation between duration and loss.
The drop between August and October 1987 was 36 percent, the same
figure recorded in the 17-month, 1968–1970 event. (Refer back to Table
4-1 for details of 25 major declines.)

Chart patterns and day-to-day action have varied widely near lows.
Most bear market turns have come from a strong V formation and
good volume. A few have been slow and wimpy, with low activity.
Classic double bottoms have blessed the patient observer on seven
occasions; the 1974 and 1987 W-looking bottoms both tagged up in
October and December.

Serious Money Again

Serious money is made mostly by the early identification of opportunity. This may not be important if the Dow is headed for a 500 percent
advance, as it was in 1921. But since the end of World War II, only two
bull episodes have gained over 100 percent.

Of 25 bull markets in the past century, less than one-third were dou-
blers; reflecting the modest index gains, the big paper profits have
been made in the first 12 months. Four bull markets were actually
completed within less than a year. But there were still large profits for
early buyers. In the 1938 intrayear move, Sperry Corporation spun up
from 16 to 49, as defense stocks drew a following.

At least in 1938 there was a decent second chance: The Dow hit 108
at the end of May, after an April peak at 121. The last high-speed turn
came in August 1982, as huge volume pushed the Dow 20 percent
above the 777 low within a month. In October, the average crossed
1000.

Belabored turns are always suspect. Some hesitation is normal, but
too much time spent in a consolidation not far above the initial low is
usually followed by a further collapse. It is far better to have a vigorous rally, followed by a serious attempt to knock out the low. If that
fails, the market promises good things.

The most tedious holding pattern of this century occurred following the October 1957 bottom. Recession gripped the country, and the Dow could not get out of its own way, trading in the 420–456 range (with one day's exception) for six months.

The 1978–1981 advance lasted three years, but 58 percent of the gain was achieved in the first six months, which is why speculators willingly take a chance on probable bear trend reversals. Investors are more deliberate, but lose big leverage unless the uptrend lasts for years. In about one year after the 1970 low, Johnson & Johnson, one of the leaders of the high-multiple "rat pack," raced from 37 to 95, up 193 percent. In the following 18 months the gain was only 37 percent. The advance pattern for Avon was similar.

In the 1932–1937 escalation, many stocks shot up five- to 10-fold in the first 12 months, but then failed to gain materially in the next few years. Among them were Illinois Central, American Sugar, Celanese, Columbia Gas, Goodyear Tire, IT&T, Olin Mathieson Chemical, Pan-American Airways, Union Bag, and Western Union.

General Motors had sped from $7\frac{1}{2}$ to 63 by February 1934, but it could not "even" double that high in the balance of the long Dow advance. Regardless of the trend's duration, first-year gains have usually doubled the best figure for any succeeding period. The serious money in bull markets is made by early identification of cyclic lows, not in the second or third upleg.

The boom following World War I seems to provide the only exception. Through most of 1918, the market only limped along, despite improving prospects for Allied victory. Peace, in November 1918, turned out to have been discounted, and at Christmas the Dow was no higher than in February.

A brief recession was followed by fierce inflation, and the market's hysteria—sparked by booming auto fuel demand—fixed upon the crude producers. Mexican Petroleum struck it rich in its "golden lane" oil concession near Tampico and gushed up to 264, having doubled during the year. The speculative mania for the oils and autos assisted the Dow to a second-year advance almost the equal of the initial period. Such tardy brilliance, however, is the exception.

More typical was the last year of the 1982–1987 bull campaign. On huge volume, the Dow whistled past 100-point milestones from Dow 2000 to 2700 as it gained 44 percent. Despite the sensational numbers and volume through August, the advance fell short of the 58 percent gain chalked in the first eight months of the sequence.

It's not only the serious money, but the easy money, that comes with the turning of the tide.

How High Is High? How Low Is Low?

If vision were granted us to know the exact earnings of the Industrials some years ahead, it would still be impossible to translate that knowledge into any accurate estimate of the Dow level.

Assume that the DJIA earnings will be a record $250 in some bull year. At what level could the average trade, based on the range of enthusiasm at past market peaks?

Dow 5875 if the market equals 1961 P–E ratio of 23.5×.

Dow 3900 at 1956 P–E ratio of 15.6×.

Dow 2250 at 1981 P–E ratio of 9.0×.

The difference between the high and low possibilities, based on the range of bull market P–E ratios since the end of World War II, is over *3500 Dow points.*

On the down side, guessing is not much easier. Assume that the Dow earnings fell back to the level of 1986, when the figure was $115. How low might the average fall, if it duplicated the extreme ranges at bear troughs since the war's end?

Dow 2024 if the market duplicated the 1960 P–E ratio of 17.6×.

Dow 1507 basis 1987 panic P–E low at 13.1×.

Dow 667 if the average fell to 1974's low figure, 5.8×.

Interest rates, recession, inflation, and consumer confidence are just some of the unpredictable factors which have caused these huge differences in P–E ratios. Earnings for major stocks are easy for competent analysts to forecast, often for several years ahead. What those earnings will mean in price terms is impossible to forecast. High or low? No one knows.

The Price–Earnings Ratio Is the Market Wildcard

The scorecard statistics of bear market troughs, as shown in Table 8-1, vary widely. The price–earnings ratio is the market wildcard. Earnings and payout ratios can often be reliably estimated several years in advance. But how will the market evaluate them? Are they already discounted? The price–earnings range for individual stocks is much wider than for the averages.

IBM earned $2.70 in 1973 and sold over 90, adjusted. By 1980, a bull year, the stock fell to 50, although earnings had doubled. Its 1981 dividend far exceeded 1973 earnings. Frenzied bulls in late 1972 had correctly forecast Big Blue's growth, but none had foreseen the shrinkage in esteem—from 33 times earnings to 9×.

Good—or bad—earnings are not consistently translated into price, which reduces the value of fundamental scorecards at either bull or bear extremes.

In 1929, the Dow earnings were up 25 percent from those of 1928. We all know what happened.

The two biggest bull markets in history began in 1921 and 1932. In both years the Dow's composite earnings were in the red—the only losses ever shown by the average.

In 1916, the Dow earned nearly $25 and was cheaply priced at an average of 4 times earnings, its lowest ratio in history. A major decline started late in the year.

Since the end of World War II, Dow earnings have fallen in 17 years. In 12 of those years, the average advanced, often dramatically, as in 1975. In the seven years when earnings fell materially—by 10 percent or more—the Dow closed higher six times.

The worst panic in generations struck the Exchange in the fall of 1987. It proved a poor barometer. The Dow earnings advanced 62 percent in 1988.

In 1965, the Dow earned $54 and had a high of 970. In 1982, the Dow *paid* a composite dividend of $54 and its low was 777.

Fundamentals seem like the solid foundation of price. They are not. Earnings are fairly predictable; the market's reaction to them is not. The numbers are gay deceivers, and the investor must not fall in love with them.

Frustrating the Analysts

If one could precisely forecast a stock's future earnings and dividends, it would be of no help in predicting future prices. Scores of capable analysts on Wall Street routinely come up with amazingly correct forecasts of earnings two and three years ahead. But the market wildcard, the price–earnings ratio, defeats their computers.

What happened to IBM in the late 1970s was not unique. Shareholders of Minnesota Mining, best known as the manufacturer of

Scotch tape, were baffled in 1980 by the market's indifference to its splendid record. Earnings and dividends had quadrupled since 1968, but the share price of 46 was slightly lower than it had been at the 1967 year-end. Inflation, high interest rates, and a jaundiced view of growth stocks had conspired to rob shareholders of brilliant results.

The yield in December 1967 was barely 1 percent; the return in the spring of 1980 was over 6 percent. But, as inflation waned later in the decade, the 6 percent dividend buyers prospered. The stock advanced to the equivalent of 167 in 1987, having been little troubled by the 1982 recession.

One would think that the fundamental evaluations for the Dow would be more susceptible to forecast, but that is not the case. Table 8-1's score-card displays the inconsistencies which have been part of the average's statistics since it was first computed. A recent example can be seen in the figures at the bull market peak of 1981. The Dow was valued at only 9× earnings, while in 1987 the multiple was 20.5×. If the earnings multiplier in that latter year had only duplicated the figure of the early 1980s, the Dow peak would have been 1197, not 2722.

Investors in 1949 were spoiled for the events of the next quarter-century. Yields would never again approach the 8 percent return available in June of that year. Return had also been rich in 1942, and the 11 percent dividend yield of 1932 remains the highest modern figure for the series.

So the postwar depression mindset had difficulty in adjusting to the skimpy fundamentals which would accompany troughs for the next 20 years; a bargain, single-digit P–E ratio would be missing until 1974. Inflation and then deflation ruled out any consistency in the 1980s. In 1987, the worst panic in history could only boost the Dow yield to 4 percent, compared with the 7 percent return at the low of 1982.

Fundamental comparisons prove nothing, for each market cycle writes its own ticket. It is possible to prove that a P–E ratio of 20× allows for no disappointments and that it indicates an approaching top. But it may stay in place for months or even years. And it can be proven that a single-digit P–E ratio and a 6 percent Dow yield are rich values. Long-term investors will go to the bank with such figures. But the statistics won't automatically jump-start the market. The values may get cheaper before the market reverses.

Don't Overdose on Stocks

The problem for most speculators at bear market troughs is that they have already OD'd on stocks. Overdosing is the fatal flaw

Table 8-4. Major Stock Market Advances
Percentage Gain of Leading Dow Average

1921–1929	497	1907–1909	90	1900–1901	48
1932–1937	372	1962–1966	86	1893–1895	47
1982–1987	250	1917–1919	81	1978–1981	38
1949–1956	222	1974–1976	76	1888–1890	35
1896–1899	173	1987–1990	73	1966–1968	32
1903–1906	144	1970–1973	67	1890–1892	30
1942–1946	129	1957–1960	63	1960–1961	30
1914–1916	112	1938–1938	60	1911–1912	29
		1990–1993	50	1939–1939	28

for most individuals' market strategy. Overloaded with shares, the addict finds that the sobriety of crisis forces costly withdrawal pains. There is no halfway house for the victim who has overdosed on high-priced stocks.

Market bottoms don't blind-side investors. The glass of confidence has been falling for months, and the arrival of the storm is trumpeted by page-one headlines, boardroom TV interviews, and a glut of doomsday hype. Even investors who have overdosed in cash accounts suffer a bitter lesson. In 1982, they were frozen out of the best buying opportunity since the 1930s.

Consider the decade of the 1970s. It was the most placid, in net change, in the past century; the Dow's gain was less than 4 percent. But there were three major bull markets. And every decade since the 1890s has offered at least one bull sequence superior to any of the 1970s. (The gain for the 1949–1956 overlap, if measured from December 31, 1949, was 160 percent.) Serious money awaits investors who have not previously overdosed.

Major market advances since 1888, as measured by the leading Dow average, are shown in Table 8-4.

9
Stocks to Buy, Stocks to Avoid

Stock selection in a bear market offers the luxury of deliberation and planning. There's plenty of time to catch up with Standard & Poor's Outlook and Value Line on a trip to your broker's office. Panics offer nothing but a hipshot. It is a reflex action, for the violence is come and gone almost before the crisis is understood.

Timing at bear market troughs is more difficult than in panic. Investors should initially opt for established names with high ratings. If an apparent bottom turns out to be an illusion—as in May 1962 and October 1974—then the buyer is not stressed by quality insomnia. Blue-chips may suffer one final selling wave, but they will survive and prosper during the inevitable bull sequence to follow.

In the fall of 1974, GE bottomed at 30, rallied to 40, and then held at 32 in the December finale. A buyer who had bought at 35 in late August would not have been too alarmed. The shares, after all, had been above 60 earlier in the year, and earnings would be well over $3. It was a historically low evaluation for the stock. Institutions cannot spend their hoarded millions all in one day, and will begin to gather in selected equities at fundamental values even though they know that such prices will represent the final lows only by great luck.

At such times, quality will turn first and give a clue that the bear episode is near an end. Conservative investors will gather in the household names when they decide to test the water. General Electric has been such an easy choice for nearly a century. A portfolio of GE, U.S. Steel, and General Motors would have made the cyclic buyer wealthy. Those were never difficult selections. General Electric dominated the electrics at the turn of the century and still does. U.S. Steel was, at its formation in 1901, the world's first billion-dollar company. About a decade later, General Motors became the largest publicly owned automobile company. Buying the biggest has not always been the best investment choice, but it was the easiest in the old days. One didn't have to wrestle those enormous Moody's manuals about.

A One-Stock Portfolio

Such a no-brain, three-stock package (tabulated for panic in the previous chapter) might have been improved on by astute money managers, but a buy-and-hold strategy would not have done so well. To make the computation easier, we'll switch to a one-stock strategy—just buy America's biggest industrial concern. It's so simple that even your brother-in-law might have lit upon it.

The first major market trough of this century was touched in November 1903. U.S. Steel was America's industrial giant; it had nearly 175,000 employees—about as many as the Civil Service—and it produced 64 percent of the nation's ingots and castings. Outside the beloved railroads, Steel was the most natural buy in those days of huge industrial amalgamations, and its autumn low was 10. Disregarding transaction costs, $10,000 would have bought 1000 shares. In 1906, the stock traded at 50.

In this fantasy, $10,000 had grown to $50,000. Buying the stock at around 10 was extraordinarily easy; its low in 1904 was 8½. Sell at 50? No way. But it traded between 45 and 50 for months. If the stock had been bought and sold at a 10 percent haircut to the extreme prices, the reward would have been $40,910, but who's counting?

The 1907 bear market pulled Steel down to the 22 range, where it traded for weeks before J. P. Morgan could rally the Street's bankers to the crisis. Our no-brain investor could have purchased 2222 shares, which would be worth $211,090 at the 1909 market top. Morgan did better. He organized a pool in U.S. Steel stock which reportedly returned about $25 million during the period. Continuing the fantasy, our occasional celibate would have pushed the value of the one-stock portfolio to $1.4 million by 1919 and $11 million in 1929. A buy-and-hold program in Steel would have been worth only $123,000.

For one who wishes to continue the pleasantry, General Motors—by 1926 the nation's largest industrial—would have been the designated purchase in 1932 and the portfolio value would have exploded to $108 million at GM's peak in 1936. (Its bellwether performance topped before the Dow, which did not slow until March 1937.)

Such a financial fantasy, far removed from real life, suggests the enormous potential of any timing system which insulates your money from stock market seductions during long, dreary declines.

Selecting Stocks Used to Be Easier

Stock selection was not overly tricky in the old days, if only because choice was limited. There were only 100 active stocks at the Exchange in 1900. Big was seen as best, and U.S. Steel and General Motors would become market leaders for decades. But they have not been dominant for a generation. The former registered its all-time peak in 1959, and GM topped in 1965. Even brother-in-law would have recognized the problems on the smokestack axis.

There are now some 2000 common issues at the NYSE, and thousands of additional active stocks on NASDAQ. The winnowing of bull market prospects is more difficult than it was several generations ago, but some well-tested groups reliably repeat in each cycle.

It would have been grand to have bought the oil service stocks and the golds in 1978, or to have foreseen the retailing explosion for companies like The Gap and The Limited in 1982. But most investors turn to familiar names in times of stress. They want stocks that they understand, stocks they will not be uncomfortable with if their timing is slightly off.

Proven Rebounders

Canny investors want stock groups with proven rebounding ability and hope that the choice will outperform the market. There are always maverick high-fliers that promise to outperform the Dow, but fads, fashions, and perceptions change; RVs, calculators and double-knits disappointed in the mid-1970s. Even the once-vaunted chemical group is now seen as a victim of commodity-type pricing and has lacked relative cachet since 1965.

Patient investors who have waited out a stubborn bear trend don't want to find their new selections out of sync with the market. Fortunately, there are many groups that march dependably to the same beat as the Dow—or at least have done so for the past four decades. They are well known, made up mostly of household names, and require no special competency to understand.

Integrated oil stocks have been such a reliable group for decades. The great old Standard Oil companies have been big winners in every bull market. Sadly, they have all been rechristened with synthetic Madison Avenue monikers like Exxon, Amoco, Chevron, and so forth, but they still possess charisma and crude. The best-integrated domestic oils, such as Amoco, have done better than the internationals over the past 20 years.

Ethical drug makers have dependably outperformed the Dow since they suffered a severe fallout in the early 1950s. In the 1970–1973 Nixon market, the Standard & Poor's drug average outpaced the Dow by more than 50 percent. Between 1978 and 1981, Barron's drug average doubled, while the Industrials' gain was less than 40 percent.

Few stocks look worse at the bottom of the market cycle than those in the building trades. Yet construction always comes back, and the shares are big winners when economic hopes improve. One problem is that representative shares are all over the board—copper, sheetrock, plywood, cement, air conditioning, lumber, plumbing, and, of course, the listed home builders.

Railroad freight business tracks the economy closely, and the volatile carriers have usually posted larger gains than the DJIA. Between 1949 and 1969 they enjoyed three bull sequences where they doubled; the Dow had only one. The railroad average was enhanced and renamed Dow Rail-Transports in 1970, but the pattern has not changed. Four Transport markets have gained over 100 percent since then. Airlines, tracked by various separate averages, have outperformed the Dow in every bull market since they became a viable group in the early 1940s.

Good Names That Can Lead
Up-Side Reversals

Following are some lead stocks in the recommended groups. Lesser issues will often outperform the leaders over the course of a bull market, but the stocks mentioned are the type that lead reversal patterns. Standard & Poor's quality ratings, always subject to change, are given.

Airlines. There's a serious lack of quality ratings here; earnings are unpredictable and balance sheets untidy. AMR earned over $7 in both 1988 and 1989, but has chalked deficits in each year since. It used to be a B+, but now it is only a C. Delta was rated the top airline for years but is now only B−. UAL is only C, while the efficient regional, Southwest Airlines, is rated B. In 1982, those two led the bullish flight pattern, and UAL flew from 15 to 37 within four months.

Building materials. It's tough to find a pure play here. Crane may be typical. It is known for its plumbing fixtures and sash and door subsidiary, but is broadly diversified though only B rated. Makers of bricks (Justin) and shingles (Elcor) are among other building stocks. Homebuilders also receive attention when the economy is seen to revive. The industry's casualty list is long, but survivors like Lennar and Ryland are A− stocks. Centex, B+, is the largest U.S. builder.

Chemicals. The Chemicals are not the reliable performers they once were, but they have all stood the test of time. Dow, DuPont, Monsanto, and Union Carbide, among others, endeared themselves to investors by paying dividends through the Great Depression. Thirty years ago the major chemicals were all either A or A+. Now DuPont is tops with an A−, and Dow and Monsanto are rated B and B+, respectively. Air Products, A−, is often overlooked as a chemical and has been a sleeper. It was an eightfold winner between 1966 and 1976. In 1992 it stood 50 percent higher than its 1987 peak.

Drugs. Ethical drugs spell investment quality and have been bought with confidence in every recession. Health care will continue as one of the growth areas of this decade, though its exorbitant costs must surely slow and drugs' short-term price course will depend on political rhetoric and action. There is a glut of quality here. Merck, the best Dow performer in the boom year of 1986, Abbott Laboratories, American Home Products, Eli Lilly, and Marion Merrell Dow are all A+. They have outdone the Dow in every sequence since the mid-1950s.

Foods. These issues are popularly regarded as defensive issues. But in the aftermath of the 1980s deflation, they outperformed the Dow year after year. ConAgra, Heinz, Hershey, and Sara Lee, all A+, were among the solid winners. For a longer review and suggestions for the 1990s, see "Foods and Beverages: Perennial All-Americans" at the end of this chapter.

Energy Stocks

Wimpy politicians guarantee that America's energy problems and opportunities will be with us into the twenty-first century. Every investment portfolio should include at least one major integrated oil. Over the past century, they have provided marvelous long-term holdings. Yet in every decade they have suffered immodest corrections. Such pangs will occur again in the 1990s.

Royal Dutch and Exxon stand at the head of the international class, rated A and B+, respectively. The internationals make it one way or another in every energy crisis—by production, marketing, or downstream operations. In 1982 Exxon fell to 25, where it was valued at 5 × earnings and a 12 percent yield, the highest dividend return in its long history. Crude would lose two-thirds of its value over the next four years, with North Sea oil falling to near $8 a barrel, but the former Standard/Jersey climbed to 100 (unadjusted).

Chevron, Mobil, and Texaco are also considered internationals. Texaco, formerly Texas Company, was shanghaied from the state about 70 years ago, but a free-swinging Houston jury got even a few years back with an $11 billion judgment in the Pennzoil-Getty dispute, and the stock has never been quite the same. Amoco, the former Standard Indiana, has always boasted a strong reserve position. Atlantic Richfield, B+, Phillips, and Unocal are other well-regarded domestics that have at one time or another led the entire market because of important crude discoveries. Merger possibilities are added bait. Within the past decade, giants such as Conoco, Gulf, Getty, Marathon, and Superior were swallowed whole.

Miscellaneous Oldtimers

Dozens of antique names, around the Exchange since the 1920s or earlier, have brilliant rebounding records. Occasionally, they have lagged the market, but mostly they have proven superior, and many investors find comfort in long-tested equities. American Smelting and International Paper are true veterans; both were made part of the Dow Jones Industrial average in 1901. Like many others, they were later shuffled out and then back in.

Canadian Pacific (CP) is a proxy for Canadian investment—railroad, airline, hotel, mineral, energy, land, shipping, telecommunications, and so forth. It is the only foreign corporation ever to become part of the Dow averages and has been popular in both New York and London since before the turn of the century. Inflationary periods have boosted the shares, as in 1978–1981, but for the decade of the 1980s, CP was quite average.

Gillette is another veteran campaigner, a household name since Teddy Roosevelt was in the White House. It's razor popularity boomed after World War I, and the shares were a huge market success in the 1920s. It didn't do too badly in the 1980s, either—up nearly eightfold.

Alcoa, the nation's largest aluminum producer, joined the Dow Industrials in 1959, but the Mellon favorite had been a speculative favorite since 1929. Incorporated over a century ago, it received its first big sales push from World War I demands, including the aluminum cook kits made for the army. The shares were undistinguished in the 1960s, but have done well since. By 1992 they were 50 percent over their best price of 1987.

Every quality consumer product represented at the Exchange has developed a loyal stock following. Maytag, into washing machines since 1907 and farm equipment before that time, is such a stock. It suffers when consumers button their purses, but its washing machines and other household appliances do well in periods of confidence. Unfortunately, the consumer has not felt well since 1987 and after a nearly sixfold increase between 1982 and 1987, shares of the Iowa manufacturer have stagnated.

Sadly, two former market giants—IBM and Eastman Kodak—also have been benched. They enjoy sharp rebounds from bear troughs, but without flashy new products, they perform no better than the market. General Motors has played the game for the past 25 years with good short-term speed but no staying power. All three lagged the Dow results in the 1980s.

Railroads

Railroad bonds, said William Rockefeller, "are the Rembrandts of investments." And good railroad common stocks were the foundation of conservative portfolios. Today, many younger investors have never traded a rail stock. They should try, and not just for old times' sake. Railroad holding companies such as the Burlington Northern and the Santa Fe Pacific (which combined the storied Atchison and the Southern Pacific) did much better than the Dow in the 1980s and have always been reliable rebounders. You won't find any Rembrandt ratings, however. Union Pacific at A− is tops; Santa Fe is B−. Both were rated higher in 1960 and 1970.

Retailing

When business sours, consumer confidence collapses and retailers wring their hands. But shopping malls and credit cards have made us into a nation of compulsive shoppers; the addict lusts to return. Retailing stocks turn early and reliably from bear markets. Allied Stores doubled in about nine months after the 1970 low, but took only five months to duplicate that win in 1974–1975. After the 1982 low, May Department Stores doubled in the same period. The proliferation of retailing sectors has changed many of the old rules, however, and you'll just have to keep your eye open for jazzy newcomers in your regional mall. But when the market hangs on disaster's lip, you may feel safer with proven A+ winners like Dillard, The Limited, May, Nordstrom, and Wal-Mart.

Drafting the "Best Athlete"

Professional sports franchises, frustrated by difficulties in selecting draft choices, often opt for the best athlete. Investors, when puzzled by the legion of bargains offered at market troughs, should also draft for the best athlete—which means the highest quality at a reasonable P–E ratio.

There will be available cheap, speculative stocks which will outperform the blue-chips. But which ones? The true investor should forgo high risk and possible high reward for the coziness of high quality and low price–earnings.

The returns are higher than one might imagine. Investors will capture more of a move from a stock like General Electric than they might from a high flier. With the high flier, the temptation is to grab the money and run. If you had bought General Mills at five times earnings in 1980, you would probably still have the shares. It's easy to forgo quick profits when you've laid up an A+ rated stock at bear market multiples.

The system will work as well in the 1990s as it has in every decade observed since the 1920s. The investor drafts only the blue-chips—preferably stocks rated A+ by Standard & Poor's; the ratings are available in their monthly stock guide and in their looseleaf reports. Only dividend-paying stocks are considered. The investor concentrates on quality and timing and, to the extent possible, forgets preconceived opinions about which stocks are the best investments.

The conservative stocks to buy in the market troughs of the 1990s will be those issues of excellent promise and quality, regardless of industry affiliation. A lot of us passed up Bandag some years back; it owned sort of a funny name for a company in a dull business—retreading truck tires—but it dominated that niche industry. It wasn't quite an A+ then, but it is now.

Thus the investor might be into auto parts and tire retreading, for they have proven more rewarding in the past few decades than the best that Detroit and Akron had to offer. The auto parts industry is fragmented, but it offers two quality entries. Genuine Parts distributes; the Pep Boys operate large discount centers. They retail seven days a week and are known to millions of amateur car fixers and repair shops. Certainly they are much better known than an A+ rated medical firm like Block Drugs, which specializes in oral care and professional dental products. Its drug division manufactures Nytol, so it's a sleeper of sorts. Durr-Fillauer was another small A+ medical firm, but it merged out before we could set type on it. Such small, quality jewels are logical candidates for a buyout.

Some Incognito, A+ Blue-Chips

Other blue-chip firms that are more or less unknown to the speculating public include Rubber Maid, which manufacturers rubber and plastic items, Schulman Corporation, which is into plastic resins, and Sigma-Aldrich, the largest distributor of biochemicals. Valspar is well known as a maker of paints and coatings, but its stock gets little hype, though it is popular with institutions. The firm's long-term debt is unstylishly low, only $10 million.

Loral is in defense electronics, a real growth area, as we learned during Operation Desert Storm. The firm's sales have increased from $281 million to $3 billion since 1982. It's not a big-ticket area, however, and the publicized defense dividend isn't expected to come out of Loral's pocket. Hillenbrand, also A+, is a little-publicized purveyor of caskets, funeral insurance, and hospital furniture; it recorded a record high only five months after the 1987 meltdown.

Financial quality doesn't necessarily come with colossal size, as we have all learned. And it can come in widely diversified niches—dental products, caskets, paints and resins, auto parts. Expand your industry horizons when the next serious buying opportunity arises. Draft the best athletes for your team portfolio. They will quickly rise from market troughs and are a lot easier to live with than speculative hot dogs.

Entertainment Stocks

The individual consumer, not some corporate purchasing agent, casts the final vote on entertainment. The election count is devastatingly swift at the box office, stadium, or video store. And it's an even faster thumbs up/thumbs down with the TV switcher at home.

Stock followers who have ridden the entertainment trends of the past have prospered mightily. But fickle public tastes make it a restless portfolio; its product mix swirls like a kaleidoscope. The only certain advice for the entertainment buff near market bottoms is to be on the lookout for radical and surprising developments in form, product, taste, and presentation.

Special-event pay-per-view expands with each new sport season, and maybe Broadway pay-TV will be next. A new cruise ship format or design might make such elegant vacations even more popular. Or maybe President Clinton will take Yellowstone National Park public in order to help reduce the budget. If so, ignore your prejudice against IPOs and opt for the Wyoming theme park.

Popular entertainment concepts have produced dazzling market winners in many decades and have provided easy-to-analyze opportunities for the amateur investor. The trick has been to get off the investment stage before a bored audience shouted for the "hook."

Parlor stethoscopes, the Victrola, player pianos, and the Nickelodeon were kingpins earlier in this century. But the first entertainment blockbuster—radio—did not arrive until the 1920s. Victor Talking Machine quickly gave way to Radio Corporation as the best-known entertainment stock.

Talking pictures and Al Jolson pushed Warner Brothers into the spotlight in 1927. Shares of the motion picture company ran from 10 to 138 within a year. But both radio and motion pictures bowed to the magic of TV in the years after World War II. The annual output of sets exploded from 6000 to 7.5 million between 1946 and 1950.

Officially, such manufacturers were listed under "Physical Output of Selected Manufactured Commodities—Electrical Machinery," but in the broadest sense they were as much a part of the entertainment industry as Desi and Lucy.

Gambling, cable TV, the VCR, video retailers, and the timeless Mickey Mouse have all made fortunes for stockholders. Disney stock sprinted from 11 to 137 between 1982 and 1990. In every instance, the small investor was able to see, hear, and judge the new entertainment stars as capably as Wall Street's analysts.

The Next Winners

Where will the new winners come from? Sports franchises continue to prosper and expand, but by the time the public gets a piece of the action, the leverage is gone. Even Larry Bird and the super-successful Boston Celtics scored poorly for IPO investors.

One thing seems certain. Electronic entertainment will work new magic in both software and hardware. An easy-to-work VCR would be a starter. And there would be a billion-dollar TV curtain call for a cheap flat-screen receiver. The Japanese, among others, are working on it. They have already bet billions of yen on American entertainment. Sony bought Columbia Pictures and CBS records. Matsushita acquired MCA. And the lovely Pebble Beach resort and golf course was sold to a Tokyo mafia chieftain who planned $750 greens fees before he was ruled out-of-bounds.

The winning Nintendo for the 1990s has not been identified. But TV addicts can put syndicate distributor King World (*Wheel of Fortune, Jeopardy,* and *Oprah*) on their prospect list. Ninja Turtle buffs will like New Line Cinema, an independent producer and distributor of movies and home videos, which carries no debt. Generally, however, investors should beware of Hollywood tinsel except in deep economic troughs. Product is inconsistent, and even pinpointing next year's Academy Award winners won't help much, as Orion Pictures proved. The industry's multiple layers of skimming are just too much.

Gaming remains an obvious growth industry as state after state opts for lotteries, riverboat gambling, dog and horse tracks, and electronic poker. Some say the dice craze will crap out, a victim of overbuilding, but International Game Technology should remain the hardware leader. It is a leading maker of casino gambling machines and is a strong player in casino services.

Circus Circus's themed properties will allow it to continue as a top casino operator. It has avoided the Atlantic City quicksands.

Those who opt for quieter surroundings should check a brochure from the Club Med. Its unique vacation resorts and Asian growth probably deserve some sort of franchise value; there is really no competition for the concept, and the U.S. company, a subsidiary of the original French Club Med, operates 25 distinctive resorts in the United States, Mexico, Asia, and the Indian and Pacific Oceans.

Show biz's shooting stars are quickly come and gone, but their brilliant passages are visible to the amateur eye and their traverses are long enough for mercurial profits.

Predictable Winners: Cheap Stocks

There is no way to guess which stock will prove the greatest bargain at the next bear crisis. But it can be predicted that cheap stocks will achieve the largest percentage gains.

Early on, such issues are mostly the province of small speculators, who find really cheap prices irresistible. Value is no guide to profitable stock selection in the early stages of a bull market. Worthless issues easily outpace blue-chips, and a cheapie with a "story" may perform heroics. These "cats and dogs," as they have been known for decades, are never the best values in the market; they are just the best speculations.

Cheap-stock action after the bear market low of December 1974 illustrates the group's rewards. Over the next six months, 18 of the 20 best performers at the NYSE were stocks which had been under 10 on December 31. The "high-priced" exceptions were Tandy, 12, and Fairchild Camera, 17.

Several of the issues were really cheap—below 2—but 12 were priced between 2 and 10; the best performer in that group was Loral, up 472 percent in the six-month period. Buyers of Loral came out splendidly if they held on. Since 1974, the electronics defense stock has bloomed from a B− rating to A+ and gained a hundredfold. Menasco, a maker of aircraft landing gear, jumped 455 percent in that earlier period. Quality is never the gauge of early bull market success. Of the 20 leaders in the first half of 1975, only one was ranked higher than B by Standard & Poor's.

The cheap performance was brilliant compared with the Dow, up 43 percent. Coca-Cola led the big-cap stocks, up a fat 71 percent in just six months, while IBM became a secondary performer for the first time since the late 1930s, gaining only 24 percent in the first half of 1975.

In the volatile autumn rise of 1982, low-priced technical issues skipped higher, but few outperformed the Detroit phoenix, Chrysler. From a low near 6 in August, it tripled by year-end. The shares had been 3½ earlier in the year.

Still, the new bull market was only a few months old, and in 1983 the performance of low-priced issues was nearly identical with that of 1975. Seventeen of the 20 best percentage gainers at the NYSE had been below 10 when the year started. APL, an obscure purveyor of tissue paper and plastic curtains, was the biggest winner, up 318 percent. Its ascent, it was said, had been encouraged by such market operators as Victor Posner and Ivan Boesky. At the Amex, 19 of the 23 big winners started from a single-digit base; Marshall Industries, a distributor of electronic components, held on for an advance of over 400 percent from a low near 5. Other super rebounders were Gerber Scientific, Wyle Laboratories, and Arkansas Best.

Superior performance for most high-techs in 1983 was blighted by their last-half collapse. Technicom had quadrupled its January low, running to 34 within a few months, but was smashed below 9 by October. Speculative fever is not forever.

Which Cheap Stocks to Buy

Most cheap stocks are outrageously overpriced in terms of value. Which cheapie should you buy? The list of big winners in 1975 offers a few clues. Most had small capitalizations. Of 12 big gainers priced at 2 or higher in December 1974, 10 had less than 5 million shares outstanding; the average was close to 3 million. There was not a huge, cumbersome amount of stock to manipulate.

And the stocks, while low in price, were not dogs. Nine of the issues had posted earnings in 1974, as well as in the two previous years. E-Systems, an electronic defense issue, fell below 8. It was priced at less than four times earnings, with a yield of over 10 percent—rich numbers for a cheap stock. Other issues spurted in anticipation of a return to profitability in 1975. One of them was American Bakers, $3\frac{1}{2}$ in December. It would earn $3.25 in 1975.

Penny stocks and issues bought only because they are cheap-cheap will usually disappoint. Reasonable earnings won't keep a stock from going down, but when perceptions change, they will spur quick recovery. A random survey of 50 stocks which fell below 10 in October 1987 shows that the greatest gainers over the next nine months, issues up threefold or more, all carried reasonable earnings. On the other hand, Coleco, the toy maker, fell from 9 to 4 in October, but with a huge trailing deficit, just kept on sliding, finally dropping below 1.

Buying cheap stocks in periods of great market stress during the 1990s will be a reliable speculative play. They will outleg the blue-chips and whistle up some startling gains. But the player must buy a package, at least four or five. There is no way to prejudge which issue will be the next Loral. Additionally, the cheapies will not be jump-started until speculators sense some stability in quality issues.

Looking for "Hundred Baggers"

Relying on proven, quality market leaders is the most conservative route for crisis investing. Perfect industry selection will improve on such choices and, it is now claimed, will outperform perfect market timing. Imaginative investors should try even harder and search for those issues which have the *potential* of being long-term "hundred baggers," or 100:1 winners. Even if the final reckoning is only 5:1, the investor has made up for the inevitable market dullards we all find ourselves stuck with. A focus on industry selection helps narrow the search for home-run stocks, although many of those issues are quietly unique, as we shall see.

Industry success no longer repeats decade after decade. In the 1950s the rubber issues were the strongest industrial group. Drugs and office equipments led the parade in the 1960s, and the gold-mining issues were tops in the inflation-wracked 1970s, followed in the next decade by a boom in retailing stocks.

Forecasting group strength a decade ahead is impossible. But new leaders will emerge, and they can be spotted by down-home research. It may not be of great help during moments of panic, but there will be other, slower, turning points. Unfortunately, we all tend to make the research task too difficult, dreaming of a high-tech, rocket winner in the field of medicine, biotechnology, or electronics. Home research should concentrate on the ho-hum field of broad consumerism, which is where the big market winners of the past 50 years developed. And we all have Black Belts in consumerism.

Millions of investors have bought a hundred bagger, but no one that we can name predicted such success or held on for the entire trip. Patience was the problem. Most of those winners, like Topsy, just grew and grew, but the process was often slow and unexciting.

We all should give attention to stocks that we think *might* be big winners in the next 5 or 10 years. It's surprising how often such issues manage to double in the first year or 18 months. Such a fast start is a big up on large gains. In the meantime, those dicey speculations bought to make a quick 5 or 10 points—a little vacation or Christmas money—turn into losers.

Patience and common-sense observation, not brilliance, are the keys to selective profits. Since World War II, simplistic market picks have provided the rich rewards. No computer maker or high-tech issue is on the big-winner list for that period.

Exercising Consumer Imagination

Thinking about possible long-term winners is a splendid exercise for consumer imagination, and requires little financial experience. Most of the 100:1 stars since World War II have been generated by uncommonly common household products that we all use on an almost daily basis. We all dream of the next Polaroid or Xerox, but such sensational new technical products are quite rare.

If 100:1 odds seem extreme, broaden the focus to some product where you visualize sales increasing by, say, fivefold over the next few years. The stock price will probably outperform the sales graph. The clue is when most of your neighbors are happy new customers. Let's think of some of the products we might all have guessed were going to have broad sales appeal. There were zippers (yes, that was long ago), Kleenex, processed orange juice, Velcro, Neutragena soap, Scotch tape, to name a few. Certainly no secrets there. The problem for most of us was that we were looking for a marvelous scientific breakthrough, not a 50-fold increase in sales, as happened to Tropicana.

The Making of a Hundred Bagger

The sensational winners of the 1990s and the first 20 years of the next century will be similar to those seen since World War II. They will be issues which make life or work easier, or more fun, or tastier, or more entertaining. Ninety-five percent of these upcoming winners can be discovered by kitchen table research, which is adequate to identify the honest homespun of simple success stories. High-tech is more difficult to understand. And its glitzy *haute couture* frequently lacks staying power.

Often the research involves little more than a simple awareness of those products everyone seems to be using with satisfaction—in the home, the garden, the workplace, or even on the jogging path. The dazzling market stories of the past 40 years have involved products which made one feel better, in the broadest sense of the word. Household brands, seen in every drug chain, supermarket, hardware store, or trendy mall, dominate the listing of 100:1 winners. Their names are promoted in print, on billboards, and over the airwaves every day. No insider cabal hid the success secrets. Only rarely did some radical new technology capture stock market profits equal to those of tire retreader Bandag.

When such potential winners were passed over, it was most often because they seemed unexciting. For years, even conservative investors looked for a little more action than Campbell Soup displayed. But patience did win out. Anyone cruising today's supermarket aisles will observe that on soup row, Campbell cans stretch a quarter-mile, six shelves high, while competing brands are lucky to snare a few feet of display space. Campbell is up over 1300 percent since 1981.

Just who were those get-rich-slowly 100:1 winners during the mid-century years? Not long ago, faced with a long plane trip to the Pacific Northwest, we packed a few dog-eared Standard & Poor's stock guides and spent the flying time tabulating the 100:1 advances recorded between the 1940s and 1973. In that period the Dow advanced by a factor 11.4×. A hundred bagger was a true "10."

About 250 names crowd the list of blue-chip performers. Many were so commonplace that one failed to think of the product in stock market terms.

Every mother is acquainted with the convenience of Gerber Products's baby foods. We wonder how many bought the stock, with which $5000 mushroomed into $530,000 in about 30 years? My excuse is that one of the kids eternally gooped the Gerber veggies all over me.

Household Names

Scores of everyday household names crowd the honors list. Basement names such as Black & Decker, Skil Corp., Maytag, and Whirlpool. Bathroom-cabinet names such as Gillette, Tampax, Noxell, and Johnson & Johnson. Parlor entertainment names such as Magnavox, Sony, and Zenith. Kitchen names such as Carnation Milk, Oscar Meyer, and Interstate Brands. Home desk convenience entries such as Minnesota Mining & Mfg. (Scotch tape) and Dennison (tags and labels). Thirst quenchers such as Pepsi, Royal Crown, and Bud.

Famous cosmetics makers dot the list as do multiple names in air conditioning, where sales exploded after World War II. Vacation and business flights brought millions of Americans into contact with such successful airlines as American, Delta, and Northwest, while plane builders Boeing and McDonnell prospered along with successful private-plane makers Beech and Cessna. All joined the 100:1 pie-in-the-sky club.

Hotelier Holiday Inns, known to every highway traveler, made the list, along with veteran retailers Gimbel Brothers and Lord & Taylor. Every investor knew these names, for their success was evident to all. Even a few railroads and meatpackers, survivors of a century of market wars, were in the peerage, along with popular names from the mobile-home, auto-parts, and greeting-card industries. Oil stocks were most numerous in the group listings. No special technical nor market knowledge was needed to identify any of the stocks.

But if the dazzling stock winners of the mid-century were household names, what about the later decades of this century? Did the high-tech names, given so much hype and brokerage-house attention, dominate the winners' list?

Sadly, they only made the list of also-rans. The leaders after 1970 include names like Wal-Mart, Prime Motor Inns (later a cropper), Rite Aid, and Dean Foods. Between 1971 and the end of 1990, it was Boeing—not IBM, Merck, or MMM—that was the biggest gainer among the Dow stocks. In the 1980s, yuppie retailers, not software makers, dominated the list of best-performing stocks. Neutragena's clear soap became a must in the ladies' personal-care section and made it an outstanding percentage leader. All-Americans such as Alberto Culver, Giant Food, Helene Curtis, McDonald's, Philip Morris, and Sara Lee did splendidly.

Faucet maker Masco and craft and electronics retailer Tandy were among the stock bonanzas in the 1960–1990 period, although both were poorly rated, single-digit stocks during Ike's final year as President.

The growth of television advertising has enormously escalated the branding of America, and the richest promise for the 1990s lies in those areas which can be easily identified by any amateur investor. Personal care, health items, creature comfort, convenience (in the store, workplace, or home), food and drink, leisure products—all have produced archival winners over the past century. Borden, Butterick, and Bigelow, along with Sears, Levi Strauss, Singer, and Wrigley, are trade names that have endured since the 1800s.

Such plebian success stories will be repeated. No one can predict the next 100:1 winner, but the future honors list will surely be made up of companies and products whose probability of patient success is as patent as those kitchen-table research winners of the past. If you just have to own General Motors or some other white-beard, balance the portfolio with an innovative company which might advance five- or 10-fold. Who knows, it might turn into a real winner.

"Eurekas"

Personal "eurekas," sudden insights into pockets of market significance, have hit us all. Interpreting or understanding the possible financial impact of such revelations is a matter of common sense and keen observation, not market mastery.

In the winter of 1969–1970, while driving to California, we noticed a large number of motor homes headed west. Judging by their Midwestern license plates, they appeared to be "snow birds," fleeing the arctic blasts of their native farmlands for the warm deserts of Arizona and California. The majority had a huge logo, a flying "W," emblazoned on their side.

Curiosity grew, and at a giant crossroads service station, obviously favored by the cumbersome vehicles, we asked a driver what the "W" signified. "Winnebago," he replied, "Cadillac of the RVs."

RVs? And so we got a brief lecture on recreational vehicles. Such diligent home—or rather, highway—research paid off. Upon returning from California, we bought the stock of the Forest City, Iowa, RV manufacturer, and it quickly doubled. We were even quicker, however, having sold out for a 50 percent profit a few months before the doubling ceremony. Those were perilous times in the market, or so it seemed, but not for even modestly more patient Winnebago stockholders, who saw the shares advance from an adjusted low of $2\frac{1}{2}$ in 1970 to a 1972 high at 49.

At the end of 1979, we had to look no further than the breakfast table to spot a tasty new Christmas treat, the jam-and-jelly delights of J. M. Smucker, then selling near 21 and at about seven times earnings. The firm boasted a dividend record going back to 1949 and owned a nice solid, homey address—Strawberry Lane in Orrville, Ohio. It seemed a fine recommendation for a food firm which had enough Smuckers on the board to encourage a meeting in the old family homestead. Although the product was far afield from the silver collapse of 1980, that event dropped the Smucker's stock to 17, about five times 1980 earnings. In 1991, Smucker shares were trading over 600 (before adjustment). By that time the stock was widely esteemed, at 36 times earnings, and didn't seem quite as tasty.

Every investor has experienced such precious insights into relatively unexploited market opportunities. Such amateur reckonings of taste are usually more reliable than reams of brokerage-house pulp, as they inspire more faith. But the reckoner must guard against those personal prejudices that can warp financial judgment.

Slam Dunk Inventions

Potential hundred baggers are most seductive in the field of invention and technological progress. We all dream of getting in on the ground floor of some "slam dunk" invention. The wheel would have been fine, but even now it is not too late for some recent inventions. The results of revolutionary patents have always been evolutionary in pace. Even the most dazzling inventions have required more capital, more management, more time, and more marketing than the patent genius or early investors ever expected.

Panic and bear markets have provided ample opportunities for bargain investments in new inventions. Ground-floor opportunities, almost alongside the original partners, have been available. The kitchen-table investor will have adequate time to judge those revolutionary inventions which seem to promise to open the door to stock market riches. Progress from the garage laboratory to the marketplace has always been maddeningly slow.

In the past, the rewards have been substantial. Consider the out-sized returns from the telegraph, zipper, gramophone, vacuum clean-er, ballpoint pen, canned milk, the sewing machine, cash register, and safety razor. Not to mention photography, talking pictures, tele-phones, and television. All yielded riches, and their secrets were easily deciphered. We'll exclude the mysterious world of computers and software as being beyond the reach of the kitchen table.

There have been dozens of inventive financial slam dunks which should have made observers wealthy. They required no technical expertise and only a little imagination. There will be more in the future.

Where will they come from, these new Polaroids? Probably from improvements, shortcuts, or cost-cutting developments in processes already at hand. A cheaper desalinization technique for sea water has an unlimited, worldwide potential. Maybe a young Tom Edison can devise a magic new battery to make the electric car a complete auto. Or what about really cheap solar panels to harness the sun's energy? Tokyo's Sango Electric has developed 54-square-foot solar panels to provide air conditioning.

Perhaps one of the enduring hoaxes of the automotive age—a carbu-retor purported to mix air and water into fuel—will come to be. (According to legend, the giant oil companies bought up and destroyed the patents and models.) Whenever the great discovery, the wizardry will not go from drawing board to working model to patent to manufacture to market without many problems and doubters. Investors will have ample time to appraise and act.

Here are a few former inventive "locks" of Guiness proportions to serve as models in your search for an invention of Ben Gump signifi-cance. They possess one common denominator: Recognition and understanding of the invention's impact took several years to develop but required no technical expertise. The early financial history of these classic discoveries displays, in every case, a dismal public market for shares, which traded at what would turn out to be extraordinarily low prices.

U.S. Patent No. 174,465 the "Most Valuable of All Time."
Alexander Graham Bell's telephone patent, No. 174,465, issued in 1876, has been termed the "most valuable of all time." Its value was not imme-diately apparent. The instruments were often seen as toys, and it took several years of financial and technical struggle before telephony swept the nation. Shares in the initial endeavor traded for a few dollars, and early investors were constantly importuned for additional funds.

Good reception was a major technical problem. Additionally, Western Union, with its nationwide wire system, had mounted an aggressive telephone effort of its own and was challenging Bell's patent in extensive litigation. In 1879, after some restructuring, the National Bell Telephone company was formed. Founders' shares were exchanged for the new stock, and the public was solicited for the purchase of 2000 additional shares. Early buyers paid $50, although that sum cannot be correlated with earlier values.

Legal fortune shone, and as rumors spread of a patent settlement with Western Union, the National shares rocketed from 50 to 1000 within eight months. Along the way, the 2000 shares were disposed of at an average price of $215. In 1880, a new entity—American Bell Telephone—exchanged six shares of its $100-par stock for each unit of National; this fixed the per-share basis of the average ($215)–priced shares at $36. Those who had bought early in 1879 at $50 had a cost basis of just over $8.

The telephone was certainly a "slam dunk" invention, but as with every other inventive winner, the first few years were rough, but full of opportunity for those who would listen. By 1899 the new stock had risen as high as 386, when it would be split into two shares of a new phone company called American Telephone & Telegraph. Along the way, dividends of between 15 and 18 percent had been paid. Additionally there had been valuable rights offerings to buy stock at par, always a huge discount, which had kept Victorian believers in Patent No. 174,465 richly happy.

The Right Name at the Right Time. Radio Corporation of America (RCA) was given the perfect name to capitalize on the radio boom of the 1920s. Formed in 1919 to purchase the American Marconi wireless firm, it had a blue-chip list of controlling stockholders—General Electric, AT&T, and United Fruit—and a vault full of valuable patents. The importance of the wireless telegraph business would shrink rapidly.

RCA's fortunes were quickly wired to radio when Westinghouse's shade-tree broadcast operations began in 1920. Within a year, the Pittsburgh firm was among the "controlling persons."

Radio became the home-entertainment darling of the decade, quickly knocking out the phonograph. The investment potential was there for all who would listen. Everyone was buying an RCA Radiola, or one of its competitors. The neighbors, the brother-in-law, even the kid across the street with a crystal set, were all ecstatic over a device which could bring entertainment—baseball, comedians, preachers, even politicians—into every room of the house.

But despite RCA's strong patent position, stock gains were slow. In 1924, a reverse split boosted price, but doubters and broad competition braked the advance. In early 1926, a bear attack drove the stock down from 77 to 32, and the shares lost one-third of their value in a slump about one year later. But "General" David Sarnoff was building an entertainment complex. He gathered in the dominant phonograph and record company—the Victor Talking Machine and its famous fox terrier logo—connived with Joe Kennedy to put together RKO Pictures, added Rudy Vallee to his star list, and made NBC the leading force in broadcasting.

All of this helped glamorize the company's image, which had suffered early on because the company was basically a licenser of radio patent rights and a distributor of RCA receivers made by parents General Electric and Westinghouse. Twenty-five percent of industry set sales was about tops. But revenues were growing enormously, as was the price of the stock. Gross income of $4 million in 1921 rose 45-fold, to $182 million, in 1929; it was a genuine, early growth stock. Industrywide, annual production of receivers increased from 100,000 to nearly 5 million.

It was a story everyone should have believed. The shares, 1½ in 1921 (before the 1:5 reverse split) hit 574 in 1929, encouraged by some wonderful pool manipulations by Mike Meehan, the NYSE specialist. Those who had fallen in love with radioland in the early 1920s had a fortune-making opportunity. Those who tuned in late, in 1929, would wait until 1965 to get even.

Instant Photography.   "Awful" was a common reaction to the first instant photography system, offered by Polaroid to the public in early 1949. The pictures were sepia-drab, and the camera cost $89.75, a pricey figure for a novelty.

Inventor Edwin B. Land had originally (1937) seen Polaroid's future as an auto supplier, providing polarizing sheets for headlights and windshields, but Detroit didn't cooperate and sunglasses were the firms's most widely admired product after World War II. In 1947, total revenues amounted to only $1.5 million.

Introduction of the camera in 1949 quadrupled sales, and in 1950 a new black-and-white film broadened its appeal. Although sales gained 300 percent by 1953, the slam dunk product didn't immediately make Polaroid a slam dunk stock. The shares remained cheap, for although Polaroid had a strong patent position, the market anticipated a competitive response by Eastman Kodak.

Despite its great novelty and publicity, the stock sold as low as 13 in the year of its introduction and again in 1951, when earnings were $1.64. For anyone who believed, the stock was a rare bargain at such a commonplace multiple. The $13 shares of 1950 would be worth $2,358 at the 1960 high, and would quadruple again during the 1960s as the firm's revenues climbed to nearly $500 million.

The most deliberate decision maker had plenty of time to get the Polaroid picture.

The Death of Carbon Paper. The real-time superiority of some new inventions is not always as self-evident as in hindsight. But the merits of Xerography were apparent very early. Within a few dozen months in the early 1960s, a small and awkwardly named company—Haloid-Xerox—relegated carbon paper and mimeograph machines to the list of endangered species.

The magnitude of the paperwork explosion and the legendary success of the copy machine could not have been accurately forecast in 1960. But in that year E. F. Hutton did prepare a convincing report on the future of Xerography. Did we go for the slam dunk? No.

Why? Well, the 1960 market was in a nasty slump, and by early autumn was 17 percent below the January high. But Xerox, trading near 60, had doubled the closing 1959 closing level and was selling at about 85 times earnings. In those days such an evaluation required enormous faith. Only a year earlier, the shares had traded at 21, though the Dow was considerably higher. The stock was up nearly sevenfold from its 1957 low.

By late 1961 Xerox had climbed to 172 before the Kennedy panic gave a second opportunity for what would turn out to be an easy lay-up. The shares suffered a severe drop, to 89. That still left them at 64 times earnings, a higher trough multiple than IBM's. It was a panic opportunity, for by 1962, the revolutionary coup in office procedures was proven and the Xerox trade name had been verbalized. Everyone who had ever fussed with two sheets of carbon paper or cranked a mimeograph machine loved instant copies.

True believers were richly rewarded. Unadjusted earnings climbed from 67 cents in 1960 to over $47 in 1972 as the shares rose to the equivalent of 2578. It was just that the Xerox slam dunk always seemed so expensive; the IBM miracle had proven the riches to be had from leasing expensive, efficient office equipment. Remembering the magic of IBM, the institutions were not about to pass up another such opportunity. Individual investors tended to balk, appalled by the high P–E ratio, runaway advance, and lofty price level.

Avoiding "Yesterday's Darlings"

The most seductive stocks in bear sequences are "yesterday's dar-lings," the big winners from the previous bull market. Their charms are not easily forgotten, and the discounted prices are hard to resist.

Such stocks make money when the market reverses, but they never duplicate their original success. The game is over. The market demands new leaders, stocks which can be easily advanced. Last year's favorites are loaded with losers only too happy to get out about even. Their advance has to fight through a deck of resting orders from the lambs who bought the stock at 60, 50, 40, and 35. Why bull a stock that everyone wants to sell?

One of the early speculative frenzies of this century involved the copper stocks. The immense growth in electric demand seemed to threaten a shortage of the metal, and manipulations ballooned the price of both copper shares and ingots. Anaconda gained 400 percent in the 1903–1906 advance; Calumet & Hecla was boosted from 400 to 1000. It all came to a head in 1907, when failed speculations fueled the autumn panic. Hecla was smashed down to 535, and Anaconda fell from 76 to 25. The copper mania had sown its own destructive seeds in new mines and new technologies, and romance had fled. Steels would lead the new bull market and boosted the popular Canadian, Dominion Iron, from 13 to 73. Anaconda had difficulty recovering over 50, and Hecla's peak was only 685.

The oil stocks were the inflation darlings of 1919, but they had spent their speculative favors. They were relatively poor performers in the 1920s though part of the coolness was caused by multiple new crude discoveries, from Iraq to Signal Hill to the political thievery at Teapot Dome. Jersey Standard's 1921–1929 gain was only 240 percent, half that of the Dow. Many oils tapped their highs in 1927, and domestic crude prices in 1929 were only half the levels of 1920.

Radio Corporation remains a symbol of the wild speculations of the 1920s, but it lacked much spark for the recovery, which started in 1932. Philip Morris, Western Auto, Coca-Cola, and—thanks to the repeal of Prohibition—the bottle and cap companies were the mar-ket's new darlings.

"Go-go" stocks and the conglomerates never recovered their ill-deserved popularity of the late 1960s, and the glamour sizzlers of 1972 lagged in the next two bull sequences. Despite an unblemished record of higher earnings and dividends, Disney at its 1981 bull market high was at only half the price witnessed in 1972.

The lust for high-techs spurred hot performance in 1983. Wall Street sated it with a record level of IPOs, about 10 times that of 1982. Before long, a sector panic seized the market and the scorching electronic and communication stocks collapsed. The game was over; most had already witnessed their high for the decade. Among them were such wonderfully named issues as Anacomp, Analogic, Helionetics, Kratos, Mitel, Tektronix, Tridex, and ZyMos.

When shopping for bargains in the next bear market, avoid the temptation to buy name-a-likes, such as Xebec, Xicor, and Xidex, other tech fizzlers of the mid-1980s.

The Rap on the Utilities

There was a time when panic investors scored larger gains in the Utilities than in the Dow. While their 1930s record was sporadic, after the World War II low of 1942 the Utilities ran up 87 percent within a year, nearly double the advance by the Dow. Until the early 1960s, the Utilities gain regularly equaled or exceeded that of the DJIA at the three-, six-, and 12-month intervals following a bear trough. Since then, high interest rates, tough statehouse regulators, and flawed nuclear construction have inhibited advances. Although interest rates have melted, the record indicates that utility stocks should be avoided by aggressive bargain hunters for three reasons.

1. Pricing and earning ability will remain regulated.

2. Consensus thinking is that the Utilities offer superior resistance to market declines. Actually, their performance since World War II has been only minimally better than that of the Industrials. They no longer offer the defensive characteristics associated with them in the public mind.

3. Quality for the group is far below what it once was.

Where yield is the major goal, however, investors will do splendidly. Returns are often double that of industrial issues of similar quality. But investors and speculators seeking the large rewards which should accompany the risks of crisis buying should avoid the utilities.

Every major decline since 1966 has been followed by superior gains for the Industrials as compared with the Utility average. And contrary to boardroom thinking, utilities have not displayed outstanding defensive ability. Since the end of World War II, ten major declines have cut the DJIA by an average of 28.3 percent. In the paired episodes, the Utilities lost 26.7, an unimpressive benefit in view of the limited rebounding opportunities in the gas and electric stocks.

Only in the 1981–1982 bear sequence did the Dow Utility average show great defensive strength, but then its yield often reached 11 percent. On the other hand, the depression of the mid-1970s hit the group with a loss of 55 percent compared with the Dow's drop of 45 percent.

Utilities' defense luster has been weakened because quality has eroded. In 1970, 10 of the 15 members were rated A+ or A by Standard & Poor's; the other five were given an A−. In 1993, there were no A+s and only seven A/A− ratings, but there were eight B+/B listings. Even since 1988, quality has fallen. Ten Dow Utility stocks were ranked lower in 1993 than they had been at the end of 1988.

Dividend lovers should opt for the utilities, and will enjoy the total returns. But the issues should be avoided by those seeking solid upside gains from days of perilous pricing. The defensive characteristics of the utility stocks have not balanced out their lack of up-side potential since 1966. Their rationale is high yield, not high yield *and* safety.

Defensive Stocks Lag during Recoveries

We have mentioned many safe industries in which the investor can bargain-hunt during bad times. Some of the groups mentioned, however are doomed to less-than-extraordinary gains in the new upswing. Industries which use up their strength in resisting panic and recession are never the strongest rebounders.

Foods, tobaccos, soft drinks, chemicals, and brewers are examples of industries with proven recession-resistance. Consequently, they seldom reach the deep-discount bargain table.

Such defensive issues can be blindly recommended as a safe play during black economic times, but the issues should be avoided by those seeking the largest return of capital in the upswing. The powerful cyclicals—industries such as machine tools, steels, autos, coppers, and railroads—will lead the reflex parade. Of course, they offer more risk if timing is bad. Joining them will be the popular consumer issues—home furnishings, appliances, and the like. Stocks in the consumer groups are typically among the hardest hit in bear markets, but their reflex strength is remarkable. Airlines also have a superior rebounding record.

Prospects for increased travel and consumer credit-card use helped American Express climb from 35 to nearly 100 (unadjusted) between the summer of 1982 and 1983. American Brands also has a broad consumer base, but tobacco sales are relatively immune to recession, and its share price was only slightly bruised during the 1981–1982 recession. The stock touched 37 in August 1982, but its advance into the next summer was "only" to 55.

On those rare occasions when the defensive stocks are bombed during a bear sequence, they do offer excellent opportunities. General Mills, for example, was a 66–28 loser within about 14 months in 1973–1974 but responded by vaulting up to 68 by January 1976. It was a volatile recovery for a top-rated defensive stock, but the stock had been badly oversold. In 1982 General Mills had actually advanced during a down market, and its gain from the bear market low of August to the best level of 1983, 39 to 58, was less spectacular, though certainly pleasing to a conservative investor.

In the meantime, however, a depressed railroad such as the Burlington Northern was showcasing the rewards of the cylical stocks, as it more than tripled, from 17 to 55.

Investment goals and temperament will determine which types of stocks the individual investor will chance during stormy days.

Shoot from the Hip during Panic

Unlike the often deliberate turn of a bear market, which at the very least gives the investor several weeks to analyze bargain values, a panic has come and gone before you can get some information mailed from your broker. Speculators have no difficulty with such situations; they are mercurial in their temperament and decisions. Investors are handicapped by slow reaction time.

It takes more courage than money at such moments, for prices are slashed mercilessly. And it takes quick reflexes rather than judgment. The buyer can only snap off a hipshot at the market; there is no time to eye the windage.

Panic does create bargain pricing, however, and investors should take advantage of the situation. By definition, they are not money-locked by margin calls and can make rational judgments. Many investors will just sit out the storm, of course. "I'll wait until things quiet down a bit," is a common response to a broker's call. Waiting out the storm is OK; selling will prove a disaster; buying is always profitable. When sellers offered 608 million shares on October 19, 1987, there was a buyer for every share—though only at distress prices. Basically, the sellers were all wrong and the buyers enjoyed perfect timing.

If there is uncertainty about what to buy, draft the "best athlete," as discussed earlier. Failing that, swing on some familiar favorite—a stock which has made money for you in times past. It may not be the best buy, but it's easy to pull the trigger. One has a sense for its bedrock value. Estimating future fundamentals for some recent hot issue is impossible.

Quality is essential. It's just too difficult for the average investor to pull the trigger on a cheap speculative stock when the market is falling out of bed, the tape is late, and the doom-sayers are predicting a new "killer wave."

Are the hipshots worth it? Absolutely. Hand-picking will prove up some unbelievable figures, so we have selected a commonplace choice, a stock that has represented conservative value for over a century— Standard Oil of New Jersey. It has never been the nation's largest corporation, and its credit rating isn't what it once was. But aside from faulty navigation, it has made few mistakes. Everyone knows Exxon, if only because they buy gasoline at its corner service station. It is the very type of stock which the investor will chance under storm conditions.

The figures below capsule Jersey's reflex gains after serious panics to the best available price within three, six, and 12 months following the low date. The gains are measured from nine panic lows—in 1946, 1950, 1957, 1962, 1970, 1974, 1980, 1987, and 1990.

Exxon's Average Gain after Panic

3 months	6 months	12 months
+21%	+ 34%	+ 53%
Range: + 2% to + 38%	Range: + 10% to + 58%	Range: + 18% to + 100%

The stock's greatest one-year advance came after the Korean crisis of 1950; the stock doubled, from 35 to 70. Its most disappointing performance was in 1957–1958, when the oils were struggling against eroding crude prices and an extended group bear market, which lasted until 1960.

Many stocks have regularly outperformed Exxon, but few with such impeccable and long-term references could have been chosen. General Electric has also proven a reliable refuge but has provided smaller profits since World War II. A comparison with the Dow Industrials shows a superior reflex performance by Exxon, its performance lagging only in the sequence following the 1957 crisis. There is no meaningful figure for average-quality recovery from panic, but the figures for Exxon seem fair, for the shares have been regarded as a blue-chip investment for all of this century.

Opting for
Dividends

Dividends are not all bad, as some avant-garde thinkers argue. They will finally bumper careening stocks in a bad market and don't hurt in a good market. They are real and believable. Dividends you can take to the bank.

Earnings, on the other hand, are ethereal. They are adjusted by footnotes, mirrors, fraud, and chicanery. Books are cooked and massaged. Auditors look the other way, or perhaps they are just careless. Occasionally, they are honestly deceived.

Fifty years ago, the first question a stock buyer asked was, "What does it pay?" No longer. What everyone wants now is a "good stock"— that is, one that will go up. If it pays a dividend, that's a plus, but yield is pretty much ignored. It has been proven that high dividends, even rising dividends, don't guarantee a rising stock. But a fat payout is a nice perk. Nice guys often win, and dividends don't hurt a stock.

We resurrected from the files a 1980 table of stocks that had paid continuous dividends through the two depressions of the 1930s, World War II, a half-dozen subsequent recessions, and the Watergate bear market. Ignoring the financial and utility entries, the list pretty much foretold the big, solid winners of the 1980s. Largely unknown retailers, such as Circuit City Stores, were the skyrocket gainers of the 1980s, but they were rank speculations at the end of 1979. The Gap was not rated by S&P.

On the other hand, highly rated Abbott Laboratories, which had paid dividends regularly since 1926, was an easy choice for conservative investors. Its gain in the 1980s was more than sixfold, a pace matched by the dividend appreciation. And its climb continued in the 1990s. Each succeeding market decline has found Abbott's drop bumpered by a higher payout.

Long dividend traditions are built on a foundation of earnings, and any company that has rewarded stockholders for the past 70 to 100 years has been doing things right. Further, it will probably continue to do so, though a few will stumble, as did storied International Harvester (Navistar). Its dividend history stretching back to 1910 went down the tube in 1982.

Another dividend perk besides the comfort of an immediate return is the knowledge that such solid properties are often coveted by their peers. Strong balance sheets, high cash flows, and understated asset values are typical. At the end of 1979, one could find nearly two dozen dividend veterans under the "As." Four of them were utilities, such as Atlantic City Electric. Of the remaining 18 industrials, one-third were merged out during the decade. Included were such diverse names as American Natural Resources, American Sterilizer, American District Telegraph (protection services), and Anchor Hocking.

Peace of mind comes with owning a prize property and is a secondary benefit of such dividend veterans. They don't usually turn into "worry" stocks.

Most investors can name a score of blue-chip payers. There are few sleepers in such a list, but other veterans are less than household names and also less than A rated. The Brown Group (Buster Brown shoes, among others), Carpenter Technology (high-grade steel), Eaton Corp., Enserch, Harland (bank checks), Nalco Chemical, Springs Industries, and Westvaco (papers) are among the long-term dividend payers.

Grasping the Nettle

Buying yesterday's darlings is the worst strategy when a *bear* sequence reverses. Buying *panic's* most victimized stocks provides a reliable rebound, even when the crisis reflex will be followed later by a resumption of the down move. Speculators often seek the worst "hurts," looking for ultraswift profits rather than the comparative safety of an Exxon. Profits can be quite splendid, but they should be, given the crisis conditions.

The Silver Panic of 1980 was a secondary correction of the ragged advance which had begun two years earlier. The upward course had been marked by minor October panics in 1978 and 1979, and repeatedly faulted by normally conservative commentators, who recklessly predicted a Dow collapse to the 400 level. Possibly it was the long gas lines that made them so testy.

In late January the London fixing for gold had peaked at $850 an ounce, and the price of silver, levered by the Dallas billionaire's corner, had reached $52. Insider knavery at the commodity exchange promoted some rule changes, and Nelson Bunker Hunt and friends found themselves at the mercy of the silver establishment. Prices for the precious collapsed overnight, and by late March gold was below

$500 and silver near $10, having lost 80 percent of its value within weeks.

A billion dollars in margin calls were said to be out on the Street, and trading in the shares of Hunt's principal broker, Bache, was suspended by the SEC. Stocks were sacrificed to meet bullion margin calls, and the entire list was hard hit; the climax came on March 27, when 64 million shares traded. Up to 1980, there had been only two days in the history of the Exchange when volume exceeded that figure.

Understandably, the most prominent victims were the mining shares. Within nine trading days, Hecla, the veteran Idaho silver miner, was halved, falling below 25. Dome Mines was driven down from 89 to 48. Asarco was blind-sided in a drop from 59 to 26. Every stock with a speculative flavor was dragged down, even if innocent of "diggin's."

A month of market indecision was followed by a revival of confidence, spurred by declining interest rates. The mining camps, it turned out, were in full operation; precious prices, even at the March lows, had never been as high prior to the previous winter. The battered victims provided some astounding gains. Dome led the way with a sprint from 48 to 132, but Asarco, Hecla, and Homestake easily doubled. ASA, the South African investment trust, leaped from 36 to 91 within about six months. Disbelief about bullion prices had made it an easy reversal. Most of the mining shares traded close to their March lows for several weeks, and contrarians uncovered many bonanzas.

A Superior Reflex in 1929

In the 1929 panic, Auburn Motors went into high-speed reverse, falling from 514 to 120. Mellon's Aluminum Co. was smashed from 540 to 180. Those were not only big dollar numbers, never so swiftly matched before or since, but appalling percentage figures. The reflex was astounding. Auburn, a speculative sensation because of its new front-wheel drive, made its low in October and then doubled to 255 within two days. Alcoa's low came with that of the Dow on November 13; it would bounce over 300 by December and reach 346 in the spring. Such battered panic victims always enjoy a superior reflex.

Such extreme volatiles were dealt in by only the most aggressive risk takers. The average speculator is not interested in stocks that trade only a few hundred shares a day. Far better to try something like AT&T. Its shares, 310 in late September, fell to 197 in October, but rebounded to 248 in the following month, a rich reward for a blue-chip, even in 1929.

It was all part of the biggest bear market rally in history, but lesser rebounds have also given dramatic rewards for those willing to grasp the nettle. When England left the gold standard in September 1931, panic seized the world markets. Most European bourses closed, and at New York the Dow would lose 38 percent in 27 trading days; the loss was greater than that of August–October 1987. The carnage was so severe that the Exchange banned short sales for a few days.

Among the principal victims were such volatile issues as American Smelting and Deere & Co., the farm equipment maker. Smelting fell to 20, but would recover to 36 by early November. Deere soared from 9 to nearly 23 in the same period. This violent, short-lived rally was typical of the 1930s. Both the Dow and most stocks, including Smelting, would record a new low before Christmas. Deere was not far behind.

Collapsing Industrial Demand
Causes "Roosevelt Depression"

The swiftest production collapse of the century occurred in 1937, not 1930. The "Roosevelt Depression" shattered a lot of New Deal theories. Within a few autumn months the demand for steel, autos, and other smokestack wares evaporated. Never had business turned so bad so fast. In May, steel production was over 5 million tons. In December it was 1.8 million tons. Automobile showrooms were suddenly empty, and Detroit's passenger car production in the first quarter of 1938 was down 50 percent from 1937, the worst year-to-year decline in peacetime history.

The stock market, which had struggled up to Dow 190 in August, only four points below the year's high, took a Brodie on September 1, leaving an ominous gap. The fall crash, down 40 percent, fell short of the 1929 damage, but was worse than that of 1987. Steels were ravaged, losing from half to two-thirds of their value within two months.

Unemployment increased by 2 million, and domestic worries were exacerbated by Japan's war on China and a collapse at the London Stock Exchange. No year since has recorded a Dow loss approaching that of 1937.

Stout-hearted traders who faded the panic had an opportunity for reasonable profits. United Aircraft, 10 in October, traded over 22 in December. Republic Steel, having dived from 40 to 12, rallied to 20. It was just a bear market rally, however, and only rewarded the nimble. Memories of 1930–1932's enduring collapse chilled courage.

In March, Hitler's war threat drove the Dow below 100, the average having lost 49 percent of its value in 12 months. It was a surprise bear attack, coming just as the nation seemed on its way back to normalcy. Within 12 months, the Nickel Plate, which had taken five years to steam from 2 to 72, was crushed to 7. Crown Cork & Seal, the Prohibition-repeal favorite, had run from 8 to 101. It was smashed to 22 and would not equal its 1937 price for decades. Still, panic pricing allowed it to double within the calendar year, and the Van Sweringens' former railroad toy would romp to 26.

For those who grasped the nettle in the face of a doubly inspired panic—by industrial collapse and the threat of war—the profits would be easy and quick on the way to the Munich high, which came in the autumn. But new faces would lead the steep upswing, which marched the Dow up by 60 percent in seven months. Heavy industry was forgotten. The steels, motors, and rails lagged severely in the rally to autumn's Munich peace peak. The Atchison's 1938 top was less than half that of 1937, even though it doubled from 22 to 44 in the brief bull sequence. McIntyre Porcupine, the Canadian gold, and Homestake were back in style, but could not match the new glamours, the aircraft manufacturers.

Aviation buffs got a lift when Howard Hughes circled the globe in a Lockheed Lodestar; defense needs also encouraged strength in the aircraft stocks. United Aircraft reached 43, up fourfold in just a year. Bendix tripled the spring's low price.

The 1937–1938 decline, like all the market adventures of the decade, was lethal. There was only a two-month breathing space between the low of November and the collapse of the following winter. The one-year ordeal was a straightforward, old-fashioned crisis caused by black economic statistics which developed with chilling swiftness.

Dunkerque Panic Discounted
Black War News

Dunkerque, not Pearl Harbor, dealt the American stock market its most brutal blow of World War II. The Dow's decline in 10 trading days was 23 percent, the most intense slippage between 1933 and 1987. The Dow Rails fell by 29 percent.

Dunkerque was an epochal event, a trigger for both the market and history. Blitzkrieg and the evacuation of the beaches changed the course of World War II and threatened the survival of Britain. Not for four years, until D Day, June 1944, would the Allies return to France in numbers. And not until January 1945 would the market rise decisively above its level of early May 1940. Despite the enormous implications of the evacuation of Allied troops from the Continent, it was a time to grasp the nettle. The black war news, as then understood, was already discounted by panic.

Until the second week of May 1940, World War II was often labeled the "phony war." Hitler had invaded Poland in September 1939, but that one-sided contest, which forced both England and France to arms, was quickly done. France's military might snoozed behind the Maginot line, for Blitzkrieg had become Sitzkrieg.

On May 9, the eve of the German assault across the Lowland countries, the Dow was at 148, about the middle of a long line formation, as can be seen in Fig. 9-1. The Nazis struck suddenly, and within two weeks their Stukas and Panzers had driven almost to the Straits of Dover, pinning down the Allied troops on the beaches around Dunkerque. On May 24, at Dow 114, the market climaxed its vertical fall, trading nearly 4 million shares. That volume was the largest of the decade at the NYSE. Bear rumors that the Exchange would close had abetted the destruction. In a miracle of sorts, Hitler delayed further assault and a motley British fleet evacuated nearly 350,000 soldiers in the period from May 26 to June 3.

The Dow loss was severe, but the damage to individual issues was worse. Many were convulsed from the year's high to the year's low within two or three weeks. General Motors was driven down from 56 to 37, and lesser issues lost 50 percent of their value. American Hawaiian Steamship was torpedoed, 51 to 23. The news did not improve. Paris surrendered on June 14, and convoy losses to U-boats mounted. In August, Britain was besieged from the skies. But the market had already discounted the summer's frightful news, and even a possible invasion of England, widely anticipated for September. Despite massive selling of requisitioned American securities by the Bank of England, the Dow inched back. Chrysler, 54 at the May low, reached 88 before Thanksgiving. The major steels, led by U.S. Steel, made new highs, along with such diverse issues as the C&O, Macy, and Timken Roller Bearing. Bucyrus-Erie and Transcontinental & Western Airlines (TWA) doubled their lowest prices.

War and history were changed by the events of Dunkerque, the panic's trigger event. But the rewards of buying in a vacuum had again been proven. Those who chanced the rails did tremendously well, for the Dunkerque smash pushed them to their lowest level of the war years. Their action was superior to that of the Industrials, which made a new low four months after Pearl Harbor. Southern Pacific, at 7, rose to 70 by 1946.

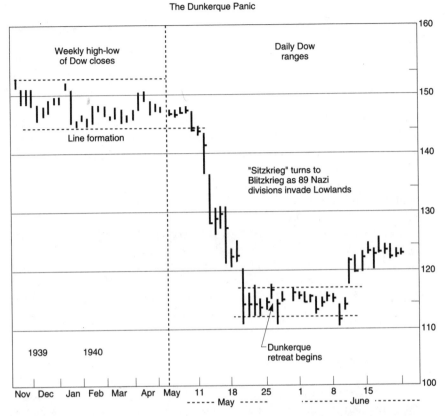

The Dunkerque Panic

Figure 9-1. Line formations mirror those unique market periods when buying and selling are in almost perfect balance. Typically, the Dow moves horizontally within a 5 percent range (from the mean figure) over a period of several weeks or several months. Generally, such movements are part of a consolidation formation. In 1940, however, two well-formed line formations reversed the market. Consider the top consolidation. We can find no other period when the Dow moved sideways for such an extended period. Actually, the consolidation had begun earlier than is shown on the chart, at the market peak of September. And the bottom reversal, which lasted from May 21 to June 12, was unique for its extremely tight range.

1946–1949: Waiting for the "Inevitable" Postwar Depression

The postwar crash of 1946, like that of 1937, got its start during Labor Day week, and the rout was later aggravated by the collapse of the Jordan cotton corner. It was the most intense decline of the years between 1940 and 1962 and followed hard on the ominous

May/August double top and a Dow theory sell signal. The worst was over by late September, although the Industrials hit a new low on October 9.

The official bear sequence did not end until 1949, but the market was mostly involved in a long consolidation movement, with key lows at 163.12, 163.21, and 161.60 spread over 32 months. It was a rare triple bottom.

Despite the long frustration which lay ahead, most stocks were well bought during the September crisis period. The automobile stocks were a freakish victim of the selling, for backlogs were enormous, and at full sticker prices. Chrysler, 71 in January and 60 in August, was hacked down to 38, but rebounded to 67 in 1947. General Motors sold at a price it has never seen since. October was also the decade's final low for the chemical group.

Not so lucky were the buyers of the airline stocks. Before the war, only thousands had flown. During the war, millions flew. The projected profits of peacetime traffic were intoxicating, and a leading issue such as United Airlines flew up from 8 to 63. But profits dived in 1946, and the shares fell to 20. They were a good trade, however, bouncing back to 29 within a few months. A final landing was delayed until 1948, when the shares dropped below 10.

Other "worst-case" groups included the motion pictures and the railroad equipments. Both had enjoyed explosive wartime advances. And both were in serious bear trends, with decline slopes much steeper than the Dow. Hollywood, as always, was tough for the outsider. Paramount had reeled off a spectacular war run, from 4 to 85. A 2-for-1 split pleased shareholders, but that was all there was. The stock fell quickly to 28, rallied to 35, and then slumped again in the bearish wave of 1947, dropping to 18. Columbia Pictures, up 15-fold between 1940 and 1946, fell stubbornly from 37 to 8. Its earnings plummeted from $5.33 to 40 cents, ruined by Britain's restrictions on motion picture imports and profit remittances.

Meanwhile, the dependable chemicals, motors, and steels did their usual good things for buyers, despite a flat market. A few new leaders showed up, as usually happens, and these would be among the best stock picks for the next few decades. Abbott Labs and IBM both doubled by 1949. Superior Oil, 102 on $4 earnings in 1946, rushed up to 235 and earnings of $35 in the next two years.

Fundamentalists found it difficult to cope. Earnings and dividends kept rising, but stocks went nowhere. The public's mindset was on the "inevitable" postwar depression, and issues such as Gulf Oil, Jones &

Laughlin, and Atchison all traded around four times earnings, but stirred little excitement. Meanwhile, the Dow's P–E ratio edged lower, to 6.9, at the June trough in 1949.

Watergate

"New Watergate Revelations" was a standing head in late 1973, but even the White House scandal couldn't halt the market reflex which followed the oil embargo crash. The Dow had fallen from 985 to 788 within a few weeks, and the high-multiple stocks, which had previously escaped the bearish harassment, finally caved in.

Texas Instruments, at an all-time high of 139 in October, was deflated to 92 in early December. Vending service growth and multiples were suddenly suspect, and ARA tumbled from 134 to 69. Much lower prices were in store, but the panic was overdone and an automatic rebound followed. Texas Instruments rallied to 116 and ARA to 101. Between December and the rally high of March 1974, the Dow gained 13 percent, intraday.

Though the market was only half-way through the worst decline since the 1930s, the swift rebound was predictable and typical of a bear market rally. The Dow did not turn lower until March, but stocks needed to be sold on every advance. ARA, after again touching par in June, was cut in half by December.

Even in bear trends, as in 1973, it is a dependable speculative play to go against the grain in panic conditions. The experiences of 1946–1949 were unusual because the only true panic came early, and the market then churned in a sideways formation for years, lacking any true psychological climax. The grade-B behavior of the motion picture stocks is cited only because of its exceptional sullenness, which reflected the end of the movies' semimonopoly on amusement opportunities during the war years.

Early in the century, the heavy-industry stocks were the most reliable issues to purchase under panic conditions or when bear market reversals seemed probable. But the shape of the American economy changed, and they lost leadership qualities. Drugs and retailers have been standouts, along with the airlines, in recent decades. Hopefully, the carriers will overcome deregulation and not enter Chapter XI *en masse*. Cheap stocks have always done well, but you need a package of them; don't bet the entire purse on one horse.

If you are really in doubt, "draft the best athlete"; its quality will reward you.

Foods and Beverages: Perennial All-Americans

Really conservative investors will add food stocks to their portfolio in deep panics and under mature bear market circumstances. The only catch is that such defensive issues never suffer the large percentage hits of the industrial group and lack brilliant reflex possibilities.

The merits of the food stocks are obvious. Modern lifestyles dictate easy-to-prepare foods, at least partially processed, and the prize dishes will capture big market profits. The products are essential, and the stocks possess low volatility along with recession-proof characteristics. Additionally, the group is a natural for kitchen-table research.

The big players are household names, perennial All-Americans, and those famous names will not be overtaken by Japanese imports, or domestic competition. Who could challenge Campbell's tomato soup, Heinz's ketchup, Kellogg's corn flakes, or Quaker Oats' Aunt Jemima breakfast products? The ability of the major processors to market and distribute is legendary, and they dominate the supermarket shelves.

Food and beverage stocks are never exciting, but they are soothing portfolio members. Though they are not completely recession-proof, they are clearly recession-resistant. Even in the 1930s, the industry posted decent earnings; and in the last six recessions, the foods and beverages have mostly marched earnings stubbornly ahead, although this has not insulated them from price punishment. But their contra-recession earnings performance has made it easy for patient owners to maintain investment positions

There is a great deal more to food stocks than just meat and potatoes, but even those mundane entries have run up big market profits. Iowa Beef Processors was a 100:1 gainer in the 1960s. Ore-Ida dominates the market for frozen potatoes; the division's success helped Heinz to a 16-fold gain between 1974 and 1991.

Placing meat-packing stocks under a food and beverages label is generalizing, but it's all part of what packs 'em in at the supermarket. A curious shopper will sniff out a half-dozen new products there every few months. Some are doomed by unattractive packaging or flavor, but the right stuff will ring up big stock market tickets.

Think back on some of the right stuff you stumbled into in the grocery aisles: Tropicana orange juice, frozen yogurt, microwave popcorn, Stouffer and Sara Lee delectables, Fritos. You liked the products and so did a lot of other folks, many of them on Wall Street. New bakery products come out all the time, and not just from Nabisco. Many are from smaller, regional bakers, and some are publicly owned.

The food-processing industry outperformed the market averages for 11 straight years, and their earnings are expected to advance through the balance of this decade. Processors add significant value to their products, a neglible price for American shoppers to pay for the added time and convenience put into their lives. The big processors were the food-market kingpins in the 1980s; look to the smaller, speciality firms for larger percentage gains in the 1990s.

And while you're checking the supermarket aisles, take a look at the store itself. See it as a food-sector retail play. In Houston, the top supermarket chain is a local organization with only 37 stores. But they all employ a pair of off-duty cops just to control the traffic. Sound like a winner? It is. Unfortunately, it's still privately owned. But there may be a similar elite group in your town headed for public ownership. The up-scale Quality Food Centers of Seattle boasts only three dozen stores, but the stock is up 12-fold since its public offering in early 1987.

You'll find plenty of new shelf names in your supermarket, perhaps one to replace the popular Valley Microwave (popcorn), which was bought out. Names already in place, but worth investigating, include Michael Foods (liquid pasteurized egg products), Tyson, Chiquita Brands (the old United Fruit banana trust), Smithfield, and McCormick (spices). Interesting nonretailing food processors include hybrid PENWEST and Midwest Grain Products.

Compared with the variety of food names, beverage stocks offer a limited field, but success for the winners has been rewarding. A great stock portfolio could have been made up 10, 20, even 40 years ago by just buying the popular labels in your 'fridge—Coke, Pepsi, and Bud. They will not be overcome, but some bottler will concoct a sparkling new flavor and that young challenger will capture a profitable niche market. Watch for it. Taste it. If you and most of your friends like it, buy the stock. A&W Brands (root beer), founded in 1919, was a six-bagger between 1987 and 1992, showing a lot more fizz than world-famous Coke and Pepsi.

The 1990s lifestyle, along with microwaves, working wives, and a growing population, promise solid performance by food stocks during this decade. And takeovers should remain popular. Even Borden, an industry *grande dame,* has appeared as a blushing merger candidate.

The gravest threat to the market pricing of the food stocks is the possible return of virile inflation. Consider the discouraging performance of H. J. Heinz in the inflation-ridden 1970s. Per-share earnings shot up from $1.54 to $3.95, but inflation sapped the value of that increase. The stock climbed a bare five points, 14 percent, during the decade, despite the fact that dividends in 1979 exceeded the earnings of 1969.

10

The 1929
Syndrome

The worst year in stock market history was 1931, when the Dow lost 53 percent. September rolled out the worst monthly loss, 31 percent, and a record smash in the week ending October 3 still stands.

But "1929" gets the blame. It is the digital printout for the agony of the depression days and for everything that can go wrong with the stock market. Rational investors still freeze with fear at the mention of "another 1929," and doomsday alarmists wave that skull-and-cross-bones on every serious decline.

There is no evidence that the autumn crash of that year caused the Great Depression. But it has been widely blamed, for it tilted the market and wrote the "sell" tickets for some gigantic losses. And yet, at the end of that year, the Dow was down only 17 percent and many blue-chips, including American Can, AT&T, General Electric, and Jersey Standard, were higher. The meltdown of 1987 was in many respects quite similar to that of 1929. Both followed years of bullish success and wrote the records that dominate bear archives. Both were implosions. No significant event triggered either. But there was no 1931 lurking behind 1987, ready to mug bargain-hunting buyers.

In 1929, the biggest-ever bear market rally began in November and seduced autumn skeptics back into the market. The advance was frothy, but April's volume was more than in any bull month except November 1928. It was typical of the deceits which would plague the market.

The first bear leg down, in the fall of 1929, and the rally into April 1930, were pretty much by the book, except for their extreme ranges. Many issues, including Deere, Standard Oil, and the major movie makers, scratched out new highs in 1930. Quality stocks revived hopes with brilliant rallies. General Electric, smashed from 101 to 42 the previous autumn, made it back to 95.

But that was the last time the market would go by the book. A cascade of panics would dominate trading for the next two years, and only the most nimble of traders would benefit from the frequent crises.

In June 1930, over the unanimous protests of the normally disjointed economists' fraternity, the Smoot-Hawley Tariff bill was passed. It encouraged a beggar-thy-neighbor trade policy and would be blamed for the widening worldwide depression. It was also the excuse for another serious panic; the Dow fell by 23 percent within three weeks.

Multiple Downlegs in
1929–1932 Decline

Major bear markets tend to develop with three downlegs, separated by intermediate corrections to the up side. There would be seven in the 1929–1932 ordeal; some market students count more. Each time the market seemed ready to stabilize, the ground fell away. In October 1930, the Industrials observed the crash anniversary with a chilling dive below the worst figure of 1929, Dow 199. Quite suddenly the bear market, barely one year old, was the worst in history—down more than 50 percent from the 1929 high of 381.17. No other decline in history has cost the Industrials more than 49 percent.

In December, New York's Bank of the United States was padlocked by state authorities. At least the stock market was not blamed for the largest bank closing in the nation's history. Crooked bank officials, third mortgages, and cooked books were at fault, but it aggravated the falling market, with the Dow recording the year's low at 158 in mid-December. Unemployment figures were ballooning, and Christmas retail sales were awful; Sears' December figure fell 22 percent below that of the prior year. Ominously, the retailer's shares had already lost 76 percent of their peak price.

It should not be presumed that stocks fell in a straight line. Rallies were frequent and volatile. Bull pools could still manage surprising successes. Auburn, which had fallen to 61 in 1930, was strong-armed to 296 in the spring of 1931. The advance was overdone, but there was some fundamental news; the Indiana manufacturer produced a record 28,103 autos during the year. Even then, the cars were admired for their sleek beauty, but they were costly, and money was increasingly hard to come by. Auburn shares would fall to 29 in 1932. The only stocks which could hold gains were the golds. Gold's selling price,

$20.67 at the treasury, was fixed, and mining costs were deflating. By December 1931, Homestake was at 138; the 1929 low had been 65. Earnings had more than doubled, to $9.70 since 1929.

The 1930 failure of the Bank of New York had been one of 1350. The problem would become epidemic worldwide in 1931. In the United States, nearly 2300 institutions would close, and deposits of the troubled banks doubled the 1930 total. In May, Austria's Kreditenstalt, the Rothschild bank, suspended, rolling havoc across Europe. New lows were seen on all the world bourses. But another vicious rally followed, sparked by President Hoover's proposed moratorium on war debts. Like all the rallies of the 1930s, it developed quickly, excited by high-volume short covering. The June push advanced the Dow by 29 percent within three weeks. On one strong day, volume topped 5 million shares; until mid-1928, there had never been so active a session. Such frenetic activity was typical of the period's short-covering rallies, and by August, when the market was again eroding, volume was half the June figure.

Sterling Crisis

The Labor Day week brought another of its patented migraines, and in the third week of the month England abandoned the gold standard, turning financial turmoil to panic. The "Sterling Crisis" destroyed currency rates; the pound, a solid $4.87 for decades, crashed to $3.25. In the United States, aside from the Dow's sharp drop—below 100 for the first time since 1924—the immediate result was a large emigration of gold and a sharp increase in interest rates. In two steps, the Federal Reserve Board more than doubled the discount rate, from $1\frac{1}{2}$ to $3\frac{1}{2}\%$. It may not seem like much to the present generation, but it was a shocker in those days.

European stock prices, which had mostly started down in late 1928 or early 1929, had not been as inflated as those at New York, and had suffered less damage. The aftermath of the Kreditenstalt crisis had forced Berlin to close in July, however, and when it reopened two months later, prices were sharply lower. The gold shock closed most of the world's bourses temporarily, which increased selling at New York and Paris. At London, inflation fears rallied stocks following the reopening, but New York and Paris continued to fall. Berlin, closed once again, remained shuttered until April.

The crisis of the early 1930s was worldwide, reflected not only in the collapse of stock prices but in falling employment, industrial production, and world trade. In Scotland's John Brown shipyard, work was completely halted on Cunarder hull "No. 534." Thousands of workers were laid off, and construction did not resume until 1934. When it was launched, the vessel would be christened the *Queen Mary*.

Falling Volume Erodes NYSE Membership Value

Work at the NYSE never stopped, but it certainly slowed. By the second quarter of 1932, volume was only one-quarter what it had been in the final period of 1929. Million-share days had become rare, and the value of memberships had fallen in lockstep with the Dow, to $68,000 from $625,000. Rally volume had also declined consistently, and bullish gambits had grown increasingly difficult. Violent downdrafts offered excellent trading turns, but were difficult to handle because new lows were never far distant.

The 1931 bank problems in Vienna climaxed on June 2, and a brilliant rally carried the Dow up by 29 percent before month-end. But that was it—three weeks and it was over. The "Sterling Crisis" ended October 5, and the Dow raced up 35 percent within five weeks. American Sugar bounced from 35 to 52. But by early December the average was at a new bear market low. On December 18, 1931, the Rails gained over 14 percent, their best-ever "regular" advance, in reaction to the probability that the rail unions would agree to lower wages; the Chicago, Rock Island doubled the index gain. The unions gave in, but the Rail average fell 62 percent in the next six months. In early 1932, another admirable rally gave way to new Dow lows in only four weeks.

There were investors, of course, who mostly bought and held on. They eventually benefited, but it was a long trail. Odd-lotters were net buyers in every month of the bear sequence. They bought over 6 million shares in the Crash and took down over 2 million in the gold panic. The investor base broadened for most companies. AT&T's shareholder list increased by 25 percent during the Depression. Its dividend remained at $9 all through the period, and those who bought the stock near 70, its 1932 low, were rewarded with a yield just below 13 percent and a splendid total return. Earlier buyers, stuck with $200 stock, would not get even until the 1960s.

The 1929 Syndrome: Still Frightening

The 1929 syndrome remains frightening because it symbolizes all that went wrong in the depression years—unemployment, closed factories, human suffering, the Dust Bowl, the loss of new-era illusions, and relentless deflation. The stock market has never suffered such a loss, down 89 percent for the Dow Industrials. But seen step by giant step, the march from Dow 294 in April 1930 to Dow 41 was not that frightening. Hopes were continually reignited. Memorable rallies achieved record results. Many blue-chips, including Allied Chemical, American Tobacco, the C&O, Coca-Cola, Dow Chemical, General Mills, the Guaranty Trust, Liggett & Myers, R. H. Macy, Monsanto, National Lead, the Norfolk & Western, Procter & Gamble, Standard of Jersey, Woolworth, and the operating utilities, maintained their dividends close to the 1929 figures.

The Dow's dividend, however, was $3.40 in 1932, compared with $12.75 in 1929. Most companies were forced to cut deeply, though all tried to reward their loyal stockholders within the limits of prudence. AT&T's reported earnings did not cover its dividend in any year from 1932 through 1935.

Soup lines and sidewalk apple sellers are a part of every documentary film about the depression years. Each crisis since has revived memories of those scenes and provoked deep and often unreasoning investor fear. Alarmists have always been quick to exploit those fears.

These recurrent 1929 nightmares have kept many an otherwise astute investor from taking advantage of the opportunities offered in times of price panic. Risk is what the market is all about, and, paradoxically, panic has already removed a great deal of risk. But one had to be quick-handed in 1931.

"Bulling" the Bond Market

The first indicator of a bear market reversal showed up in May 1932, as foreign markets made a slow turn. On June 1 the S&P index made a low. At the same time, a Morgan pool went to work on the bull side of bonds. To the shock of the bears, it became apparent that there were no anxious sellers left. A buying panic, the biggest, fastest advance in bond history, burst upon the market. New York Central 4½'s of 2013 were pushed from 31 to 72 within weeks. The Dow Jones Bond average, at its depression low of 65.78 on June 1, reached 71 in a few days, 75 in July, and 83 in August. Encouraged by scheduled tariff increases on gasoline, many oil stocks made their lows in April. Commodity prices appeared to be shifting direction, and the farm equipment stocks leaped up at mid-June. The Dow's turn was next. On July 8, 1932, its ordeal came to an end. It was a quiet ending, almost as if no one cared. Certainly the unemployed did not. Nor did the thousands of busted speculators who had hung on too long. Nor did the floor brokers, for volume was only 720,000 shares. Not even the bears were whooping it up. There were 118 advances at the Exchange and 214 declines, a slim climax differential.

Investors simply weren't that interested. Stocks had truly become too cheap to sell, but such cavalier judgment toward value had repeatedly cost investors dearly. Besides, it was too early to buy; there would be plenty of time. Scores of stocks had lost 95 percent of their 1929 value—good names, such as American Smelting, the B&O, Bethlehem Steel, Caterpillar, Chrysler, Deere, Goodrich, Montgomery Ward, and Westinghouse. And then there were the Democrats to worry about; they might even win the White House and wreck the budget.

But hope did revive, almost overnight, and the market launched a rocket move. The Rails tripled in eight weeks; the Industrials doubled. Volume leaped to a high of 5.5 million shares. Investors suddenly realized that if one-quarter of the working force was unemployed, three-quarters were getting paychecks. Hoarded money came out from under the mattress. It didn't take much.

Building a Diversified Portfolio with $1000

A thousand dollars would buy a nice, diversified portfolio and leave plenty of change. How about Phillips Petroleum at 2, U.S. Rubber at $1\frac{1}{4}$, and Black & Decker, Louisiana Land, Maytag, Square D, and Warner Brothers, all for $1 a share or less. Atlantic Richfield, the C&O, General Motors, Gillette, Kresge, Otis Elevator, Pillsbury, Standard Brands, and Texas Company all sold in the single digits and paid at least a $1 dividend. General Electric was below 9, but paid only 40 cents.

IBM, even then regarded as rather special, was not low priced, but was "cheap." At 53, it yielded 11 percent—a figure that Big Blue hasn't equaled since—and earnings for the year would be $9.01.

The previous pages have been jammed with horrendous bear market numbers, stretched over nearly three years. The bulls would take 25 years to recover the Dow loss, but they made a spectacular start in the summer of 1932. It was the most dramatic advance in market history. While the Dow doubled, scores of popular stocks gained fourfold. Issues which advanced even more spectacularly in the summer rally included the following market leaders, shown with their multiple of gain:

Airlines—Trans World, up 7 ×

Amusements—Warner Brothers, 9 ×

Autos—Studebaker, 5.5 ×

Farm equipments—Oliver, 8 ×

Metals—Anaconda, 6.4 ×

Office equipment—Remington Rand, 7.5 ×

Rail equipment—Budd Mfg., 7 ×

Rails (quality)—Southern Pacific, 5.8 ×

Rails (spec)—Chicago, Rock Island, 11.2 ×

Retailers—National Dept. Stores, 9.8 ×

These volatile gains were achieved between the early summer and September. In most instances, investors had plenty of time to make buying decisions. Southern Pacific's low was $6\frac{1}{2}$, but the shares traded below 7, off and on, for six consecutive weeks. The September high was 38. General Motors, whose low was $7\frac{5}{8}$, traded at 8 or below in 17 sessions. It was a laggard, but it would advance to 25 shortly after Labor Day. Recovery then slowed dramatically; see Fig. 10-1.

No Market Strategy Is Perfect

Wall Street's ubiquitous disclaimers regarding "future performance" also apply to panic. There can be no perfect market strategy, and panic buying has suffered occasional performance failure. Its long-term statistics suffer in lengthy declines, as in the 1930s, when panic values, no matter how carefully chosen, seemed always to show red ink after six months or a year. The profits, while reliable, were mercurial.

The notorious 1929 crash also blackened the short-term record of panic buying. Its chilling second attack, in November, was one of the many anomalies of the period.

On Monday, October 28, the first storm surge smashed Wall Street. The Dow lost 12.8 percent of its value, a record which stood for all the years from 1896 until 1987. On the following day, on 16 million shares—a volume record which stood until 1962—the average fell nearly 12 percent. By every standard, speculators could safely charge the market.

Morgan's banking pool was throwing millions into the support of leading blue-chips, and stocks appeared enormously attractive. Earnings were excellent across the board, and prices were at a fraction of the previous summer's levels. General Motors' sales had slipped a bit, but the stock was at less than half its spring high. Radio

A DANGERFIELD DECLINE

Bull-bear market tabulations seldom agree precisely.

A consensus sees the 1932–1937 uptrend as a bull market for the Industrials, but that sweeps a very nasty decline under the carpet. One problem is that if the serious slump of September 1932–February 1933 is granted status as a bear sequence, then the previous bull advance lasted only two months, a duration inconsistency.

In any event, the 1932 boom peaked at Dow 79.93 on September 7. Still beset by depression headaches, including a new rash of bank failures, the average was cut to 50.16 by February 27, a drop of 37 percent. Chrysler, 33 in September, fell to 12. IT&T lost two-thirds of its value. Southern Pacific dropped from 17 to 6. The numbers were painful enough to qualify as a bear market, but like Rodney Dangerfield, the sequence gets no respect.

If inserted in the tabulation of major price movements, as seen in the Appendix, the 1932–1937 series is changed as follows:

From	To	Average	Percent
July 8, 1932	Sept. 7, 1932	41.22 to 79.93	+ 94
Sept. 7, 1932	Feb. 27, 1933	79.93 to 50.16	− 37
Feb. 27, 1933	Mar. 10, 1937	50.16 to 194.40	+ 288

Figure 10-1. The bull market that began in 1932 is remembered mostly as a very easy ride, one that did not end until 1937; the advance remains the second largest in history. But a nasty, five-month interruption occurred early on. While little remembered, the collapse of prices amounted to 37 percent for the Dow. Only one decline since World War II has exceeded its severity.

Corporation had fallen to 26; it had been 114 in September. All of the Dow gain since August 1928 had been erased in weeks.

Technical signs were bad enough to encourage contrarians. On October 29 there had been 551 new lows and no highs, and the NYSE tape did not stop running until 7 p.m. Joe Kennedy was reported to be among the speculative bulls, and John D. Rockefeller bought Standard Oil heavily. Surely, it was enough on the down side.

It was—brilliantly, but briefly. The Industrials rallied by 33 percent, intraday, within two sessions. But in a failure of precedent, the Dow reversed and within two weeks dived to a new low, 13 percent beneath what had appeared to be the classic panic low. Woolworth, beaten down to 72 in the October crush, descended to 52. U.S. Steel, supported at 180 a week or so earlier, fell to 150. General Electric was smashed to 168, versus a 221 low at the end of October. Only a few former favorites held above their October low points; RCA, General Motors, and American Tobacco were among them.

JFK versus U.S. Steel

Such deceptive double dealing would not be repeated until 1962, when the May panic ended with an apparent classic reversal day. It came on the largest volume since 1929 and with statistical overkill: There were 937 new lows and only five new highs, while 74 advances matched against 1212 declines.

Stocks had been mangled because of the pricing confrontation between President Kennedy and the steel industry. U.S. Steel had been a leader in the failed battle for a price increase and was a natural selling target, but richly priced favorites of the previous year were treated as badly. The extreme decline of late May, however, seemed the clue to an important low.

Unfortunately, IBM, which had not taken a heavy hit in years, and Xerox, the other great market leader of the period, were headed for serious new lows. IBM had dropped to 355 in May, down from the year's high at 579. After a quick reflex, it slipped badly in June, casting a pall over the market, and did not stop until it hit 300.

Xerox, already a 166–105 victim of the bear, also rallied but then dived to 88 in June. Big Steel, having fallen to a May low at 50, down from a bull market peak at 91, slumped to 40 in the second-stage attack of June.

Other stocks behaved in a more traditional fashion. General Motors gave comfort by holding its May low, despite a court order requiring DuPont to divest its long-held control of the company. Meanwhile, volume declined significantly and technical indicators improved. It was the last instance of such dismal performance following crisis.

Hitting on Capital and Other Anomalies

Large bear operations in March of 1907, aimed mostly at the Harriman rail stocks, stirred a classic panic. But the spring recovery was brief, and the Dow was lower in both the six-month and one-year spans following the event, for it had to struggle against the autumn's commercial crisis, which blighted banks, the economy, and the market. During the year, politicians the world around were hitting on capital, and President Theodore Roosevelt was seen as an implacable foe of the railroads. The Industrials did manage a rally of 13 percent following the March crisis, but it was unimpressive and lacking in vigor.

The collapse of a single, manipulated trust company stock—National Cordage—in May 1893 led to a fearful assault on the new industrial trusts and set the stage for the downfall of the entire market only two months later. The unraveling of the Twine Trust, a mutinous amalgamation of binder twine and rope firms, was the result of failed monopoly hopes and of the dissolution of a pool in the stock managed by James R. Keane. Cordage had been a winter feature, puffed up to 150. A 2-for-1 split, unusual in those days, and a dividend increase in April spurred public excitement. In early May the company ran out of cash and sought to recoup working capital by offering a preferred issue. It didn't fly, and within days the firm was in foreclosure, unable to refinance a $50,000 bank note.

Cordage, trading near 70 after the split, appeared to have split again, for the stock dropped quickly to 10. Other trusts, many no better than blind pools, were suddenly suspect. American Sugar, 104 on April 28, was melted down to 62 by May 5. General Electric was a 101–58 loser in the same period, and Distillers, the Whiskey Trust, was halved.

A study of price records shows that an index of leading industrials—even excluding Cordage—lost 25 percent in six trading days. The intensity was far worse than the commercial crisis which would follow two months later. The reliable profits of panic would follow, but were available for only a few weeks. U.S. Rubber, a 50–33 victim in the first week of May, rebounded to 45.

The June–July crisis which cut short the rally was triggered by Europe's demands for a return of her credits and a melting gold cover in the United States. Europe feared that the Sherman Silver Act of 1890 would allow America to repay her debts with 60-cent dollars.

Perhaps the panic of May had not been broad enough; it had been specialized, a sector attack aimed primarily at the industrial shares. But none would escape in July, when the new crisis stunned the entire country and not just Wall Street. Not until September 1895 would the 20-Stock average return to the level of late April.

Manipulating the Hocking: From 20 to 93 to 3

James Keene's final major manipulation, in Columbus & Hocking Coal & Iron, ended in another market panic in January 1910. The Hocking shares had been miraculously levitated from the low 20s to 93 within less than a year. They were "pegged" near 90 as Keene hastened to slip out of the position. When the "peg" melted, there were no buyers, and the stock fell from 89 to 24 in a single day. Three stock exchange firms failed, including the specialist. The Dow lost 10 percent in a month, and Hocking, bereft of friends, fell to 3 in September.

As in 1893, the reflex was poor, and a major rally had to await the dropping of a second shoe, which occurred amidst a forced rail liquidation in the summer. The ICC was squeezing rates, and an undermargined pool undertaken to capture strategic lines and control a true transcontinental route was suddenly struck with margin problems. The British-Canadian group had collected a strange menage of carriers, starting with the Lehigh Valley and ending with the Western Pacific. Also included were such lines as the Wabash and the Chicago, Rock Island.

The Railroad average slipped below its worst level of 1907, and the ambitions of the new rail barons melted away. Finally, their position was taken over by stronger hands, as Kuhn, Loeb—the longtime Harriman bankers—relieved the adventurers of a "too heavy burden of stock."

The transportation average made a solo bear market low at this time, and the Industrials slipped 13 percent beneath the worst level of the Hocking fiasco. They would make a modest new low about a year later.

In these special instances, 1893 to 1962, panic was followed by decent reflex pricing, but a second shoe would drop, forcing the market to a new low and clouding the short-term profit picture of panic buying.

The lengthy decline of 1919–1921, as we shall see, was marked by panic in its early course; as in the 1930s, the long-term-rebound figures were unimpressive.

1920: Squeezing Inflation Out of the Economy

World War I's price-doubling inflation was broken by tight money and a firestorm of deflation. In its course the stock market was badly burned in one of the century's superbear moves, down 47 percent between the November peak of 1919 and the summer of 1921. It took about 18 months to squeeze inflation out of the economy, and in the meantime the rebounds from recurring crises were quite modest.

For the only time in history, the stock market plunged into panic directly from a historic peak, a true steepletop formation. The Federal

Reserve Board, concerned about the inflation mania, tightened the fiscal screws in November 1919, and the Dow fell over 10 percent in seven trading days. Not until 1924 did the average recover the peak level.

Disinflation has washed over the economy a half-dozen times in the past century, but never more swiftly than in 1920. It depressed the market in five steps, and bottom pickers were hard-pressed to capture profits. There was a series of hard downers, but most lasted too long for true crisis conditions. In November and December 1920, however, a pair of high-volume panics struck, encouraged by aggressive bear pools and the problems at General Motors. The overall decline lasted for about seven weeks and wrote a loss of 19 percent; Goodrich fell from 52 to 27 in the period.

It wasn't that stocks hadn't been able to rally, they just couldn't rally for long. A true panic had fallen on the market in early February 1920, when a huge drop in the value of currency exchange caused a cancellation of foreign buying orders. General Motors was driven from 345 to 226 as the Dow fell by 13 percent, but a super reflex got the loss back and a bit more, aided by a pair of infamous manipulations. In March, William Crapo Durant, president of General Motors, and Allen A. Ryan of Stutz Motor Car, cornered the shares of their respective auto companies and gave the bulls a great whirl. Stutz, maker of the famous Bearcat roadster, was squeezed from par to 724 within weeks, the most notorious corner since the Northern Pacific. Rallies later in the year lacked such sponsorship, and market gains, like business profits, were then hard to come by.

The depression put Harry S. Truman's Kansas City haberdashery into bankruptcy, and he immediately deserted to the public sector, linking up with the Boss Pendergast Democratic machine. In 1921, for the first time in history, the Dow earnings slipped into the red. Commodity prices had been halved and then quartered after the Fed hiked the discount rate again. Coal, $9.51 in the spot market in September 1920, fell to $2.40 nine months later. Unemployment seized the nation. Ford laid off 60,000 at the nation's largest auto plant just before Christmas. Flying squadrons of price police patrolled New York City, and the Justice Department pursued "profiteers" with great media success. Lunchtime parades and placards praised the merits of second-hand clothes.

In a prospectus for its 10-year, 7 percent gold notes, offered in January 1921, Armstrong Cork plaintively briefed the deflation problem when it noted that 1920 profits were a record, except that millions had to be written off "to adjust present inventories to current market conditions."

Wall Street was not spared. On September 16, a bomb exploded outside the Morgan offices, killing 30 innocents. Trading volume fell 43
percent between 1919 and 1921, and turnover was halved. Sears fell
from 243 to 54, and Atlantic Refining, the highest-priced issue at the
Exchange, toppled from 1650 to 820. Durant lost control of the beleaguered General Motors for the second time in his career, after dropping nearly $100 million in a fruitless effort to peg the share price.
Adjusted for a 10:1 split, the stock fell from 42 to 12 in 1920 and ended
below 9 in 1922.

Crucible Steel, one of the market's most volatile stocks, illustrates
the disintegration of prices. The specialty steelmaker had reached an
all-time high of 279 in April 1920. By August it had fallen to 116, but
then it blew away the shorts with a stunning move to 162. Back to 118,
up to 135, down to 70 in December, and then up to 108 in January.
And 49 the following August. Panic contrarians found it a very fast
game, where profits came fast, but faded faster. There were no contrary winners after six months or a year.

There were several reasons why the market failed to make a strong
stand until early 1921. First, the downward drives between February
and November 1920 lacked intensity. Second, the hard lessons of
deflation were long forgotten, buried in the archives of the mid-1890s.
Manufacturers had hoarded inventories of rubber, cork, silk, lumber,
steel, sugar, leather, cotton oil, and wool. Everyone was protected
against inflation, ready to fight the last war. No one was prepared for
deflation and the shrinkage of export demand. Business and commerce
were shocked by buyers' strikes launched against the "HCL," or high
cost of living. Silk shirts at $16 were a thing of the past, as Harry
Truman learned.

In May 1921, U.S. Steel announced a wage cut of 20 percent, the first
general reduction since 1904. The Railway Labor Board proposed a
pay slash, which was initially applauded by the market. But in the
broad band of pessimism, it was quickly turned into a bear argument.
The cut was too low, or too late, or would only encourage strikes. In
June, stocks plunged into their third serious panic of the sequence, but
again the rally was sullen and the Dow scraped out a final low in
August. The firestorm of deflation cost the market dearly. Over 84 percent of the entire World War I gain, July 1914 to November 1919, was
dissipated. The Rails, laggard for years because of government restrictions and ownership, had fallen completely out of their range for the
twentieth century, back to the level of August 1898.

The recurrent slumps of 1919–1921 were not breathtaking and did
not produce the brilliant rallies of the early 1930s. The first crisis, in

November 1919, was followed by a miserable rebound, and not until February was the market clearly oversold. The following advance pushed many issues to record highs in March and April. Vanadium Corporation, a bull pool fancy, was propelled from 42 in February to 97 in April. The downturns of late spring and late summer uncovered few bargains, but the double hit of November–December finally produced panic pricing. Studebaker, 38 at the end of the year, raced to 93 the following spring.

The Inevitable Exceptions

Every rule of stock market behavior has inevitable exceptions. The profits of crisis were exceedingly slim in 1920 and 1931, among a few other exceptional years. But success has generally followed the efforts of investors and speculators who chose to "gut up" and buy during the storms of panic.

The most painful experiences have occurred when a two-stage bear attack routed early buyers. None was more testing than the industrial collapse of late 1937. That unique three-stage affair cost the Dow 34 percent between the first day of September and Thanksgiving eve. It was relieved by a monumental rally of 25 percent, intraday, which lasted less than two weeks. In that period, Phillips Petroleum rebounded from 30 to 48. But that was all. The war panic of the following spring dropped Bartlesville's pride to 27. Still, there had been reasonable profits for the nimble, as there would be immediately again. Phillips arced up to 44 by mid-summer.

11
The 1990s: Another Meltdown?

There will be panics and bear markets in the 1990s. But Meltdown II seems unlikely, if only because market history indicates that such light shows, like Haley's comet, occur only rarely.

To date, the decade's disaster record is unremarkable. In every decade since the 1890s, except for the 1950s, the first and/or second year has involved a bear sequence. The Kuwait invasion in 1990 raised some alarm, but the August–October decline was minimal. Scholars will argue as to whether it was a secondary correction or mini-bear, but it makes little difference. The decade has experienced low volatility and already presents a different economic and stock market profile from that enjoyed in the 1980s. We expect the slower pace to continue, which means less likelihood of record declines.

Arguments against Another Meltdown

Violent market collapses generally follow extended periods of heated speculation, and the outlook for the 1990s seems to argue against a repeat of the fever of the mid-1980s. Saving, not spending, is the surprising new gospel for baby boomers, the largest segment of our population.

Spiraling health and education costs and the realization that home ownership is not an automatic wealth maker, even in California, have increased the pressures to save. Furthermore, little government stimulus can be expected, as mushrooming deficits at every level of government preclude any broad-based tax reduction or spending increase. The painfully slow recovery from the 1990s' first recession already offers one clue to the decade's slower pace.

The stock market, which enjoyed its second best decade in the 1980s, will not benefit from the conspicuous consumerism of that yuppie era. While the Dow has achieved a new high, economics and history suggest that the pace of the 1990s will fall far short of the exceptional advance of the Reagan-Bush years.

Any challenge to the archival records of the 1987 crash should take some years to develop. Big scores on the down side are uncommon. The climactic loss for the Dow 20-Stock average (forerunner of the Rails) in the Venezuelan Panic of 1896 was not exceeded by that latter average until 1931. A large loss by the Industrials in the Boer War smash of 1899 was not equaled for 30 years.

The dismal record of October 1929 stood for nearly 60 years, and the worst month ever at the NYSE remains a forgotten September 1931. Horrific down-side figures are not every-year occurrences. It will require a new era of wild speculation to breed a challenge to the meltdown statistics of 1987.

Poor Blockbuster Follow-ups

Records following previous blockbuster decades argue against high market expectations. The top three decades since 1860, in terms of performance, recorded remarkably similar gains and were each followed by a decade of meager performance.

In September 1929 the Industrials were up 255 percent for the decade, though that gain was eroded by the October panic. The 10-year advance of the 1950s ended with a Dow gain of 239 percent, while that of the 1980s was 228 percent. Look what happened next. The 1930s were a disaster, and in the 1960s the gain was only 15 percent, although at the peak (1966) the Dow was up by 32 percent. What if the 1990s could avoid the dismal action of the 1930s and match the maximum gain of the 1960s? That would put the DJIA at the 3634 level. We don't expect back-to-back blockbuster decades.

Fundamentals Are No Longer Cheap

Fundamental valuations also favor a decline in momentum. At the beginning of the 1980s, the Standard & Poor's 500 yielded over 6 percent, and the price–earnings ratio was less than 8. Prices could expand significantly without becoming overheated.

At the start of the 1990s, the S&P ratio was at 14.9, the second highest decade-end level in history; the dividend return was barely 3 percent. Additionally, low interest rates—excluding those on credit cards—lacked the improvement potential of the early 1980s, when the prime rate was often above 20 percent. By 1991 the prime had already fallen 63 percent from its record high level of a decade earlier, and with further sharp declines unlikely, one powerful catalyst for a boom in stock prices was shelved.

A new American trade rival, the European Community, adds another caution flag. If Fortress Europe does not cave in to French insurrection, American manufacturers will find themselves besieged from both East and West.

The stock market will not self-destruct in the 1990s, unless it first goes on a speculative binge. But that seems unlikely, since the gains—and ease of gains—will not match those of the 1980s, for the reasons previously mentioned. Remember the easy money of the mid-1980s? Between July 1984 and September 1987 the DJIA did not suffer a single correction of as much as 10 percent. Money could be profitably put out to rent in a hundred enterprises, spurred only by whispers, rumors, inside tips, and buyouts and buyins.

To make money the old-fashioned way—slowly—was a lesson forgotten. But the market has a way of reviving such homilies. The easy-money days are as surely gone as were the "new era" days of the 1920s when the tide finally turned.

Other Trends
for the 1990s

The economists may finally be right: The decade's recessions should end in "soft landings," for shorter, gentler recessions will be one reward of the painful deflation which has swept over the economy since 1981. Oil, metals, farm prices, real estate, bloated corporate staffs, unprofitable subsidiaries, and so forth have all suffered from a painful but rolling readjustment. The firestorm of deflation is over, and the dangers of an overheated expansion seems some years away.

Twenty-four-hour global markets will also shorten the time span of market cycles, for news and information are discounted overnight in the world's bourses. Consider the foreshortened bearish episodes of the past 10 years. In 1984 the Dow's slump lasted for only six months, while the 1987 ordeal was finished in less than two. The Persian Gulf war triggered a slide which sliced the Industrials from 3000 to 2365, but the decline, like Saddam's bravado, ended quickly, lasting less than three months.

Greater stability in interest rates and lowered inflation will help maintain liberal P–E ratios and make it easier for investors to hold well-chosen stocks through the inevitable market downers. Exclusive of the 1929–1932 tragedy, the historic measure of a severe market collapse has been a figure slightly below 50 percent, a penalty exacted in eight other great declines between the 1890s and 1973–1974. But that most recent collapse—45 percent—required an oil embargo, rocketing gold prices, hallucinatory P–E ratios, OPEC blackmail, and the scandalous resignation of a President to fold the market. We don't look for a conjunction of such bad news again in this century.

A volatility level below that of the past decade does not mean that the opportunities of crisis will be lacking. There will continue to be violent short-term swings. The Dow's net advance in the 1970s amounted to only 37 points, but the decade witnessed three bear markets plus conditions of panic pricing in five years. Instant globalization of news will continue to compress the time frame of corrective movements. And intraday volatility will continue to be aggravated by program trading. Air pockets of 40 or 50 points can be expected when computer selling rises to a frenzy. And such spasms, often seen as akin to the "pool" activities of an earlier era, will probably continue with only the loosest of supervision. There will always be opportunities in such minor crises.

Do not expect knavery on Wall Street to diminish, either. Just when Ivan Boesky, Mike Milken, et al., had vanished from page one, John Gotfreund and his Salomon partners were caught rigging Treasury bond auctions, a new high—or low?—for Street chutzpah.

Build a Patient Portfolio

Looking forward toward a slower pace in the 1990s, the investor should focus on a patient portfolio concentrated in easily understood companies whose products are broadly popular with consumers. Leave the volatile high-techs to the deep pockets of institutions.

When the next wave of great prosperity rolls over the stock market, the brutal restructuring of American industry, which has stretched over the past half-dozen years, should work wonders for the profits and prices of quality corporations which are able to compete in the global economy.

In the meantime, take a chance when panic does stalk the market. The last solid opportunity was during the Kuwait crisis. The slowdown in the 1990s has kept the market unnaturally restrained since then; the Standard & Poor's 500 set a record with its narrow trading range in 1992.

No Laws against Panic

There will be numerous opportunities of crisis. There is no law against panic, and a downward course will not be halted by circuit breakers, specialists' cash in the till, or a billion-share computer system. The market will do what it must in the 1990s to accommodate the forces of financial stress. SEC regulations against rumors, phony reports, short selling, pools, manipulations, and the selling of "blue sky" have never stayed the bear's course, nor slowed panic.

Financial excesses can be cured only by the shock of dramatic decline. Despite a generally bullish trend, and a circuit breaker used scores of times, there have been many frightening downstrokes since 1987. The market has been hit twice by daily losses of 7 percent, falls not equaled since 1937, except in the meltdown.

The urgencies of panic will repeat in the 1990s, for their triggers are often independent of the market. Every decade except the 1950s has logged at least one short-term crisis which slashed the Dow by 15 to 20 percent within a handful of trading days. There is no reason to think that we will escape such trials in the 1990s; such a hard-case decline would amount to something like 500 to 700 Dow points, given the now-popular Dow 3600 readings. Panics of the 1990s will be no more orderly than those of a century ago, as was proven in the first post-1987 crisis, in 1989.

The rout of Friday, October 13, 1989, urged on by program trading, was for 191 Dow points, and was the first to "learn" from the 1987 lessons. Its origin lay in the airline merger madness. William J. O'Neil, Chairman of *Investor's Business Daily*, critically analyzed the panic on October 16 in a page 1 editorial for his paper. "The stock exchange was routed and converted into a commodities trading pit." he wrote. "Is this what America's leading corporations pay a listing fee for, to be kicked around like soybean futures....Is this recurring circus fair to the American public?"

What Could Change?

Legendary crashes have usually followed periods of manic speculation. The railroad booms gave way to a rolling madness for steels, coppers, war babies, autos, radio shares, trusts, conglomerates, glamours, and so forth. All those manias were followed by sector or broad panic.

The wounds of 1987 are now forgotten, and while reason points to a less volatile decade in the 1990s, there has been plenty of time to raise a new crop of speculators. By 1933, some lessons of 1929 were forgotten, and the craze for repeal's "whiskey" stocks was as high-proof as anything recorded in 1929.

Manias have seized the market in every decade of its existence, though some—as in the 1950s—were modest. It is possible that the growing passion for mutual funds carries the seeds of future trouble for this decade.

"Cash Is Trash"

When CD rates crumbled in the early 1990s, "cash is trash" became a favorite Wall Street bromide. Low-paying certificates should be ditched, it was argued, and the monies rolled into mutual funds.

And so an incipient mania was born. In 1992, $87 billion was plunked into stock funds. It seemed a cinch. Four-color sales brochures featured charts of past performance showing asset values rising like the Himalayas, year after year. And, what with chart sizes shrink-wrapped, any embarrassing financial valleys along the way were well camouflaged.

The long bull market which began in 1982 made the tabulations of gains and distributions seem as safe as government bonds and vastly more rewarding. Fund Pied Pipers picked up an immense following. In the first half of 1993, over $60 billion in new money went into the investment pools. Suddenly, there were more funds than equity listings at the NYSE. Sector funds proliferated until some management groups had several dozen specialty portfolios in the house. Dozens of foreign country funds, guaranteed to broaden investor currency sophistication, if not wealth, were added.

A score of newsletters sprang up to feed the fad. Wall Street wanted the restless billions to find a proper new home, and underwriters lined up a record amount of stock offerings to feed the ravenous demand. By 1993 it was the best of all times: the Dow at 3600; record mutual funds sales; record underwriting volume.

From perfect bliss, however, comes disappointment. In the first place, the mania will cool. And when it is sated, the self-leavening impact on the market will end. Second, it will be found that the quality of professional management varies enormously. Few managers will equal Peter Lynch, the legendary Fidelity guru. Some will be less than professional in their aptitude for managing others' money. And third, the psychology of the market will change. When that happens, many shareholders will forget that rainbow dream of long-term financial success and opt back to cash.

Far from offering group insurance against bad market action, many funds only mimic the averages. In the 12 months ended September 1974, a very nasty market period, 181 funds tracked in *Barron's* declined an average of 38 percent; the Dow lost 36 percent in the same period.

Manias End in Disaster

Alan Abelson, editor of *Barron's,* wrote in his column of May 10, 1993, "It has been our deepening conviction...that mutual funds will be at the heart of the next great stock market catastrophe." Just when this rumble will start is not clear. But every financial mania in history has ended with disaster, and mutual funds will not be exempt.

A hysteria for the investment trusts helped push the 1929 market over the edge, when such infamous promotions as Blue Ridge and Shenandoah were promoted into "hot" deals. Lesser speculative fevers have gilled the public into untimely enthusiasm with heavy net buying of the trusts in late 1961 and early 1962, and again in 1968–1969—both bad-timing periods. In 1986, a craze for closed-end funds, particularly one-country funds, was an early indicator of the coming storm.

Despite the marvelous upward slant on all those long-term charts of investment results, every stock fund has posted some horrendous quarters and years. Professional management cannot insure against the short-term convulsions of the market. Perhaps it will be Dow 7000 by the year 2000, as some say, but there will be some dicey times along the way. And even professional management can't insulate fund buyers from market fear, which will cause some investors to cash in their shares at the worst possible moments. Fund holders were untimely sellers, for example, in August 1990, when the Kuwait war broke out.

Assuming that the mania for a managed portfolio continues, one can bet that by the time the last "trashy" CD is rolled into a mutual fund, the market will be on the skids.

Other "Hot" Spots

One can toll a half-dozen alarums for market stability. Rogue Russian states, Iran, and North Korea all threaten nuclear proliferation. The bloody Balkanization of Yugoslavia has caused political, if not financial headaches. But the Serbian assassin in Sarajevo 80 years ago caused no immediate concern, either, and World War I followed.

Inflation, while widely discounted as a serious bear threat, lurks behind every price increase. A solution to the "energy crisis" of the mid-1970s never got beyond rhetoric, and the nation's dependence on foreign crude has increased dramatically. Natural gas prices had no trouble in doubling in the spring of 1993 as the value of gold, a natural inflation indicator, showed surprising vigor. High price–earnings ratios and bonds will be the first victims of a revival of inflationary thinking.

A gambling mania could overwhelm Wall Street, as in 1929. Margin debt, already at a record, continues to increase—a bullish sign—but it could be signaling a spastic swell of speculation. The gambling mania which has seized the country may be an indicator of trouble. Million-dollar lotteries and riverboat gambling have been institutionalized by state treasuries and are now part of everyday life. It's no longer Las Vegas once a year. New Orleans and Chicago compete in planning the nation's biggest casino. Horse tracks, not content with win-place-show tickets, have added saliva-test wagers such as Twin-Trifectas, Exactas, and Pick Nines.

Wall Street (and the Chicago Board Options Exchange) have hyped gambling's free lunch since the introduction of listed options. Program trading, asset allocation, and portfolio "insurance" all seem to promise something for nothing. Index futures and options thereon afford high-leverage bets, most generally lost. Artificial derivatives and synthetics are fabricated to increase the "play."

Unlike some gambling crazes, Wall Street eschews public vulgarities of phraseology. Its products are introduced by prospectus and fancy brochures which promise to "enhance return and improve portfolio flexibility while controlling and reducing risk"—akin to walking on water. Does such seductive nonsense forecast a return to wide-open gambling at the Exchange?

The devil is always at the gate.

Appendix

About the Dow Averages

The principal gauge of panic, and other market sequences, in this book is the Dow Jones Industrial average. Before it was first compiled in 1896, the Dow 20-Stock average is generally used. The sometimes confusing record of the Dow averages deserves a brief explanation.

The first Dow average, compiled in 1884, was made up of 11 stocks. All were railroads except for the Pacific Mail steamship company and Western Union. About a year later, the roster was increased to 14 by the addition of three more rails. In 1886 the list was cut to 12.

Bowing to demands for a broader index, a second average—of 20 issues (18 rails)—was added in 1888; both indices were maintained until 1896. At that time the first Industrial index was established, comprising 12 stocks, mostly the early trusts. This was the forerunner of the modern Dow. In 1916 the list was increased to 20 stocks, but prices were computed back to the reopening of the NYSE after the war "holiday." At that time, the old 12-stock list was priced at 74.56 and the new 20-stock list was 54.62. This leaves continuation charts with an apparent huge gap to the down side, which has often been misinterpreted. The average was expanded to 30 stocks in 1928.

In 1896 the 20-Stock average had become a pure rail index, and the changes melded perfectly. In 1970 the Rails evolved into the Dow Jones Transportation average when nine rails were replaced by a cross section of other transportation issues. It should be noted that the major cycles of both the Rail and Transport averages have frequently diverged from those of the Industrials.

The Dow Jones Bond average was added in 1915 and the Utility average, originally 20 stocks but now 15, was first compiled in 1929. The 30 Industrials, 20 Transports, and 15 Utility stocks make up the Dow 65-Stock average.

Dow Jones & Company has always been the sole arbiter of membership listings, and changes have been frequent, sometimes even whimsical. Thus, leading stocks such as Coca-Cola, General Motors, and

IBM have been in and out and in. A number of popular, if not leading, issues have also flitted in and out of the Industrials list. Only General Electric has maintained its position since 1896.

Readers curious as to the current makeup of the averages will find them listed on the daily charts published by *The Wall Street Journal* opposite the "Abreast of the Market" column.

Table A-1. Major Price Movements, 1888–1993

Leading Dow Average

From	To	Average	Percent
Apr. 2, 1888	June 4, 1890	58.18 to 78.38	+ 35
June 4, 1890	Dec. 8, 1890	78.38 to 58.10	− 26
Dec. 8, 1890	Mar. 4, 1892	58.10 to 75.68	+ 30
Mar. 4, 1892	July 26, 1893	75.68 to 43.47	− 43
July 26, 1893	Sept. 4, 1895	43.47 to 63.77	+ 47
Sept. 4, 1895	Aug. 8, 1896	63.77 to 41.82	− 34
Aug. 8, 1896*	Sept. 5, 1899	28.48 to 77.61	+ 173
Sept. 5, 1899	Sept. 24, 1900	77.61 to 52.96	− 32
Sept. 24, 1900	June 12, 1901	52.96 to 78.26	+ 48
June 12, 1901	Nov. 9, 1903	78.26 to 42.15	− 46
Nov. 9, 1903	Jan. 19, 1906	42.15 to 103.00	+ 144
Jan. 19, 1906	Nov. 15, 1907	103.00 to 53.00	− 49
Nov. 15, 1907	Nov. 19, 1909	53.00 to 100.53	+ 90
Nov. 19, 1909	Sept. 25, 1911	100.53 to 72.94	− 27
Sept. 25, 1911	Sept. 30, 1912	72.94 to 94.15	+ 29
Sept. 30, 1912	July 30, 1914	94.15 to 71.42	− 24
July 30, 1914†	Nov. 21, 1916	51.88 to 110.15	+ 112
Nov. 21, 1916	Dec. 19, 1917	110.15 to 65.95	− 40
Dec. 19, 1917	Nov. 3, 1919	65.95 to 119.62	+ 81
Nov. 3, 1919	Aug. 24, 1921	119.62 to 63.90	− 47
Aug. 24, 1921	Sept. 3, 1929	63.90 to 381.17	+ 497
Sept. 3, 1929	July 8, 1932	381.17 to 41.22	− 89
July 8, 1932	Mar. 10, 1937	41.22 to 194.40	+ 372
Mar. 10, 1937	Mar. 31, 1938	194.40 to 98.95	− 49
Mar. 31, 1938	Nov. 12, 1938	98.95 to 158.41	+ 60
Nov. 12, 1938	Apr. 8, 1939	158.41 to 121.44	− 23
Apr. 8, 1939	Sept. 12, 1939	121.44 to 155.92	+ 28
Sept. 12, 1939	Apr. 28, 1942	155.92 to 92.92	− 40
Apr. 28, 1942	May 29, 1946	92.92 to 212.50	+ 129
May 29, 1946	June 13, 1949	212.50 to 161.60	− 24

NOTE: See page 286 for footnotes.

Table A-1. Major Price Movements, 1888–1993 (*Continued*)

Leading Dow Average

From	To	Average	Percent
June 13, 1949	Apr. 6, 1956	161.60 to 521.05	+ 222
Apr. 6, 1956	Oct. 22, 1957	521.05 to 419.79	− 19
Oct. 22, 1957	Jan. 5, 1960	419.79 to 685.47	+ 63
Jan. 5, 1960	Oct. 25, 1960	685.47 to 566.05	− 17
Oct. 25, 1960	Dec. 13, 1961	566.05 to 734.91	+ 30
Dec. 13, 1961	June 26, 1962	734.91 to 535.76	− 27
June 26, 1962	Feb. 9, 1966	535.76 to 995.15	+ 86
Feb. 9, 1966	Oct. 7, 1966	995.15 to 744.32	− 25
Oct. 7, 1966	Dec. 3, 1968	744.32 to 985.21	+ 32
Dec. 3, 1968	May 26, 1970	985.21 to 631.16	− 36
May 26, 1970	Jan. 11, 1973	631.16 to 1051.70	+ 67
Jan. 11, 1973	Dec. 6, 1974	1051.70 to 577.60	− 45
Dec. 6, 1974	Sept. 21, 1976	577.60 to 1014.79	+ 76
Sept. 21, 1976	Feb. 28, 1978	1014.79 to 742.12	− 27
Feb. 28, 1978	Apr. 27, 1981	742.12 to 1024.05	+ 38
Apr. 27, 1981	Aug. 12, 1982	1024.05 to 776.92	− 24
Aug. 12, 1982	Aug. 25, 1987	776.92 to 2722.42	+ 250
Aug. 25, 1987	Oct. 19, 1987	2722.42 to 1738.74	− 36
Oct. 19, 1987	July 16, 1990	1738.74 to 2999.75	+ 73
July 16, 1990	Oct. 11, 1990	2999.75 to 2365.10	− 21
Oct. 11, 1990	?	2365.10 to ?	

*Dow Industrial average replaces 20-Stock average.

†Dow average increased from 12 to 20 stocks in 1916, but has here been computed back to the crucial 1914 date.

Table A-2. Almanac of Stock Market Panics and Panic Episodes
Measured by Leading Dow Average

Year	Dates	Percent lost and duration*	Causes and comments
1890	Nov. 5–Nov. 18	11.7%, 11 TDs	England's "gaucho speculations" sour and London must sell heavily in New York. Northern Pacific suffers bear raid.
1893	Apr. 29–May 13	11.2%, 12 TDs	Nouveau industrial trusts ravished after collapse of National Cordage pool.
1893	July 8–July 26	21.1%, 15 TDs	Silver collapse, dollar doubts, credit stringency bring sudden commercial crisis.
1893	Dec. 4–Dec. 29	10.2%, 20 TDs	Lower tariff proposals worry market. Atchison unexpectedly seeks receiver.
1895	Dec. 16–Dec. 21	15.9%, 5 TDs	War scare erupts as Cleveland seems to threaten UK on Venezuelan dispute.
1896	July 11–Aug. 8	20.0%, 24 TDs	Sound money runs for gold after Democratic silverites nominate W. J. Bryan.
1897	Oct. 12–Nov. 8	9.9%, 23 TDs	Spanish war fears. Yellow fever hits South. Reflex after 14-month advance.
1898	Feb. 15–Feb. 24	10.7%, 7 TDs	Explosion sinks *U.S.S. Maine* in Havana.
1898	Sept. 6–Oct. 1	12.7%, 22 TDs	World bourses stressed by Anglo-French confrontation at Fashoda, Egypt. U.S. worries about tight money, peace treaty.
1899	May 3–May 31	11.2%, 22 TDs	"Flower" panic. Bears attack stocks of ex-governor Flower, a leading bull operator.
1899	Dec. 2–Dec. 18	23.0%, 13 TDs	"Black Week" in London as Boer War crisis worsens. Selling spreads to New York. Dec. 18 worst day until 1929.
1900	Apr. 16–May 15	12.1%, 26 TDs	Panic in iron trade. "Bet a Million" Gates closes American Wire. Longish episode.

*Duration in trading sessions (TDs).

Table A-2. Almanac of Stock Market Panics and Panic Episodes (*Continued*)

Measured by Leading Dow Average

Year	Dates	Percent lost and duration*	Causes and comments
1901	May 8–May 9	10.2%, 2 TDs	Northern Pacific cornered. Stock squeezed from 160 to 1000. Dow falls 20% in four sessions, intraday.
1901	July 2–July 15	9.9%, 10 TDs	Drought causes Corn Panic. Santa Fe RR threatens freight rate war.
1901	Sept. 7–Sept. 25	8.3%, 14 TDs	President McKinley shot Sept. 7, dies later. By early Oct., Dow loss 12%.
1903	July 8–July 25	15.3%, 15 TDs	Rich Man's Panic. Banking underwriters and friends choke on unsalable trustification offerings.
1903	Sept. 24–Oct. 15	11.5%, 19 TDs	Depression gloom sharpened by Steel's dividend cut Oct. 6.
1904	Dec. 6–Dec. 12	10.2%, 6 TDs	Writer/speculator Lawson spurs bear raid (Lawson Panic). Dec. 6 volume is largest between 1901 and 1916.
1905	Apr. 19–May 22	14.5%, 26 TDs	Insurance scandals. Lawson strikes again. Longish.
1906	Apr. 17–May 3	10.7%, 14 TDs	Heavy portfolio liquidation by casualty firms after San Francisco quake.
1907	Mar. 2–Mar. 14	14.9%, 10 TDs	Rails battered as bear operators hit stocks Harriman had bulled; Union Pacific a 172–120 loser.
1907	Aug. 3–Aug. 24	11.8%, 18 TDs	Indiana Standard fined $1000 on each of 29,000 rail rebate charges. Worldwide credit crisis.
1907	Oct. 21–Nov. 15	12.8%, 21 TDs	Copper scams collapse. Banks suspend. Morgan's pool rescues Street from commercial crisis.

*Duration in trading sessions (TDs).

Table A-2. Almanac of Stock Market Panics and Panic Episodes
(*Continued*)
Measured by Leading Dow Average

Year	Dates	Percent lost and duration*	Causes and comments
1908	Jan. 15–Feb. 10	10.1%, 22 TDs	Reflex from two-month 53% gain. Railroads seen threatened by ICC. C&GW, Seaboard enter receivership.
1910	Jan. 13–Feb. 7	11.6%, 22 TDs	Hocking Coal bubble bursts. Stock plunges from 91 to 22 within days.
1910	June 25–July 26	14.4%, 24 TDs	ICC rate cut stuns rails, triggers transcontinental merger collapse.
1911	Sept. 6–Sept. 25	9.1%, 16 TDs	Antitrust fears wreck U.S. Steel, which trades over 50% of NYSE volume on several days. Intraday loss over 11%.
1914	July 23–July 30	11.3%, 6 TDs	World War I begins. Enormous selling from Europe forces NYSE to suspend. Reopens Dec. 12.
1915	May 6–May 14	11.5%, 7 TDs	*Lusitania* torpedoed. Nearly 1200 perish. War with Germany feared.
1916	Apr. 6–Apr. 22	10.1%, 13 TDs	Belated news of *Sussex* torpedoeing. Wilson to Congress on sub threat.
1916	Dec. 11–Dec. 21	13.9%, 9 TDs	Wilson's peace scare rocks market, followed immediately by Secretary of State Lansing's war scare remarks.
1917	Jan. 31–Feb. 2	8.8%, 2 TDs	Loss a little shy, but unrestricted U-boat campaign sparks largest daily decline between 1907 and 1929.
1917	Oct. 27–Nov. 8	11.8%, 9 TDs	Bolsheviks overthrow government in Russia. Allies fear separate peace with Germany.
1917	Nov. 26–Dec. 19	10.9%, 19 TDs	Bond market panic. Bear market climax. Railroads to be taken over by government.

*Duration in trading sessions (TDs).

Table A-2. Almanac of Stock Market Panics and Panic Episodes
(*Continued*)

Measured by Leading Dow Average

Year	Dates	Percent lost and duration*	Causes and comments
1919	July 28–Aug. 20	10.5%, 18 TDs	German trade embargoes lifted. Fed warns against speculation.
1919	Nov. 3–Nov. 29	13.4%, 21 TDs	Fed hikes discount rate to chill inflation. Postwar bull market ends overnight.
1920	Feb. 2–Feb. 25	12.6%, 18 TDs	Foreign currency collapse cancels overseas buying. Call rate: 25%.
1920	Apr. 10–Apr. 29	11.5%, 16 TDs	Bond market crash. Dow falters after March's bull manipulations, including Stutz, GM corners.
1920	Nov. 4–Nov. 19	13.4%, 13 TDs	GM in turmoil; stock down 68% since March. Founder Durant ousted.
1920	Dec. 7–Dec. 21	13.0%, 12 TDs	Second-stage panic. Liberty bonds make new lows. Ford lays off 40,000 at nation's largest auto plant.
1921	May 23–June 20	14.4%, 22 TDs	Retroactive dividend tax feared. Psychological low for 1919–1921 market.
1926	Feb. 27–Mar. 30	12.5%, 26 TDs	Nickel Plate merger axed by ICC. Bears raid crippled pool stocks.
1927	Oct. 6–Oct. 21	9.8%, 13 TDs	Car output slumps as buyers await Ford's Model A. GM's value suspect. Dow earnings slump.
1928	Nov. 28–Dec. 8	13.0%, 8 TDs	Treasury warning scares specs. RCA falls, 405 to 296 within three days. Huge margin calls.
1929	Mar. 1–Mar. 26	7.7%, 21 TDs	Small drop deceiving; intraday loss 13%. Record volume Mar. 26. Call rate highest figure of 1920s.
1929	May 6–May 27	10.0%, 18 TDs	Serious price cracks. Chrysler at 56, down from 135 Jan. high.

*Duration in trading sessions (TDs).

Table A-2. Almanac of Stock Market Panics and Panic Episodes (*Continued*)

Measured by Leading Dow Average

Year	Dates	Percent lost and duration*	Causes and comments
1929	Sept. 19–Oct. 4	12.1%, 13 TDs	Hatry swindle stirs London. Public drowned by mutual fund IPOs.
1929	Oct. 22–Nov. 13	39.2%, 15 TDs	The Classic.
1929	Dec. 7–Dec. 20	12.4%, 11 TDs	Harsh reflex after 16-day rally of 32%. Many new lows recorded. Business stats increasingly bad.
1930–July 1932			See Chap. 9 for discussion.
1932	Sept. 7–Sept. 19	18.6%, 10 TDs	Commodity price break triggers slide. Market had run too far, too fast.
1932	Oct. 4–Oct. 10	17.8%, 5 TDs	Second stage. World wheat prices collapse. Bonds fall sharply.
1932	Nov. 12–Nov. 30	17.2%, 14 TDs	Second thoughts about FDR election. Bank crisis deepens.
1933	Feb. 11–Feb. 27	15.6%, 11 TDs	U.S. banking system on verge of collapse. Multiple bank holidays and suspensions.
1933	Mar. 16–Mar. 31	12.0%, 13 TDs	Downward reflex from record markup following FDR bank holiday.
1933	July 18–July 22	18.6%, 4 TDs	Dow had doubled since Feb. Whiskey Panic smashes "repeal" fancies.
1933	Sept. 19–Sept. 27	11.9%, 7 TDs	Market had far outrun outlook for improved business prospects.
1933	Oct. 11–Oct. 21	16.1%, 10 TDs	Germany withdraws from League of Nations. FDR rachets price of gold.
1934	Apr. 25–May 14	12.6%, 16 TDs	SEC advent feared. Labor troubles anticipated.
1934	July 19–July 26	11.7%, 6 TDs	San Francisco general strike. Austrian premier assassinated by Nazis.

*Duration in trading sessions (TDs).

Table A-2. Almanac of Stock Market Panics and Panic Episodes
(*Continued*)

Measured by Leading Dow Average

Year	Dates	Percent lost and duration*	Causes and comments
1935	Feb. 18–Mar. 14	9.8%, 20 TDs	Dollar attacked. Guaranty Trust cuts $20 dividend. Hitler rejects Versailles.
1936	Apr. 13–Apr. 29	10.6%, 14 TDs	Severe market break in Berlin. Ethiopia near defeat. Sitdown strikes multiply.
1937	Aug. 31–Sept. 22	16.9%, 20 TDs	Hitler, Mussolini confer. Japan wars on China. Sudden business collapse.
1937	Oct. 2–Oct. 18	17.4%, 11 TDs	London hit hard. War scare. Intraday loss is 25% to Oct. 19 reversal.
1937	Nov. 1–Nov. 24	16.4%, 18 TDs	Industrial production, commodities in depression. Dow's autumn loss 40%.
1938	Jan. 20–Feb. 3	10.5%, 12 TDs	Bonds and utilities lead liquidation and fall beneath panic lows of autumn. Intraday loss, 11.6%.
1938	Mar. 15–Mar. 31	22.2%, 14 TDs	Bonds smashed following Hitler's move on Austria.
1939	Jan. 6–Jan. 26	10.8%, 18 TDs	New Hitler demands rumored. Heavy selling from London.
1939	Mar. 14–Apr. 8	19.6%, 21 TDs	Munich betrayed. Czechoslovakia invaded by Germany, Mussolini seizes Albania.
1940	May 9–May 24	23.1%, 13 TDs	*Sitzkrieg* turns to *Blitzkrieg.* Nazis roll to Dunkerque. War's biggest volume.
1941	Jan. 15–Feb. 14	10.5%, 25 TDs	Experts, including General Marshall, predict Nazi invasion of UK in spring.
1946	Aug. 26–Sept. 19	13.3%, 17 TDs	Strikes, shortages, rail problems. Dow had failed mid-August test of May high.

*Duration in trading sessions (TDs).

Table A-2. Almanac of Stock Market Panics and Panic Episodes
(*Continued*)

Measured by Leading Dow Average

Year	Dates	Percent lost and duration*	Causes and comments
1948	Nov. 1–Nov. 30	9.8%, 22 TDs	Truman's upset victory stuns market in biggest volume since Dunkerque. Dow loss marginal, but Rails drop 16%.
1950	June 23–July 13	12.0%, 13 TDs	South Korea invaded. UN call to arms. U.S. troops airlifted to Korea.
1955	Sept. 23–Oct. 11	10.0%, 12 TDs	"Ike" plays 27 holes in Denver, suffers heart attack. Record volume since 1933.
1957	Oct. 3–Oct. 22	9.9%, 13 TDs	*Sputnik I* shocks West; scientific wizardry unexpected from Moscow.
1960	Aug. 26–Sept. 28	10.5%, 22 TDs	Market discounts JFK victory. Penn RR shut down by strike—first time ever.
1962	Apr. 24–May 28	16.7%, 24 TDs	JFK–steel confrontation frightens business. Biggest volume since 1929.
1962	June 8–June 26	10.9%, 12 TDs	Low-volume, second-stage decline. But psychological low had come May 28.
1966	July 22–Aug. 29	11.7%, 26 TDs	Longish. Credit crunch, sick bonds, record prime cause persistent slide.
1969	July 7–July 29	9.0%, 15 TDs	Price controls threatened. Vietnam peace hopes dashed. Moon walk ignored.
1969	Nov. 12–Dec. 17	10.1%, 24 TDs	U.S. Steel at 14-year low, "Go-go" stocks become "yesterday's darlings."
1970	May 1–May 26	14.0%, 17 TDs	Kent State tragedy, news of troops in Cambodia smash market. Penn Central in trouble. Ross Perot's EDS dives, 164–29.

*Duration in trading sessions (TDs).

Table A-2. Almanac of Stock Market Panics and Panic Episodes
(*Continued*)

Measured by Leading Dow Average

Year	Dates	Percent lost and duration*	Causes and comments
1973	Oct. 29–Dec. 5	20.0%, 26 TDs	"Nifty Fifty" surrenders en masse. Dow falls 200 points. Resignation of Nixon demanded. Fuel shortages feared.
1974	Aug. 9–Aug. 29	15.5%, 14 TDs	Nixon resignation fails to turn market. Drought fans inflation fears.
1974	Sept. 20–Oct. 4	12.9%, 10 TDs	Wholesale prices soar at 47% annual rate. Dow falls for 11 straight days.
1974	Nov. 14–Dec. 6	12.4%, 15 TDs	Justice seeks AT&T breakup. Chrysler shuts down. Israel mobilizes.
1978	Oct. 13–Oct. 31	11.7%, 12 TDs	October sees 8th prime hike of year. Inflation rate 10.8% and climbing.
1979	Oct. 5–Oct. 23	10.1%, 12 TDs	"Saturday Night Massacre" (Fed tightens) leads to "wildest week since 1929."
1980	Mar. 4–Mar. 27	11.3%, 17 TDs	Fallout from failed silver corner creates billion in margin calls. Trading halted in stocks associated with Hunt group.
1981	Aug. 21–Sept. 25	10.5%, 24 TDs	Carrier planes down two Libyan jets. Reagan asks for tax increases.
1987	Oct. 13–Oct. 19	30.7%, 4 TDs	Implosion and meltdown. On Oct. 19, Dow falls 508 points; volume 604 million. Oct. 20 will be a classic key reversal day.
1989	Oct. 10–Oct. 13	7.7%, 3 TDs	Deceptive episode. Dow drops 11% intraday. Airline merger bubble bursts and Transports fall 22% in 14 sessions.
1990	Aug. 1–Aug. 22	14.3%, 16 TDs	Kuwait invaded. U.S. sends troops to Saudi Arabia. Blockade set. Iraq takes civilians hostage. Nikkei down 23%.

*Duration in trading sessions (TDs).

Index